PHILOSOPHY AND HAPPINESS

How philosophy can bring felicity

by

John L. Bowman

Philosophy and Happiness

Copyright 2017 John L. Bowman. All rights reserved.
Printed in the United States of America.
No part of this book may reproduced, stored in a retrieval system, or transmitted by any means without the written permission of the author.

ISBN 978-0-692-96278-7

Any people depicted in stock imagery are models,
which are being used for illustrative purposes only.
Because of the dynamic nature of the Internet, any web addresses
or links contained in this book may have changed
since publication and may no longer be valid.
The views expressed in this work are solely those of the author.
This book was printed on acid-free paper.

I dedicate this book to my youngest daughter Sydney Bowman because she enthusiastically suggested I write it.

The cover is a collage of portraits of some philosophers referred to in this book. Each has been quoted on the nature of happiness and unhappiness. They are (top row left to right) Plato, Søren Kierkegaard, Marcus Aurelius and C. S. Lewis; (second row left to right) Bertrand Russell, Aristotle, Seneca and Erasmus; (third row left to right) Arthur Schopenhauer, Hannah Arendt, Sigmund Freud and Jonathan Swift; and (fourth row left to right) Boethius, Machiavelli, Epictetus and Samuel Johnson.

CONTENTS

Introduction	1

PART I: Sources of Unhappiness

CHAPTER ONE: **The Unknown** — 11
No man is happy until he is dead, until then only lucky

CHAPTER TWO: **Skepticism** — 17
Skeptics must be skeptical of their own skepticism

CHAPTER THREE: **Realistic** — 21
Do not be a Yahoo

CHAPTER FOUR: **Live Life** — 30
Do not be unauthentic or anonymous

CHAPTER FIVE: **Negative Judgments** — 38
The world is as one makes it, so fashion good judgments and make it a place that brings joy

CHAPTER SIX: **Fortune** — 43
Have proper judgments of externals and do not invest in the wheel of fortune

CHAPTER SEVEN: **Habit** — 50
Have Machiavelli's first kind of brain and develop good habits

CHAPTER EIGHT: **Passion** — 63
Do not be Sisyphus, forever having to push the rock back up the hill

CHAPTER NINE: **Desire and Appetite** — 70
How pleasant it is to ask for nothing because the man who expects nothing is never disappointed

CHAPTER TEN: **Boredom and Pain** — 82
Avoid the pendulum and live the Earth life

CHAPTER ELEVEN: **Death** — 89
Do not be Denial, Folly, Neurotic, Hermit or Forceful

CHAPTER TWELVE: **Pride and Envy** — 103
Remember each person dies and probably has average abilities

CHAPTER THIRTEEN: **Competition** — 111
Compete but do not make life a contest

CHAPTER FOURTEEN: **Fear and Trembling** — 118
Do not live in fear and trembling

PART II: Sources of Happiness

CHAPTER FIFTEEN: Simplicity and Nature — 131
Do not fight time or nature

CHAPTER SIXTEEN: Knowledge and Experience — 137
*Know thyself, seek the crown of happiness
and avoid the prison of others' opinions*

CHAPTER SEVENTEEN: Values and Creeds — 147
Take the Tolstoy Test of Values and avoid Pascal's Wager

CHAPTER EIGHTEEN: Stoicism and Epicureanism — 154
*Avoid the skeptic's dilemma, know that pleasure
cannot be increased only varied and be an unsatisfied pig*

CHAPTER NINETEEN: Blissful Ignorance — 163
*Do not take life and its troubles too seriously, lighten up, see the big picture,
put things in perspective and have a little fun through blissful ignorance*

CHAPTER TWENTY: Flourish through Love, Zest, and Hope — 167
Break the hard shell of ego, enjoy a conflagration and hope for the best

CHAPTER TWENTY-ONE: Purpose — 172
Be a ship with a rudder

CHAPTER TWENTY-TWO: Health — 178
Health enables people to worry

CHAPTER TWENTY-THREE: Reproduction — 186
Escape the isolated and barren prison of self and reproduce

CHAPTER TWENTY-FOUR: The Mean — 191
Avoid the Law of Undulation and embrace the mean

CHAPTER TWENTY-FIVE: Appreciation — 195
*Everyone can choose whether to view the glass half empty
or half full—appreciate any volume*

CHAPTER TWENTY-SIX: Virtue and Justice — 200
Do not be a Troglodyte—focus on the inner ring

CHAPTER TWENTY-SEVEN: Courage — 209
Act on one's inner voice, be authentic and escape one's cage

CHAPTER TWENTY-EIGHT: Reason — 215
Do not be a dog, cultivate reason and avoid an empty min

Conclusion — 225

INTRODUCTION

Everyone wants to be happy, but some are incapable of achieving it because they do not understand the source of Plato's crown of happiness. They are unhappy because they pursue desire like Swiftian Yahoos, invest in the capricious Wheel of Fortune, like Sisyphus forever repeat life mistakes, live in the opinion of others, live in fear of death or are unduly skeptical. They live lives worrying and fretting, fearful, melancholy and irritated. Those who understand the crown's source are happy because they live simply in nature, have salubrious judgments, create meaningful life purposes, value people, avoid extremes, appreciate what they have, are courageous, have virtue and live zestful lives. These people are peaceful, calm, dauntless, joyful and unperturbed. This book is about those who achieve Plato's crown of happiness through philosophy.

    Plato wrote in *Charmides* that (v) if one discards knowledge he will hardly find the crown of happiness. The crown is happiness, and its characteristics are discovered through knowledge, and in particular philosophic knowledge. For Plato, the crown was called *eudemonia*, which is an ancient Greek word for happiness, well-being, welfare, flourishing, contentment, health and prosperity. Philosopher Hannah Arendt in *The Human Condition* described *eudemonia* as blessedness, and Aristotle to live life well. The crown of happiness comes from the philosophic knowledge that discovers it.

    But not all philosophers agree with this assertion. Jeremy Bentham and John Stuart Mill famously debated this very issue. Bentham wrote that (v) it is better to be a happy pig than a miserable human being, to which Mill rejoined that (v) it is better to be a human being dissatisfied than a pig satisfied; better to be Socrates dissatisfied than a fool satisfied. Michel de Montaigne agreed with Bentham when he wrote that (v) too much learning only produces idle fantasies. So, the question is: does philosophic knowledge bring happiness? This book assumes that it does and gives the reasons philosophers think why.

    Unhappiness is counterproductive, useless and painful. William James once wrote that (p) the attitude of unhappiness is not only painful, it is mean and ugly. What can be more base and unworthy than the pining, puling, mumping mood, what is more injurious to others and less helpful as a way out of difficulty? Unhappiness only fastens and perpetuates the trouble that occasioned it and increases the total evil of the situation. This book assumes man can avoid the mean, ugly and puling state of unhappiness.

Readers could reasonably ask why philosophers have any advice to give on how to be happy. They could rightfully point out that philosophers are notoriously humorless, grave, intellectually unfeeling and sometimes suicidal. But, throughout history, happiness has been an enduring interest of theirs. They have pondered it and have developed many worthy ideas. Indeed, Seneca wrote that (v) philosophers' writings can bring happiness and not just far-fetched and archaic expressions or extravagant metaphors. Indeed, the ancient philosophies of Platonism, stoicism, Epicureanism and skepticism dealt extensively with happiness. Even this author's honored major professor in graduate school at Oregon State University, Bill Uzgalis, told his students that they must have some humor in their papers to get a good grade. Philosophers are only thinking people seeking ways to happiness. At a minimum, they ought to at least explain how to avoid unhappiness.

In spite of their purported ilk, many philosophers assert that humans are born for happiness. A few like Sigmund Freud believe humans are incapable of happiness, and some, like Samuel Johnson, believe man can achieve only brief interludes of happiness that make endurable his otherwise painful life. But many philosophers believe man was made to be happy. The ancient Roman Stoic Epictetus wrote that (v) men should be happy—God made him that way, life is to be happy—free from hindrance and restraint, and if one is unhappy it is his fault because God made man to be happy and enjoy peace of mind and furnished him with the resources to achieve this. John Locke believed that (v) people extend themselves from present existence only through consciousness, all which is founded in a concern for happiness. This happiness, according to Locke, is the (v) unavoidable concomitant of consciousness.

The philosophers' idea of happiness comes in many forms. They, and in particular Hegel believed happiness comes from freedom. Cicero wrote that (v) philosophy consists in the collection of rational arguments that that can lead to a good and happy life. For Cicero, happiness also comes from lack of fear, worry and covetousness. Epictetus believed (p) attending to daily activities does not bring happiness such as those who attend to their farms and do not ask what the world is. Seneca, in response believed philosophy (pe) strips the mind of empty thinking about farms and focuses on happiness. For George Santayana, (pe) heaven or happiness is to be at peace with the world.

One famous philosopher/psychologist Sigmund Freud in *Civilization and its Discontents* believed humans are constitutionally unable to avoid suffering and achieve true happiness. He depressingly wrote that humans are faced with the powerful exigencies of nature, feeble bodies and the inability to adjust to relationships with others, states, and societies and thus are doomed to live unhappy lives. Freud believed men are consigned to suffering by nature, which is epitomized by what happens to their bodies—they naturally decay and die. Further, constructs of families, states and civilizations are built on the renunciation of human instincts. These artificial constructs limit freedom, impart responsibilities and repress man's aggressive nature. For Freud, human lives are essentially one of toil, discouragement, disappointment, pain, angst and struggle interspersed with occasional bouts of pleasure.

Freud believed that humans try to overcome these sources of unhappiness in a variety of ways, none of which work. Some seek chemical intoxication with alcohol or drugs, but this only numbs the pain. Some try to kill their instincts such as in some Eastern religions, but this only brings quietness. The artists try to sublimate some instincts and heighten others like their intellectual capacity, but the benefits are only mild and of use to a few. Creative people endeavor to create illusions to escape reality, but they achieve nothing because reality is too strong. Some like hermits seek to cut off all contact with the world, but this achieves nothing. The passionate seek to enhance the sources of happiness, but passion thwarted only brings unhappiness. The final solution is a flight into neurotic illness, which only brings derangement.

Freud has some powerful arguments why humans cannot be happy, but most philosophers disagree. Epictetus wrote that (v) man can suffer and still be happy. He may be hounded by innumerable demons, but his mind, what he knows and effort can still make him happy. Happiness is not a mirage that always appears elsewhere and evaporates when approached only to reappear in the distance. This book is about how philosophy can turn that mirage into real happiness.

So what is happiness? What is its definition? Happiness is an unusually subjective term that means different things to different people. Some think it is an active state of mind, while others consider it a byproduct. Some believe happiness is derived from beliefs people hold, such as a person of faith, and others from physical pleasure, such as a sensualist. The words used to describe it are similarly disparate. It is commonly described as pleasure, tranquility, felicity equanimity or simply an undisturbed state of mind. It is also frequently defined in a negative sense such as freedom from anxiety, pain, ennui, agitation or troubles. Most agree that happiness is an attitude or some kind of mental state free from anxiety.

In classical times, the Platonists described it as a harmony of the soul that is free from internal strife. The Aristotelians called it *eudemonia*, or happiness obtained from achieving one's potential for a fully rational life. The Cyrenaic Hedonists and Epicureans described it as the presence of pleasure and absence of pain, and the Skeptics thought happiness was a trouble free mind that comes from the suspension of belief.

The Stoics' definition of happiness can be found in the distinction between two ancient Greek words: *ataraxia* and *apatheia*. *Ataraxia* is a word for happiness that means tranquility or imperturbability of mind and body. *Apatheia* means not suffering in Greek and was used by the Stoics to mean indifference to pleasure and pain, a state of tranquility, or peace of mind and body resulting from emotional detachment from the everyday world.

This book uses the Stoic definition of happiness, which is defined as tranquility, peace, contentment, calmness of mind, peace of mind and well-being. It is the state of not being disturbed, troubled, worried or driven by insatiable desires. This definition of happiness, in part, derives from two of Cicero's minimum essentials for a happy life described in his *Tusculan Disputations*. These conditions are to learn not to be a prey to anxiety and to (v) acquire the ability to control the sensations of excessive joy, fear and desire. This Stoic interpretation of happiness entails the virtues of endurance, courage, self-control and justice because to be happy for the Stoics requires humans to adjust themselves to the world and not demand the world adjust to them.

The word felicity is often used in this book in place of happiness. Felicity is a refined definition of happiness and thus often more fitting. It means satisfaction, a general state of happiness, ease, contentment or pleasure with no pain. Perhaps the essential definition of felicity comes from John Stuart Mill, when he described happiness simply as the presence of pleasure and absence of pain. This is the way most philosophers have defined it.

Certainly, some can achieve happiness easier than others due to external circumstances. Having food, shelter, health, love, a successful career, money and respect give some advantage. Also, different circumstances present different challenges to happiness. The old, young, educated, uneducated, man, woman, rich and poor all typically have different ideas of and obstacles to happiness. The old face health issues and the young and poor money issues that can detract from felicity. This said, most philosophers believe happiness is available to everyone.

However, for the philosophers, achieving felicity requires effort. The Anna Karenina principle reveals that there are more ways things can go wrong than right. Samuel Johnson in *The History of Rasselas* wrote that (v) human life is everywhere a state in which much is to be endured and little enjoyed. Happiness is not given to man; he must earn it. Epictetus wrote (pe) that, like virtue, humans are born for the good but not with it—it only come with practice. To reinterpret Epictetus, people are born for happiness but not with it—it only comes with practice. Cicero in *Tusculan Disputations* wrote that (p) the happy life rests upon the individual alone, and one proverb says that everyone is responsible for their own happiness. Happiness is not inherited, and it is a mistake to wait for it to come—an individual must achieve it. So, happiness is a kind of art that must be studied and practiced to be realized. Achieving happiness is not easy, but then smooth seas never made a good sailor.

For the philosophers, happiness is the attitude one chooses to have. If a man asks himself whether he would be better off alive or dead and the answer is alive, he has concomitantly decided that life is worth living. It is only natural then to decide that the life one prefers to live is best lived happily. With such choices people create an attitude filter that looks for happiness rather than sources of unhappiness. Indeed, Shakespeare wrote that (v) there is nothing either good or bad, but thinking makes it so, Boethius wrote (v) nothing is miserable unless one thinks it so and Seneca that the (v) world is as a person makes it. These three authors, who spanned 2,000 years of human history, described the same timeless source of unhappiness, which is the mind. The world truly is as the individual makes it, and if he wants to be happy, he needs to look to himself and shape his minds to make it so.

A few final remarks about the limitations to happiness, citations and some final comments conclude this introduction. The philosophers' prescriptions for happiness in this book do not apply to everyone. They may not apply to those with chemical, biologic or psychic anomalies. The philosophers' advice addresses the way humans think, an assertion that assumes they have free will. Some philosophers believe man's will is determined, and contemporary philosophy argues for a compatibilist view that reconciles free will and determinism. This book assumes that man has the free will to choose to think in a way that brings felicity.

This is not a scholarly work, and the citations are spare. Scholarly citations impede this author's often stream of consciousness thinking, so a new, abbreviated form of citations has been created in order to avoid plagiarism. Whenever possible, a quote or source of an idea is attributed to the original author in context. When needed, (v) is used when a source is quoted verbatim and (p) when the source is paraphrased. When a source has been embellished by this author, it is cited as (pe) for paraphrased and embellished.

Finally, this is to acknowledge that the *Stanford Encyclopedia of Philosophy* has been referenced often in this book. It is a tremendous source of philosophic knowledge for which this author is very grateful. Whenever it is used, it is always reference it with (SEP), sometimes verbatim and sometimes paraphrased.

A few final comments about this book require mention. The appellation "philosopher" is used in an expanded way. Philosophy is the love of wisdom, and philosophers are those who pursue it. Because others also pursue it, like psychologist Sigmund Freud and author C. S. Lewis, they are also considered philosophers. Unfortunately, there is some repetition because some subjects are so intimately related. For example, in chapter eight on passion and ten on boredom and pain, some comments are redundant. An effort was made to avoid repetition, but it crept in occasionally due to the nature of the topic. Finally, sometimes capitalism is criticized in this book (chapter fifteen on simplicity and nature) due to its impact on individuals' happiness. To be clear, this author believes capitalism with its vices is superior and ultimately brings greater happiness than other political systems like socialism and communism with their virtues.

This book is dedicated to my youngest daughter, Sydney Bowman. In pondering the topic of my next book, she reminded me that the relationship between knowledge, philosophy and happiness has always been an enduring interest of mine, so, she asked, why not write on that. I took her advice and wrote this book—she earned the honor.

Philosophy and Happiness has two parts. The first part is what philosophers have said are sources of unhappiness, and the second what they have said about the sources of happiness. Sometimes the sources of happiness are included in the first section and sources of unhappiness in the second. This is because the philosophers mentioned had counter examples that were best placed with their assertion.

Finally, this book is about what philosophers believe brings happiness, observations that have been expanded on and embellished with this author's views, observations, beliefs and opinions.

SOURCES OF UNHAPPINESS

Chapter One

THE UNKNOWN
No man is happy until he is dead, until then only lucky

A man is hiking in the woods and suddenly a grizzly bear appears that causes him to feel instant fear. His fear is from a known source, and his fear immediately becomes courage to confront the source or the overwhelming desire to flee for his life. This is not the case with unknown sources of fear, such as death. Many people live unhappy lives in constant fear of uncontrollable unknown things that cause harm—like the fear of death.

Many prefer to remain fearful of unknown things because they lack courage, fear unpredictability or, as Shakespeare wrote, would rather bear those ills they have than to fly to those they know not of. Remaining in fear of the unknown is a choice, and the better choice is to confront and conquer one's fear. Two historic ways to influence choices and ameliorate fear of unknown things have been faith and reason. There is nothing necessarily wrong with faith balming one's fears. Indeed, philosopher Kierkegaard would say without Christian faith, man lives in despair. The image of an afterlife is comforting. The problem too often is the diviners conceive of imaginative alternate unknown sources like hell or a vengeful God to maintain faith. This just replaces one fearful unknown source of unhappiness with another.

Philosophy offers an alternate solution, which is to address one's fears with reason and insight. So, this book will look at what some philosophers have said about how to deal with fear of the unknown in order to achieve happiness.

Herodotus once wrote that no man is happy until he is dead, until then he is only lucky. Just living life is living in fear of the unknown. Life is uncertain, people can get sick, injured, sued, calumniated, divorced, fired, impoverished or innocently sent to prison for manslaughter—the list is endless. Fortune is fickle, life is full of chance, and the future bears down upon each person with all the hazards of the unknown. Plutarch once wrote that to congratulate a man on his happiness while he is living and contending with all perils of the mortal state is like proclaiming an athlete the victor and crowning him before the contest is decided.

Bertrand Russell pointed out that one source of the fear of living is due to overstating one's importance. When humans are self-consumed, they become self-serving individuals who are easily troubled by trivial misfortunes, which puts them into a state of dreading what fate may have in store. Russell's solution was to develop an expansive view of the world—to put troubles in perspective. It is edifying to observe others' troubles that are far greater than one's own. Another solution is to explore what positive alternatives the world has to offer, like others' love, rather than focusing on one's immediate troubles. Living ought to be enjoyed and not endured— the end of life is not the grave.

Philosophy's ability to help navigate the fear and uncertainty of the unknown can be seen in philosopher Boethius's writings around 520 CE. Boethius was charged with treason and condemned to death, perhaps the greatest unknown and unknowable. He wrote his masterpiece the *Consolation of Philosophy* in prison while awaiting execution. He was a man suffering with the knowledge that he would soon enter eternity, which he endeavored to escape the fear of through philosophy. In his darkest hour, he reflected on some sources of fear, such as chance, poverty and rejection.

On endeavoring to overcome the fear of the unknown, Boethius wrote that humans all are, in a way, like him, facing execution. Anything can happen to anyone for no apparent cause— only by chance or luck do lives progress. Life is unpredictable, and anyone can find themselves in the same circumstances as his at anytime. No man is happy until he is dead because chance can make him unhappy tomorrow, and there is nothing he can do about it. Happiness thus cannot exist under things governed by chance— indeed her very mutability often leads to unhappiness. The constant fear of loss itself keeps man unhappy.

So, humans cannot control chance, but they can control whether they invest in her and what they think about what she dispenses. As Boethius and the Stoics admonished, humans should remain indifferent to that which remains beyond their control and properly judge that which is within it in order to preserve happiness.

Boethius wrote about the fear of poverty. Financial fortunes are fickle, so people can find themselves in want at any time. Indeed, the fear of not having the means to obtain food, shelter or medical care stalks everyone. This is a justifiable fear, but Boethius says to consider the other side of the coin—the consequences of having money. He wrote that money is created by man and thus is transitory and short-lived. It is of value only because it can be transferred to someone else, which then makes it no longer one's own. Because it is of value only when transferred, it has no inherent value. What ultimate value is there in looking at a pile of gold metal? Thus, being artificial, money can be alienated at any time, unlike a beautiful countryside that fortune can never take away.

Boethius also described the fear of losing money if one has it. With money, one fears losing it to the highwayman, whereas if one has no money, he just whistles by. Further, money makes one dependent, which robs his freedom. People think money makes them self-sufficient, but in reality those with it need others to hold and protect it, which makes one dependent on another. Being dependent robs one's freedom because others' actions determine one's fortunes and not one's own. For Boethius, once riches are won, a man is never free again. Most importantly, money brings the never-ending desire for more money—it never fully satisfies. He who has too much wants more, and he who has little measures his wealth according to the need of nature and not excess ostentation.

The solution is to not fear being poor, do not be avaricious, and live simply. Nature truly is easily satisfied. There are innumerable other ways to happiness that do not require money, many of which have been discussed throughout this book. Having good judgments, limiting desire, controlling passion, suppressing appetite, flourishing, having purpose and virtue, and appreciating what one has are just a few things that limit desire for money and mitigate fear of not having it. As Cicero wrote, philosophers are not afraid of poverty, and Socrates observed how much he did not need.

As social creatures, it has been said that two of the greatest unknown fears are the fear of not being accepted and the fear of being rejected—two sides of the same coin. For many, happiness depends on being part of the social group, but integration into society can go awry for many reasons. Unfounded damaging rumors about one's character, silent enemies who endeavor to subvert one's reputation and political correctness that impugns one's independent views can turn others against him unbeknownst to him. Even friends are fragile sources of human connection. Those one acquires through fortune usually abandon him in misfortune, and those one acquires through personal qualities sometimes abandon him due to their own lack of character. Indeed, it has been said that there is no greater evil more able to cause injury than a friend turned foe.

The solution comes from Ralph Waldo Emerson, who advised men to live lives of self-reliance and independence. Succor dignity, maintain self-esteem, and let the hisses of the world slide by.

Like death, competition naturally exists for the living. Many fear competition because they fear falling behind their competitors, which Russell wrote is really a fear of the future. This seems only right because nobody is prescient. The future is opaque and uncertain. But why bother? Each person will be dead soon and forgotten in fifty to a hundred years, and nobody really cares except each person about himself. Ultimately, it does not matter what the future holds.

Unlike competition, death is the greatest unknown. C. S. Lewis in the *Screwtape Letters* speaking through the devil wrote that because focusing on death increases fear, the devil endeavors to knit man to this world. The devil wants man to feel human troubles and believe death is the greatest unknown evil. This keeps him in fear of the unknown and suffering fearfully within the devil's control. The devil reasons that if humans begin to believe in a religious afterlife, they detach from worldly problems and lose fear.

Put competition in perspective and realistically accept death because one only begins living when he does. Smile at the devil's silly tales.

Lewis's most insightful observation about fear of the unknown is the fear of fear itself. Screwtape the devil tells his minion

Wormwood that (v) fear becomes easier to master when the patient's mind is diverted from the thing feared to fear itself. Indeed, President Roosevelt in the 1930s told Americans that the only thing to fear about the Depression is the fear of the Depression itself.

This is the ultimate fear of the unknown because fear itself has no object that allows one to discern whether it is worthy of fear. Fear becomes a free-floating emotion detached from reality. It becomes a feeling that can be magnified exponentially when in reality what one imaginatively fears may not warrant it. He becomes blinkered and ends up fearing only for the sake of fear and no other reason.

This kind of fear has no boundaries, truncates any effort to seek solutions and demonstrates a lack of control of emotion. The solution is to understand the fear of fear, the consequences of emotionally indulging in fear and to use reason to keep one's passions aligned with reality.

Fear of an unknown future can be conquered with courage, reason and philosophy. Seneca wrote in his dialogue *On Tranquility* that fear is a significant but avoidable source of human unhappiness. He admonished men to be like Socrates who lived life as a free man walking unafraid amid the thirty tyrants of Athens. With the use of proper judgments one can (v) move and not freeze in the fetters of fear. Indeed, Epictetus once said that a tyrant is only master of his corpse. It is a waste of life to fear that which one has no control over, so have courage.

Using reason enables one to overcome fear of the unknown in many ways. Putting life in reasoned perspective—connecting causes with consequences—brings many benefits. People come to see that self-reliance places happiness within their control—when they are other-reliant, their happiness is controlled by others. Indeed, no one can make someone unhappy without his consent. One learns to control emotions, and in particular fear. Finally, one comes to understand the nature of fear and why it necessarily has no object of which to be fearful.

Adopting a philosophic attitude toward life, people who see it more catholically broaden their perspectives and lessen their fears. People come to see how utterly insignificant they are, so the fear of loss lessens and the value of money becomes clearer. This is advice that Boethius dispensed over 1,000 years ago that is as true today as it was then.

When man fears, he must remember that no man is happy until he is dead, only lucky. Accept that unknown things will happen, appreciate that much of life's success is due to luck, face demons, accept change, live life to its fullest, and do not fear the unknown.

CHAPTER TWO

SKEPTICISM
Skeptics must be skeptical of their own skepticism

There is a lawn sign that says *Everybody Sucks and the USA Is Going to Hell*. This is the ultimate skeptic sentiment—everybody is wrong, all things are going awry and no solutions are offered. Put in philosophic terms, this skeptic formula means there is no right or truth. No matter how humans try, there will always be opposing propositions and doubt, so remain skeptical. One sees this skeptical sentiment throughout modern society with statements like "nothing works," "things are broken" and "civilization is going to hell." Most significantly, it asserts that humans cannot make matters better, which collaterally makes philosophy a discipline that does not bring happiness.

In ancient Greek philosophy, three philosophies were offered to achieve happiness. They were stoicism, which preached controlling the passions; Epicureanism, which believed passions should be indulged; and Skepticism, which believed happiness comes by suspending judgment. Two founders of Skepticism were Greeks Pyrron of Elis, who established Pyrrhonism, which is an extreme form of skepticism, and Sextus Empiricus who is the best-known ancient skeptic. This chapter is about the skeptics and happiness.

The skeptics believed that one can know nothing for certain; therefore, people must suspend all judgment in order to attain a state of *ataraxia*, or peace of mind, which was their idea of what constitutes happiness. Their reasoning goes like this: to claim truth presupposes one knows truth, which has either been approved or not. If it has not been approved, then it is not truth, and if it has been approved, that which has approved it must have also been approved, and so ad infinitum. In short, there is no ultimate judge of what constitutes truth; therefore, one should suspend judgment about all beliefs nor affirm anything true or false. To achieve happiness, man should simply give up belief.

Skepticism is not a formula for happiness. It is a negative, inert, listless philosophy that leads to resignation and the nihilist view that nothing matters. It offers no search for happiness or hope of achieving it—when one gives up belief, one gives up hope. In the end, it can only result in cynicism. C. S. Lewis's devil Screwtape advised Wormwood to make humans skeptics because it causes them to suspend judgment about how things really exist. Certainly, joy can be had from folly, as Erasmus pointed out, but enduring happiness does not come from illusion. If the devil is right, everything is relative, and ethics are mere conduct, habits, laws, legendary beliefs and dogmatic conceptions. Hail the assassins' creed under skepticism, where if nothing is true, everything is permitted. Morality becomes a social fact, and under its aegis, empty utilitarian Byronic pleasure may ascend, which necessarily insatiably seeks new and more pleasure without enduring happiness.

Skepticism is not a normative philosophy that tells one how to act, and as such it offers no roadmap to happiness. It offers no ideas or solutions to felicity. When one gives up belief, as Sextus Empiricus advocates, he gives up hope. There is an old proverb that says when things are the worst they begin to mend, and the reason they do so is because people in very black places seek solutions, which skepticism denies. It is a negative philosophy that does not offer solutions to people in black places; it does not discriminate and thus ignores sources of happiness such as some of the simple pleasures of just living.

Sextus Empiricus suggests that to be happy, one should simply go along with appearances, like a child blindly following a teacher. Live naturally, non-dogmatically, follow feelings, obey the laws and customs of the times, and learn arts and crafts. In contemporary lingo, this means just go along and do not rock the boat. But this is not happiness, it is contentment; it is living like a satisfied pig. Contentment is satisfaction, ease and gratification that may bring peace of mind but not necessarily happiness. Indeed, many would feel unhappy being a satiated pig when there is so much in the world to learn and do. *Ataraxia* may bring ease and satisfied pig–like pleasure, but not necessarily happiness.

Skepticism is essentially a concept without content. It is more a mental attitude or therapy than a theory or concept. It is a framework idea with no ideas inside it, like a jug without water. Indeed, if one is a skeptic, then he must be skeptical not only of his own skepticism but also the kind of happiness it professes.

Revered philosopher David Hume was a skeptic to the extent he raised the *post hoc ergo propter hoc* (Latin for "after this, therefore because of this") or a logical fallacy argument against knowledge. As a skeptic, he asked why a sequence of events in the future will always occur as they have in the past. This form of inductive reasoning falsely assumes that because event Y followed event X, then Y must have been caused by X.

But Hume moderated his views on the value of skepticism, as people should on its ability to bring happiness. Even though Hume believed human reasoning is inherently contradictory, he argued that one must reject extreme Pyrrhonian skepticism because it brings no durable good, which could include happiness. Instead, he advocated exercising caution and modesty in judgments, using naturally instilled beliefs and restricting skepticism to speculations of abstract reasoning. Skepticism has a function, but people must keep their minds open to positive judgments for happiness that skepticism would deny.

The skeptic's *ataraxia* is not happiness. Peace of mind, mental suspense, unperturbedness, and quietness are not happiness but rather numbness. It is rather a state of suspended numbness bereft of joy or hope. Would man be happy being numb to his family, nation or God? To be happy, it is far better to care, believe, seek, hope, strive and look for solutions than numb oneself. If man is unhappy, numbness only perpetuates his state, whereas striving offers the opportunity for a better, happier state.

Perhaps Diogenes, the ancient cynic, had the answer to skepticism. He was for sure cynical, but he was not a skeptic. He sought to challenge conventional standards and beliefs, unlike Sextus Empiricus, who believed man should live non-dogmatically in accordance with laws and customs. For Diogenes, to be happy, one needs to challenge stifling conventions that make him unhappy and live a simple, natural life. Indeed, one can be happy being cynically skeptical of false conventions, immorality and politics, but not when one suspends all judgment in order to become numb. For Diogenes, happiness and independence are possible even under reduced circumstances. Like the Stoics, he believed people possess within themselves all that they need for happiness.

Skepticism does not bring happiness because it is resignation—it is like giving up. Happiness is an emotion, and when one gives up judgments, he gives up that which can direct his emotions to happiness. David Hume was right: skepticism offers no durable good or happiness. It is better to modify skepticism, accept the faults of a flawed world and inconsistencies in knowledge and seek solutions to happiness rather than become numb to them.

Chapter Three

REALISTIC
Do not be a Yahoo

When young, Prodigal did not want to worry about money and played tennis, whereas Thrift did worry and worked. The irony is now in old age Thrift rarely thinks about money, and Prodigal thinks about it all the time. Thrift is happy and Prodigal is not. Certainly, a degree of illusionary blissful ignorance can be salubrious, but one foot must always be firmly planted in reality to be happy. Those who live in perpetually unrealistic worlds are forever at odds with the way things are and forever being disappointed when their experiences do not match their expectations.

There is a spectrum of perceptions of reality. It is a continuum that could be described as positive to negative, optimistic to pessimistic or rose to black prisms of perceptions. All perceptions may contain some truth about reality, but where individuals' perceptions concentrate on this spectrum has much to do with their felicity. Unlike Prodigal, it is important to understand this spectrum of perceptions realistically in order to avoid illusion and remain realistic. If one falls on the extreme negative pessimistic side, the odds are they will view the world as a hostile place, a view that is conducive to melancholy. Conversely, if they inclined to the positive rose prism, they may also be unhappy because reality rarely meets their expectations.

Consider the human characteristics of goodness and empathy. Some thinkers like Mahatma Gandhi and Jean-Jacques Rousseau believed in the goodness of man. However, Gandhi was a deeply depressed soul. Nassir Ghaemi in *A First Rate Madness* described him as a supremely empathetic and suicidal man who was often deeply depressed and prone to negative and pessimistic moods. Rousseau was a philosopher who believed humans are inherently good and only corrupted by society. Human nature for him was innately good like a noble savage that was enchained by civilization. Interestingly, Ben-Ami Scharfstein in his book *The Philosophers* attributed this to Rousseau's childlike effort to recreate his serene and happy childhood.

Gandhi was often depressed and Rousseau paranoiac to the extent of insanity. The reason these two great thinkers were troubled was because they were not realistic—their perceptions were grounded in one extreme end of the continuum of perceptions of reality.

In contradistinction to Gandhi and Rousseau, consider seven past misanthropically inclined philosophers and literati whose ideas cluster at the pessimistic end of the continuum. Their observations offer a different view of human nature. Both of the optimistic and pessimistic viewpoints contain some truth and many omissions. It is only a realistic outlook that puts all of these thinkers' perceptions of reality in proper perspective that in turn enables happiness.

Psychologist Sigmund Freud in various writings including his *Thoughts for the Times on War and Death* and book *Civilization and its Discontents* wrote that people are not gentile creatures or good at heart, rather they unconsciously want to kill and be cruel and brutal. Instinctually, man is a wolf to man. Indeed, Freud believed humans want war in order to both work off the intolerable burden of civilization and avoid boredom. Charles Van Doren in his *A History of Knowledge* echoed Freud's with his view that human nature is fundamentally selfish and not altruistic.

Sixteenth century French nobleman Francois de La Rochefoucauld wrote *The Maxims*, in which he explained how men all deceive. He wrote that (v) men would not get on for long in society if they did not fool one another. Indeed, it has been said that people would have no friends if they knew others' thoughts. He believed everyone wears a mask and the world is a congregation of masks where (v) on all occasions men assume the look and appearance they want to be known for.

Some of the emotions men cover with a mask include envy and pride. For La Rochefoucauld, they do so because (v) envy is so sneaking and shameful that they never dare confess it. Those who scorn others wealth, for example, use a mask as a (p) strategic way of avoiding the humiliations of poverty and a roundabout way to gain the esteem they cannot obtain through wealth. Like envy for La Rochefoucauld, all humans are all prideful—pride (p) exists in all men. Pride, for example, (v) plays a greater part than kindness in one's remonstrating with those who make mistakes; man points out their faults less to correct them than to indicate they are not his, which is his way of deflecting blame of his faults and inflating his ego. If the band of perception consisted of vice at one end and virtue at the other, La Rochefoucauld would counterintuitively say that (p) faults are more attractive than virtues. Some people's faults are becoming and other's virtues drawbacks; the solution is to (p) skillfully mount one's faults and make them shine brighter than virtue.

Juvenal was a first-century CE Roman who wrote *On the Vanity of Human Wishes*, in which he claimed that the most fundamental human characteristic is desire. For him, (p) humans are all foolishly led by blind desire, which only brings them unhappiness. They, for example, (v) wish for power that only brings others hatred because people hate people with power. Everyone also wishes for good looks, which only brings dissoluteness and problems like envy. People also wish for a long life, which desire only brings unhappiness when they must endure the miseries of old age. With old age, (p) faces become unshapely, foul and disgusting; they get wrinkles, doddering voices and limbs, bald heads and runny noses like children; they become impotent, sick and unable to make love; they get fever and diseases forming in a column marching and countermarching; minds weaken, unable to remember their children and wives; brothers, sisters and friends all die. This may be melancholic, but it is a realistic assessment of old age. Many euphemistically call old age the golden years when, in truth, in order to be happy, it is more important to suspend such illusion and confront what it really is—decay and eventual death. Happiness comes from acknowledging this reality and thus deciding to accept the process and do what one can, while one can, now.

Machiavelli, in his famous book *The Prince*, asserted that all men are essentially evil, and his message was how to deal with it. He advocated deception, vice and rashness, to name a few ways. He wrote that (v) since men are wicked and do not keep their promises, one likewise does not have to keep his to them, so he must become skillful at pretending and dissembling. For him people are (p) so simple and so subject to present needs that he who deceives will always find those who will let themselves be deceived. For Machiavelli, virtue is a mistake because (v) he who is good must come to ruin among so many who are not good; therefore, one must learn how to be not good when it is required. Because it is the crowd that determines one's reputation, one must, for example, act only in such a way to appear generous rather than stingy. Men should appear virtuous but do what they have to in order to get what they want. To succeed in life, one also should be rash and bold because fortune favors the brave and not those who (v) proceed slowly, consistently and carefully. Thus, it is better to be rash than cautious because (v) fortune is a woman, and if one wishes to keep her down, one must beat her and pound her. It is evident that she allows herself to be overcome by men who treat her in that way rather than by those who proceed coldly.

Jonathan Swift's *Gulliver's Travels* satirized the idea of human goodness. In it, he derides human's excess passion in the form of lust, envy, avarice, greed and rage. Humans arrogantly assert that they can control their passions with reason, but for Swift, they are so driven by their emotions and desires that reason has little chance of mitigating them. He also finds humans hypocrites who are always willing to compromise their ideals for practicality and social necessity. They profess moral ideals but in the end pursue passions that make human society morally intolerable. Hypocrisy may be the homage that vice pays virtue, as Francois de La Rochefoucauld famously said, but for Swift, humans are animals incapable of understanding the hypocrisy. In his mythical land, Yahoo humans and Houyhnhnm horses trade places. The disgusting Yahoos represent the degraded human form and embody characteristics of humans beings deprived of all rational capacity. They act on the basis of pure and ugly passion and universally practice lying. Females (v) of the species practice lewdness, coquetry, censure and scandal. Yahoos are creatures that are uncivilized and use reason only to (p) improve and multiply vices. For Swift, they are detestable and embody vice. The Houyhnhnms, on the other hand represent what humans should be—rational and civilized. They lead orderly lives without disagreement or excitement. They control their passions with reason, never lie, are not greedy, and do not rage. They are not hypocrites, and they understand La Rochefoucauld's maxim and embody virtue.

Famous twentieth century newspaper pundit H. L. Mencken scathingly derided humanity both individually and collectively. He believed that (p) the masses are animals and beyond salvation. Individually, he wrote that (v) and (p) failures are all incompetents—that God had marked them for the ditch, only the strongest survive, and inequality is natural. He believed that life was a struggle for survival to which some men are ill suited by accident of birth. For him, the best way to make men better is not to throttle ambition and competition but to let generation after generation fight it out, with the unfit perishing and the fit surviving. Collectively, he was a Nietzschean deriding both Christianity and democracy, both of which attenuate the strong. Indeed, all government for Mencken is in essence a conspiracy against the superior man; its one permanent object was to oppress him and cripple him. Democracy in particular (p) arises from the envy felt by the inferior man for his superiors; the peasant craves security, the gentlemen fights for liberty, and since there are more peasants than gentleman, the inevitable result of universal suffrage is to make the peasant persecute the gentlemen, which impedes human progress. Democracy (p) is a governmental system based on the organized hatreds of the lower orders, and politicians are those who pander to the prejudices of the peasants, which is something gentlemen are too principled to do. For Mencken, placing power in the unlettered and envious majority threatens two of man's greatest intellectual possessions: personal freedom and the limitation of government.

At the optimistic end of the spectrum of perception are Gandhi and Rousseau, and at the pessimistic end are Freud, La Rochefoucauld, Juvenal, Machiavelli, Swift and Mencken. Is human nature essentially altruistic or selfish? Certainly, some are avaricious while at the same time other-regarding. Altruism may be a good ideal, but in reality it can only lead to disappointment, disillusionment and unhappiness because as Machiavelli wrote, he who is good must come to ruin because so many are not good. Alternatively, the pessimists only see the worst in human nature, which mitigates disappointment but denies hope. Any happiness that may be derived from the improvement of humanity is dashed on the rocks of negative pessimism, which also leads to disappointment, disillusionment and unhappiness.

It would seem both optimists and pessimists are unhappy because they see reality through biased lenses. The real question is not who is right but rather who is happy. Both extremes contain some truth, some half-truths, some unacknowledged truths and some falsity. In reality, humans are some of these things but not all of them. The astute student of felicity would observe that neither is a comprehensive picture of human nature and conclude that the gaps ought to be filled with realistic assessments. Philosophy offers a solution, which is to seek truth unencumbered by dogma, biases or historic thinkers. It just so happens that one of the imperatives of truth seeking is to remain realistic. So to be happy, philosophy tells men to put the spectrum of perception in perspective, be realistic and seek a mean. This enables them to better navigate the band of perception adroitly to achieve happiness. With this, man comes to understand how the extremes are unreal.

So what are some of the solutions that help one remain realistic and thus happy? Adopting the ancient Greek maxim elucidated by Plato, "know thyself" is one. If one knows his strengths and weaknesses, kind of mind and proclivities, he develops realistic opinions of himself, which in turn enables him to better navigate the tremendous amount of information received every day. From this perspective, one is better able to discern patterns in life and predictable ways of the world that help forge a realistic perception of reality. Indeed, Thomas Hobbes believed that one learns more by studying himself than others. Without knowing himself, an individual gets whipsawed from public opinion to orators' latest proclamation to an unsure state with no foundation on how to think and live. Reality becomes an illusion in which he is continually reacting to rather than organizing and acting on.

Seneca believed that denial and self-deception may disguise sources of happiness, so it would only seem logical that they would also disguise sources of unhappiness. Holding harmful and self-defeating beliefs that one is not aware of because he does not know him obfuscates the band of perception and blinds him to the true sources of happiness as well as the causes of unhappiness. Seneca believed that philosophy, with its pursuit of truth, is the ideal vehicle to disabuse one of harmful and self-defeating beliefs that cause unhappiness. The flip side then is that philosophy, which helps one know oneself and navigate reality, also helps one appreciate the sources of happiness. If a person is prideful and arrogant and does not know it, he will live in an unrealistic, self-imposed fog, forever wondering why he has no true friends that just might have brought him happiness.

Seventeenth century French dramatist philosopher Molière's play *The Misanthrope* contrasted two characters, Alceste, who did not know himself, and Acaste, who did. Alceste is prideful, arrogant, extremist, conceited, petty and condescending. He loves to hear his own opinions in his own voice and is contemptuous of other opinions. He moralizes and is intolerant of others' views. For Molière, these qualities make Alceste a misanthrope and hater of human nature. Pride, arrogance and extremism engender hatred of humans because they make perceptions unrealistic. Acaste is different because he knows himself and thus has a more realistic outlook on life. He escapes misanthropy by being true to himself and freely admitting that he flatters himself and practices self-deception. Molière endowed him with the attributes of humility, honesty, understanding and moderation that are the tools for realistic thinking and the antidote to misanthropy. Acaste is happy because he knows himself and thus has a realistic outlook on life. Certainly all people have vices, but some conceal them from themselves and then accuse others of the same vices. Unrealistic people like these only see the weaknesses of others because their lens to reality is bent. Seneca states in his *Letters from a Stoic* that this kind of ignorance is a kind of running away from oneself, which will never bring happiness because a person is only running away in his own company.

Realistic thinking entails abandoning self-serving beliefs. Seneca wrote that self-serving beliefs are not the route to happiness because they disguise the sources of happiness (and, this author would add, the sources of unhappiness). For him, philosophy is unique in its pursuit of truth because it disabuses harmful, self-defeating, wrongful and unrealistic beliefs. At one end of this spectrum is Jean-Jacques Rousseau, who, according to Ben-Ami Scharfstein in his book *The*

Philosophers was forever unsuccessfully trying to recreate his happy childhood through philosophy in order to be happy, and at the other is Molière's character Philinte, who believed people should be honest with themselves, avoid self-deception and expose their vices. Doing so enables them to exercise the natural right to virtue and achieve happiness.

Machiavelli described three kinds of minds. From worst to best the first kind is one that cannot learn, the second can learn only from experience and the third learns unassisted. For this author, the first is ignorant, the second is unrealistic and the third is imbued with realistic thinking. To achieve happiness, philosophy tells one to cultivate the third kind of mind. It is a mind that tells one to stoically consider the worst that can happen and that successes and failures ultimately do not matter, which are realistic perspectives that lessen worry and result in happiness.

Thinking realistically also causes one to limit desires and live simply, which promotes happiness. Many think, for example, that they must have a certain level of material wealth to be happy. With this perspective, the significance of money becomes magnified and other sources of happiness diminished. The pursuit of wealth too often becomes an unrealistic, imaginary need that is never satisfied. A person's spectrum of reality again becomes skewed, and he forgets that little is truly needed to be happy. Indeed, Diogenes once said that a man's happiness is measured by what he does not want. It seems much of human nature pursues unquenchable desires, which are a great source of unhappiness. Samuel Johnson wrote that people cannot fill a cup at the same time from the source and mouth of the Nile, which means one person cannot have it all. The solution then is to be realistic, limit desire, live simply and be happy with what one has.

Passion is often the source of unrealistic thinking for a variety of reasons. It can bring single-minded obsession, enhance unquenchable desires and cause unrealistic beliefs. Reason controlling passion mitigates these tendencies and causes one to think more realistically. Unreasoning Swiftian Yahoos are rarely happy—to be happy do not be one. Reason also teaches good principles, which are another source of realistic thinking. In the case of honesty, for example, the first principle is to be honest with oneself. Self-honest thinking belies Molière's view that individuals have vices that they conceal from themselves yet accuse others of—he wrote that people may have one hundred good qualities, but people only notice their weaknesses. The second principle is to be honest with others. Do not be a Swiftian hypocrite. Rather, remain square with the world and avoid the tangled webs that are woven when one deceives. The third principle for realism is to be consistent. Consistency tells one to tell the truth even when it is not in one's interest because it builds trust, integrity, loyalty and friendship. Untrustworthy, inconsistent people are not trusted, welcome or happy.

Perhaps it was Juvenal who offered the best advice on how to deal with the spectrum of perceptions of reality. He believed that man should accept fate because in the end he will get the things most suitable for him. One should wish for health in both body and mind, to be unafraid of death, to bear up under trouble, to be free from hate and to have the ability to work. He believed above all to have virtue because it is the only way to have a happy life. He wrote (v): "I show you what you can give to yourself; only through virtue lies the certain road to a life that is blessed and tranquil." To be happy, take Juvenal's advice and think realistically, like Thrift.

CHAPTER FOUR

LIVE LIFE
Do not be unauthentic or anonymous

Philosophy advises to live life to be happy. It is a mistake to live a life others think one should live or, more importantly, one that a person mistakenly thinks he or she should live. Authentic was a young man in college taking science courses in order to become a doctor. He studied hard but was supremely unhappy because physics, chemistry and biology did not interest him. His liberal arts college required that the take courses in other disciplines, so one semester he took a class in philosophy, and it changed his life. He was struck by its pursuit of truth and relentless investigation into human nature. Authentic pondered Socrates's admonition to know thyself and his self emerged. What he found was that he hated science and loved philosophy, so he changed course in life and became a philosopher and not a doctor (supported by a career in commercial real estate). He learned to live his life and not another's.

People do not live their lives when they succumb to the empty gods of convention or unvetted beliefs acquired in childhood. Society often says that money, power and social prestige are gods to be worshiped and pursued, and parents tell their children they must be doctors. As people age, many come to realize that the vetted beliefs are empty treadmills, and those things parents and society told them they must be are self-imagined, life-draining beliefs. To be happy, people need to know themselves because doing so will clarify conventions and allow them to understand what they want rather than what someone told them they want. Jettison empty gods and live life.

Two philosophers, Søren Kierkegaard and Martin Heidegger, shed considerable light on why many do not live their lives. Kierkegaard was a nineteenth century Danish religious philosopher regarded as the founder of existentialism. He wrote *Either/Or*. Ernest Becker, in his book *The Denial of Death*, interpreted Kierkegaard's philosophy of man, and in particular his description of the inauthentic man from a psychological perspective. For Kierkegaard, to avoid the fear of death and other life challenges, humans create strategies. There are essentially five; the first three cause the unauthentic man, and the last two bring the authentic one.

The first is to block off perceptions of reality that result in character defenses and armor, and ultimately the inauthentic man. These men avoid developing their own uniqueness and live with automatic styles and uncritical living. They do not belong to themselves, they are not their own person, they do not see reality on its terms, they are one dimensional and they are totally immersed in fictional games being played out in society. They are unable to transcend their social conditioning. They do not know what it means to think for themselves and therefore shrink back from audacity and exposure. They are confined to culture and a slave to it and are lulled by the daily routines of society and content with its satisfactions. They are tranquilized into the trivial.

The second kind of inauthentic man comes from having too much possibility, and the result is a madhouse. In this response, man succumbs and is beaten by the world and the existential truth of his situation. He is bogged down by daily duties and the demand of others like family, children and friends, which narrows his horizon. He cannot see alternatives, cannot imagine any choices or alternate ways of life and cannot release himself from his network of obligations. He is defrauded by others, forgets himself and is a depressed coward because he will not stand alone on his own center and cannot draw from within himself the necessary strength to face up to live. So he embeds himself in others. He chooses slavery because it is safe and meaningful but then loses the meaning of "I," out of which he fears to move. He has died to live but must remain physically in this world.

The third is the normal neurosis. Most people avoid the extremes and follow a middle course, which Kierkegaard called Philistinism. Breakdown occurs because there is either too much or too little possibility. These men figure out how to live safely within the probabilities of a given set of social rules. They tranquilize themselves with the trivial. Kierkegaard's solutions to be an authentic man who lives his life will be discussed later in this chapter.

Martin Heidegger was a twentieth century philosopher who wrote *Being and Time*. He made famous the "anonymous one," who shares many traits with Kierkegaard's inauthentic man. The anonymous one is a depersonalized man who moves in the realm of the customs, habits and conventions of everyday living. He succumbs to the everydayness of existence. He takes on mechanical habits and the established customs and accepted conventions of everyday life. He is characterized by averageness. He lives by a golden mean in which social behavior is based on the social laws of average. He opens himself to the public and conforms to its demands and opinions. He accepts its standards and thus retreats from personal commitment and responsible decisions. He becomes leveled and reduced, thinking what the public thinks, feeling what the public feels and doing what the public does. His condition Heidegger calls fallenness, which represents the present and man's universal tendency to lose himself in his present preoccupations and concerns. He alienates himself from his unique and personal future possibilities. He engages in gossip, which is simply the accepted everyday conventional and shallow interpretation of the public repeated. Gossip is only concerned with reiteration of clichés that reflect the present and restricted world horizons of the anonymous one. The anonymous one is reduced because he sacrificed to the present.

Kierkegaard's unauthentic men and Heidegger's anonymous one are unhappy individuals who do not live life. Next will be a discussion of the solutions to their ways of thinking and how to live one's own life.

The first thing a man must do is ignore what others think of him. There will always be those who will not like a person, perhaps even hate him. People are a rainbow of characteristics, each with their own biases, prejudices and proclivities. Who knows where their judgments come from—some come from reason and others from emotional caprice. Collectively, it often gets worse when emotion becomes fashion, political correctness and sometimes law. To live life trying to satisfy this roller coaster of human opinion will only make an individual what he is not. One must listen to his inner voice, mine his feelings, use his intellect and discern what is right for him rather than listen to what others think.

It is particularly important to understand the nature of gossip in order to completely ignore it. Everyone is familiar with the game where the first in a circle of people tells a story that is whispered from person to person until the last one. The last rendition of the story is never true to the original because everyone in the circle reinterpreted it, hindered by ability, desire and sometimes prevarications. Gossip is like this. Gossip is rumor, misinformation and often-malicious wrongful projections. An individual is not what gossip makes him, so ignore it.

Identifying with gossip invites the questions: Who are we? Is each individual truly something unique, individual and special, or is each a composite of what others think he is? In truth, people have two identities that they cannot escape; the one the individual thinks he is, and the one others think he is. Marcel Proust, for example, wrote that (p) none could be said to constitute a material whole because one's social personality is a creation of the thoughts of other people. Like Proust, Heidegger's anonymous one also is a composite individual created by society who does not exist. So, which is the real individual?

Much of living and maturing is the process of getting back to the true inner self and living life. Some mature and achieve happiness and others do not and live conventional lives of duplicity. The truth is there is a real individual, like Authentic, who must be learned, as Socrates admonished. With this he got to know himself; he became more comfortable, confident in his skin and happy. Ignore gossip; it only detracts from one's true self and happiness.

It is also a good idea to not take society and its conventions too seriously. One of people's deepest fears is to be an outcast from the herd—to not be accepted. People fear rejection, and society demands conformity. Society uses this fear to control people for some good reasons. It is a powerful force, but when people assimilate its control too much, they become fearful, timid and guilt-ridden. It brings a kind of irrational fear that causes remorse, strips individuality and uniqueness and brings unhappiness. Assimilating societal conventions and accepting collective disapprobation suppresses living life. If one is virtuous, he has no fear of society's disapproval because he is living an ethical life; if one is viceful, he should fear because he has no defense.

Early American thinker Ralph Waldo Emerson wrote that one way to escape convention is to be self-reliant. He wrote that society everywhere is in conspiracy against the manhood of every one of its members where the virtue in most requests is conformity. He believed that (p) centuries have conspired against the sanity and authority of the soul and that the coercive, collective group thinks it knows what a man's duty is better than he does. He believed collective society draws out the sinew and heart of man, and men become timorous, desponding whimperers afraid of fortune, afraid of death, and afraid of each other.

Emerson's solution was to become self-reliant. He wrote that (p) it is easy in the world to live after the world's opinion, but the great man is he who in the midst of the crowd keeps with perfect sweetness the independence of solitude. Being independent and self-reliant helps men live their own lives, resist the enervating and numbing norms of society, avoid others' efforts to control them and achieve happiness. Self-reliance is freedom.

Ancient Stoic Roman Emperor Marcus Aurelius in *Meditations* similarly advised to cultivate a self-directing mind. For Aurelius, people should use rationality in order to make proper decisions when under the influence of the primal contest between pain and pleasure. Humans want pleasure, but pleasure does not always bring happiness, so the directed mind must recognize the right thing to do and cultivate the right judgments of impressions—and, collaterally, the right course of action. For Aurelius, (v) the directing mind is that which wakes itself, adapts itself, makes itself whatever nature it wishes, and makes all that happens to it appear in the way it wants. Developing a directing mind helps people see through society's stifling artificial conventions, understand the pull of pleasure, live their own lives and achieve happiness.

Living life avoids the inauthentic and anonymous ones and brings freedom and potential. Aurelius' self-directed mind enables people to avoid self-thought oppressive obligations, allows them to imagine alternatives and gives them courage to change their lives in order to live them. The responsible, overworked, burning-out executive Authentic's directing mind kicks in at some point in his career and tells him he must change his life to be happy. It tells him he must measure his obligations and imagine alternatives like a summer in Greece with his family, and it tells him to summon the courage to do it. If he does it, he has engaged his Aurelian directing mind and will live his life and not others'.

With this new freedom of thought, Authentic will also come closer to his unique human potential. He will because he set himself free to mine his talents and their potential rather than continuing to live in conformity with others. This new freedom also gave him the courage to imagine success and to reach for it. To borrow from Alfred Lord Tennyson, he decided that it is better to try and fail than to never have tried at all. Authentic is living life to his potential—living life brings potential.

French philosopher Albert Camus wrote that (v) what a man accepts with the most difficulty is to be judged, to which Virginia Woolf added, (p) the eyes of others are prisons and their thoughts, cages. Others judge constantly, which can be a great source of angst and deterrent to living life. Seneca believed that one reason for this was the fear of non-acceptance. He wrote that (p) the need to be accepted causes men to maintain a careful pose because they are tormented by the thought of being caught out of character and constantly feel as if they are being assayed every time they are looked at. He believed that men who fear others would not like who they really are, so they never reveal their natural selves. The consequence is that they live like (v) people in a fiction, polished up for exhibition. Because of this, Seneca believed that men live their lives under a mask, which La Rochefoucauld in *The Maxims* universalized: with a world is a congregation of masks.

Camus, Woolf, Seneca, La Rochefoucauld (and Shakespeare) are right. In many ways, life is a play in which all men wear masks because they fear judgment. But living one's own life requires a different perspective that understands much of life is a masquerade. It is perspective that tells one to be civil but also brave and free; it tells one who he is. It tells man to live life being honest with himself because, as Seneca wrote, (v) it is better to be scorned for simplicity than tormented by permanent hypocrisy. Do not fear others' judgments and be free.

Earlier, three of Kierkegaard's five inauthentic kinds were described who did not live their lives. In this author's view, his final two do resist convention in order to become authentic. Even with their faults, they are paradigmatic characters who endeavor to live their lives to be happy. His fourth type has contempt for immediacy, tries to cultivate his interiority, bases his pride on something deeper and creates a distance between himself and the average man. Kierkegaard calls this man the introvert. He is more concerned with individuality and uniqueness. He enjoys solitude and withdraws periodically to reflect and nurse ideas on what might be. He asks what his true authentic vocation is. He holds himself somewhat apart from the world but not completely. He is a university man, husband and father, competent in civil matters and seldom goes to church. He prides himself on vaguely felt superiority.

The fifth and final character type is the one who asserts himself. He tries to be God, is self-created and is master of his fate. He plunges into life with a restless spirit, which often manifests itself in wonton sensuality and perhaps debauchery. He sometimes becomes demonic in his revolt against existence.

From Kierkegaard, it seems then to become authentic and live life entails contempt for convention, introspection, looking for truth, eschewing conformity, liking oneself for who one is, being somewhat detached, being educated and not religious, having self-esteem, asserting oneself, being self-directed, being industrious and ambitious and generally revolting against existence. This is a formula for an authentic man who resists daily dying in life but rather lives his life.

In order to achieve authenticity, it would seem then that the Stoic advise to use one's mental powers to escape other-control and living in the opinions of the world. For them, one function of philosophy is to separate socially taught opinions from true beliefs in order to rid oneself of false beliefs that obscure the good. Doing so enables an individual to live his own life and achieve happiness.

Living life is important because each person only gets one life to live. Happiness resides in authentic living and not in the shadows of others' opinions. It also means to live life to the fullest while one can. The goal of life is not the grave. Seize the day because it will be over soon. It is, as Sophocles wrote, a mistake to wait to the evening to see how splendid the day has been.

CHAPTER FIVE

NEGATIVE JUDGMENTS
The world is as one makes it, so fashion good judgments and make it a place that brings joy

Counterproductive judgments can cause unhappiness. When an individual was young, someone told him that his nose is too big, so for the rest of his life, he labors under the wrongful judgment that his nose is too big. He poses in prescribed ways that lessen the prominence of his nose, and anyone that looks at his nose for too long sends him into a fright. The truth is that his nose is an average nose, but his judgment of it is interfering with his ability to be happy.

The language is antiquated, but the ancient Stoics emphasized the need to use the proper judgment of impressions in order to live a good life. Impressions are the data or sensations that the brain constantly receives, and it is judgments of this data, or the concepts one has developed, that evaluate this data and determine reactions to them. The data are just data—they could be benign—but if judgment of them is negative, one will feel the consequences. For the Stoics, it is important to develop the right attitudes and beliefs or judgments about experience.

The implication of this is the liberating thought that things are as one makes them. How an individual views the world, what attitudes and beliefs he adopts about events, how he feels about circumstances, or what makes him happy or unhappy depends on how he judges perceptions. Indeed, the stoic Seneca wrote that everything hangs on one's thinking, which timeless advice could be described today by a psychologist with the observation that the world is as one makes it.

Seneca also wrote that what matters is state of mind, attitudes and how one can heal his mind, and fellow stoic Marcus Aurelius believed people can strip away many unnecessary troubles that lie wholly in their own judgment because things themselves are inert; it is only people who procreate judgments about them. Humans have no control over fortune and death, but they do over how they judge them. Ultimately, humans are in control because they can decide how they think about things.

This is profound advice when it comes to being happy. One could be sick, poor, angry, anxious, fearful, jealous or physically tortured, but ultimately it is what he thinks about these things that determines whether he is happy or sad. Certainly, some things, like the pain experienced in dying are difficult to master, but this does not defeat the Stoic's proposition that how one feels about them depends entirely on what one thinks about them.

It is only human to hold mistaken judgments. Whether one's nose is too big, his father was evil or there is no meaning to life, these things will impact how one feels. People unwittingly acquire learned but unevaluated judgments about many things that silently superintend their lives. Søren Kierkegaard in *Either/Or* wrote extensively on whether to live an ethical or aesthetic life, which in many ways is a false dichotomy. It may well be that it is not a matter of being either/or but rather evolving from one to the other, which is a process often called maturing. Kierkegaard lived a troubled life struggling with mistaken views.

The sources of mistaken judgments are found everywhere. Someone admired expresses an opinion, which is readily adopted; a politician makes a good speech, which influences what a person thinks; secular societal norms convince people of one thing, and religious beliefs another. Always judgments are influenced by passions and appetites topped by fear of death. Ernest Becker in *The Denial of Death* wrote that it is the fear of death that drives much of one's life, which includes judgments; one can fear it and live a life of fear or accept it, move on and live life fully while he can. The impressions one gets from these sources are themselves just inert impressions—what matters is how he judges them.

It is particularly difficult to develop sustained healthy beliefs in late democratic political environments like America. In America today, political views and norms are in flux due to the caprice of the majority, so the tyrants of wealth, power, prestige and sensual pleasure have become the filters people use to determine their level of happiness. These are poor bases for productive judgments because they pit people against the winds of fortune, which can blow any way.

Seneca wrote that the ability to remain indifferent to fortune, or matters beyond control is a requisite for felicity. Seneca knew what he was writing about because he lived under tyrants like Nero and Caligula that could have him executed on a whim—he lived under Damocles's sword. It was only by remaining indifferent to this real possibility that he was able to control his fear of death and thus live a relatively happy life. Likewise, Epictetus, who also lived under fearful tyrants, jettisoned his fear of death and adopted the better judgment that the tyrant is only the master of his carcass. It does not matter whether the source of angst is a real tyrant or the tyrant of fortune; the solution for both is to adopt good judgments.

Many self-defeating beliefs derive from childhood. When one was young and malleable, he unwittingly soaked up others' wrongful beliefs, innocently believing they were the right ones to adopt. People are the products of many pejorative covert judgments that were implanted in them, which judgments continually and silently superintend their lives. Many live under a kind of tyranny of early unvetted counterproductive beliefs. Some can be quite damaging, like an off-handed suggestion by someone once that one is not worthy that leads to a lifetime of feeling worthless. To have no sense of self worth is a damnable judgment the can only lead to a life of unhappiness. The solution is to liberate oneself from the pernicious silent judgments one acquired in his youth.

Much unhappiness derives from acceptance of others' negative opinions. An acquaintance comments offhand that a man has few friends and voila! He comes to believe he is unworthy of friendship. Eleanor Roosevelt once said that no one can make one feel inferior without his consent. Do not let others' wrongful judgments stand—do not give consent. Such advice, however, is double edged; a teacher judges that a student has not learned his lesson and codifies it with a grade, but he knows he learned the material, rejects the teacher's judgment and remains satisfied with himself. He remains happy but may not get into graduate school due to the low grade. In spite of this, it is better for one to honestly judge others' judgments of him than worry about the consequences of his judgment of them.

Many self-defeating judgments derive from trying to make reality adjust to oneself rather than adjusting to reality. Everyone has unmet aspirations. Someone may believe he should be rich and famous but is not, so the judgment makes him unhappy. One must ask himself if his judgments are realistic and worthy. He may decide that he does not have the ambition to be rich or the talent to be famous, so he moderates his conception of himself. Being satisfied with a moderate income and lots of friends may well be a better judgment. Be realistic and adjust to reality.

Consider for demonstration the great Stoic philosopher Epictetus's comparison of two individuals, one without the right judgments and another with. He wrote that the first takes pains to gain office and riches, while the other endeavors to gain right judgments and the proper use of impressions. He wrote that one gets up in the morning and looks for some powerful person to flatter, someone to address pleasing words, someone to send a present to, and to gratify one man by reviling another, while the other gets up in the morning and asks himself how he can be free from passion and enjoy tranquility and what he is? The former is forever appeasing another, while the latter is satisfying himself by developing values that ultimately bring him happiness.

The great German Idealist philosopher Immanuel Kant famously wrote that concepts without precepts are empty, and precepts without concepts are blind. Analogously, to have a clear understanding of what brings happiness requires proper concepts, or judgments, that evaluate the precepts, or sense data people encounter daily. This is important because it is concepts or beliefs that regulate what people think. For example, if one is chronically angry, the odds are that he will not be happy. With the proper judgment of the anger emotion, he is able to evaluate it and its consequences. Seneca, for example, wrote that anger is an extremely destructive emotion that only causes the vessel harm. He believed that anger is an unnecessary emotion. Like Seneca, with such a judgment of anger, people gain control of themselves and purge a destructive source of unhappiness.

In a broader perspective, with such proper judgments, people can manage their emotions in such a way to bring felicity.

The moral of this chapter is to carefully evaluate judgments of impressions. Look at them from all angles, turn them over like a globe and evaluate them from all sides. See them in the light of day; truly compare one nose to other noses and ask whether others who are rich and famous are really happy. Then ignore the injurious judgments and enhance the salubrious ones. Get the right judgments and jettison the rest.

Epictetus wrote that people should not seek happiness outside themselves, which means they must look inward for happiness using the right judgments. The world is as people make it, so fashion good judgments and make it a place that brings joy.

Chapter Six

FORTUNE
*Have proper judgments of externals
and do not invest in the wheel of fortune*

Chance is a shallow fellow. He does not think deeply about things, is easily swayed by others' opinions and has little self-confidence. He firmly believes that if he could only acquire wealth, get some prestigious governmental position or make love to more women, he would be eternally happy. In reality, he is a lucky guy with a good college education, a good job, a home and health, but he is never satisfied with what he has and perpetually dissatisfied with what he does not have. Chance is unhappy. He is so because he does not think things through. He does not understand that when he invests his happiness in externals, fortune takes over, which makes the outcomes always uncertain. Chance cast his happiness to the fate of the capricious winds of fortune. He is a man that does not understand that happiness comes from within and not from without.

Fortune is destiny, fate or kismet, and it necessarily entails luck and chance. Those who invest their happiness in her fickle grasp live under a gleaming Damocles sword hanging by a horsehair forever threatening to fall and sever their necks. They are the unlucky ones Herodotus referred to when he wrote that no man can be called happy until he is dead—only lucky. Do not invest happiness in that which is subject to fortune.

Two philosophers that have advocated this view are Seneca and Boethius. Seneca described the winds of fortune metaphorically embodied in externals and advised the use of good judgments as a shield, and, as discussed in chapter one, Boethius invoked his famous wheel of fortune and the importance of not riding her.

In a previous book, *Stoicism, Enkrasia and Happiness*, one of the key Stoic doctrines, which is that peace and contentment do not come when high value is placed on externals, is described. Stoic Epictetus wrote, for example that (v) the difficulties men face arise with externals, and Seneca that (p) peace and contentment do not come when high value is set on externals—what fortune has made is not one's own. Externals are those things in the world that are beyond human control—they are those things that can be taken. The Stoics like Seneca often mention wealth, position, power, fame, and sensual pleasure—the same list as Boethius's—as externals. Seneca wrote that they should never be trusted because they are subject to fortune and nobody has ever been (v) crushed by adverse Fortune who has not first been beguiled by her smile. This gets a little dicey, however, because health and children under this definition are externals that can be taken, so following the Stoic's advice, should one not invest in them? Exploring this criticism is beyond the scope of this book other than to say some Stoics do indeed advise not investing happiness in health and children—be prepared for them to vanish at any time.

The point is to be wary of externals governed by fortune because people have no control over whether they will endure or not. If one invests his happiness in, for example, wealth and prestige, he has consigned his happiness to fickle fate that may change, thus taking his happiness. What fortune gives, it also takes away, and with it happiness, which can scatter like a puff of smoke in a strong winter breeze.

Why do people invest their happiness in that which can bring unhappiness? For some, it is a wager in which they hope to win happiness, and for others it is a matter of ignorance—they just do not know. In both cases, it is desire that drives some into Fortune's arms; wealth, prestige and power are powerful draws to those who seek happiness. Desire and its ramifications are discussed at length elsewhere in this book, so for now it can just be said that desire is the crux of human bitterness. It is better to cultivate virtue than desire to be happy.

The Stoics had other solutions for those who desire externals. The first is straightforward—do not do it. Seneca wrote (v) that what fortune has made yours is not yours, and how pleasant it is to ask for nothing and be independent of fortune. Elsewhere he wrote that (v) once you start looking outside yourself for any part of yourself you are on the road to being dominated by fortune which means you have lost control of your happiness. For Seneca, the wise man is content with what is his. In short, one must not wager happiness on externals, and one must be content with what he has.

The second Stoic suggestion is to avoid ignorance by cultivating good judgments. Good judgments tell one not to invest his happiness in capriciously fortune driven externals. Having the right judgments entails having beliefs, attitudes, and values that enhance happiness. Both stoics Marcus Aurelius and Epictetus said if one maintains the belief, for example, that what others have should be his, he has set himself up for unhappiness, because he will forever be desiring what he cannot achieve rather than be satisfied with what he has.

Perhaps the most famous scholastic philosopher thinker in history on the nature of fortune was previously mentioned Boethius. He was a fourth and fifth century ACE Roman scholar, Christian philosopher and statesman. In his *Consolation of Philosophy*, philosophy is personified as a woman who is consoling the prisoner Boethius who is awaiting execution. Her overriding objective is to explain the true sources of happiness in order to console Boethius and edify humankind. Because Boethius was a philosopher his advice is a mix of philosophy and religion. He for example wanted to justify Christian faith, justify God and religion and show how the love of God can bring happiness, but he also wanted to show how philosophic wisdom and reason can also be sources of human happiness. However, his central theme is that happiness cannot reside in things governed by chance or fortune because ultimately happiness resides in men. Boethius is best known for his image of the wheel of fortune, which is the topic of this chapter.

It should be noted here that Boethius' criticisms of the things many desire are sometimes extreme. For sure, these objects of desire do often bring happiness, like a moderate amount of wealth or a degree of recognition. Consequently, it is better to view these objects of desire with an Aristotelian measure of moderation. Nevertheless, Boethius' criticisms are instructive because they describe the consequences of restrained desire such as unhappiness.

The wheel of fortune is a metaphor for things humans desire that are fickle, capricious and subject to change. It involves chance, inconsistency and unreliability. It is like a defective Ferris wheel at a carnival that can fail at anytime. One gets on to have fun but ends up somewhere in the air unhappily in a place he did not expect. The wheel did not fulfill his desire for a thrill.

The significance of the wheel is that it does not always take people where they think it will. Indeed, Boethius argued that it too often takes people to places that make them unhappy. Boethius used sailing as a metaphor and commented that once a boat is committed to the winds of fortune, one discovers that he must sail whichever way they blow and not the way he plotted. He finds that he must acquiesce to her ways. Further, if the wind stops blowing, he lies in the doldrums no longer sailing. Similarly, when the wheel stops turning it is no longer the wheel of fortune and life becomes static. Further, the harder one pursues fortune, the faster the wheel spins to some capricious and often unexpected end. Any way one looks at it getting on the wheel of fortune for Boethius is a mistake.

Boethius wrote that the wheel of fortune seduces and lures one into unhappiness. Those, for example, who have chosen to pursue power have unwittingly chosen to have more enemies, those who have chosen wealth have unwittingly chosen to live in fear of losing it and those who have succumbed to sensual pleasure have unwittingly chosen to perpetually desire more sensation. For Boethius, individuals are more than fortune.

Boethius' central theme is that fortune's mutability does not bring happiness. Because there is no permanence in fortune, if one invests his happiness in it, he will be subject to its caprice, and so will his happiness. Happiness cannot consist of things governed by chance because one never knows where he will end up.

For Boethius the only "good" fortune is bad fortune. Bad fortune is better than good fortune because good fortune deceives with her smiles and then lets men down. Bad fortune, on the other hand, is always honest because by changing she shows her true fecklessness. Bad fortune enlightens by showing one how fragile happiness based on fortune is.

Earlier, the wheel of fortune was described as a metaphor for human's desire for fickle and capricious things. For Boethius, this desire when thwarted by the wheel is the crux of human bitterness. In the case of wealth, he wrote that (p) no man is rich who shakes and groans convinced that he needs more—one can never be happy always wanting something he does not have, and it is in the nature of fortune to feed this desire. He who has much wants much. The solution for Boethius is to measure one's wealth according to the needs of nature and not the excess of ostentation. True happiness is a condition of self-sufficiency with no wants. This is a common theme in philosophy. Plato admonished men to moderate desires, Aristotle to achieve a mean between extremes and Socrates wrote that a man's happiness is measured by what he does not want. True happiness does not come from desire but rather that which makes a person self-sufficient, strong, worthy of respect, glorious and joyful.

Indeed, happiness based on desire invested in the wheel of fortune only results in a condition one forever wants to change. In this state, one remains fraught with anxiety because his state is never right. He is forced into a corner, always desiring another condition—the grass is always greener on the other side of the fence. Humans have set themselves up in circumstances that will never bring contentment, rather only anxiety and unhappiness.

Earlier in this chapter, Seneca listed some externals that should be avoided. These included pleasure, wealth, position, power and fame. Boethius expanded on this and explained each of them in terms of the wheel of fortune and why they do not bring happiness.

Pleasure does not bring happiness because happiness is not pleasure. Happiness is a state and pleasure is a sensual feeling that comes and goes. For Boethius, the pursuit of pleasure is full of anxiety and its fulfillment full of remorse. In excess, it often causes illness and pain. Further, pleasure depends on the flesh, which makes one a slave to the worthless and brittle human body, which is a fragile entity that can be reduced to nothing with three days of burning fever.

Wealth does not bring happiness. Indeed many wealthy people are miserable. Boethius gives many reasons for this. First, money is transitory and short-lived. It is only valuable because it can be transferred to someone else, but when it is, it is no longer one's own. Second, when one has wealth, he needs other men to protect it, so wealth, which ostensibly makes one self-sufficient, actually makes one more dependent on outside help. Third, counter-intuitively, money never satisfies because riches create a want of their own. Nature is easily satisfied, whereas nothing satisfies greed. Fourth, once riches are won, they never leave one free again. When one has wealth, he will forever be plagued by the fear of losing it. Indeed, if one sets out on life with nothing, he will whistle his way by the highwayman, but if he has money, he will always live in fear of losing it to the highwayman. Finally, money is a man-created thing that can be alienated—unlike a beautiful countryside, which fortune can never take away.

Power and prestige do not bring happiness. For Boethius, the only way to exercise power is to superintend another's body and possessions, but one will never be successful because a free mind cannot be controlled. The philosopher Zeno once bit off his tongue and threw it at a tyrant to prove this point. Further, power brings nothing but danger to those who possess it. Kings do not live free from worry; they require bodyguards and are sometimes terrorized by their subjects. The more power the king acquires, the more enemies he makes. His power is ultimately dependent on the will of those who serve him, so in reality his power comes from others.

Kings often suffer that which they inflicted on others. They also have few friends and supporters because power brings sycophants who befriend them for what they can do for them and not their personal qualities. One in power cannot depend on "friends" brought by fortune. To make matters worse, the king's friends that power brings become his foes in times of misfortune and there is no greater evil able to inflict injury than a friend turned foe.

Prestige does not bring happiness because if one wants high office he will have to grovel before those that bestow it, and if he wants high honors, he will have to cheapen and humiliate himself by begging. Further, high office often brings wickedness to light, which too often infects the office holder. Indeed, high office does not in itself make a man worthy of respect but rather makes him more despised.

Perhaps most importantly, prestige and power bring the desire for more prestige and power. With this, one can never be a master of oneself. Instead, he becomes imprisoned in the chains of the lust that pursues prestige and power.

For Boethius, glory and fame also do not bring happiness because of their fickleness. Ultimately, glory and fame mean nothing, because everyone will someday be utterly forgotten. Many famous individuals in history are unknown. Fame is worthless because it is only the common gossip of people. It is just the product of what others say about a person that can change with the wind. Men were born naked and should not wear themselves out by setting their hearts on living according to laws of others in a world shared by others. Indeed, fame is often acquired through the wrong opinions of people that make some famous for not being themselves. Happiness cannot be measured on popularity based on people's feelings. Popularity's acquisition is fortuitous and its retention continuously uncertain.

For Boethius, these are the characteristics of the wheel of fortune. Chance deceives man because he thinks he will achieve happiness, but the results are too often hate, jealousy, desire, pain, avarice, fear and melancholy. After four years of imprisonment, Boethius was executed in 524 CE in Pavia.

Ultimately, fortune does not bring happiness. In the end happiness comes from within and not from something out there governed by chance. Human happiness is an attitude or choice that determines the kinds of lives each man live. Happiness comes from how one thinks. Indeed, nothing is miserable unless one thinks it so, which makes Seneca's judgments and Boethius's perspectives on the wheel of fortune critical for happiness.

The message from the philosophers is clear: do not invest in externals that are beyond control, use good judgments and avoid the wheel of fortune. With this advice, one lives a serene life within his walls and smiles at the raging storm.

Chapter Seven

HABIT
*Have Machiavelli's first kind of brain
and develop good habits*

Chapter three on Realism abridged Machiavelli's kinds of brains. In *The Prince*, he wrote (v) that there are three different kinds of brains, the first understands things unassisted, the second understands things when shown by others and the third understands neither alone nor with the explanations of others. The first and second kinds are excellent and the third is useless. Habit and Caprice are examples. Habit connects things, vividly sees consequences from causes and learns from just thinking deeply. Habit also learns from others and endeavors to avoid the mistakes they have made. From his mind he developed good habits, which included working hard, saving, being loyal to his spouse and caring for his children. Caprice is different. He lives only on feeling, emotion and passion. He does not connect causes with consequences because his intellect is blinded by his feelings. He is oblivious to others' mistakes thinking them only unlucky. From his brain he developed bad habits, which included indolence, improvidence, drug abuse, succumbing to sexual passion with an affair and eventually divorce, thus leaving his children fatherless. Habit has Machiavelli's first and second kind of mind and Caprice the useless third.

This chapter is about philosophers' thoughts on habits and how they affect happiness. This entails their observations on how to develop good habits and avoid bad ones.

Aristotle in *Nicomachean Ethics* emphasized the importance of habit for happiness. He believed good habits bring virtue, which brings happiness. For Aristotle, emotional dispositions range between extremes, which precipitates his famous doctrine of the mean: choosing between extremes determines wellbeing and happiness. His theory will be discussed at length elsewhere in this book, so for now it can just be said that he believed where one falls on this continuum is due in part to his upbringing and habituation. In ancient Greek terms, Aristotle was discussing the concept of arête, which means virtue or excellence, because he believed it lead to *eudemonia*, which in Greek means happiness or flourishing. So, through upbringing or habituation, people develop *arête* or virtue, which lands them in a mean between extremes. This brings *eudemonia* or wellbeing, which is a source of happiness.

People cannot change their parentage, but they can change their habits, which Aristotle argued enables them to attain virtue and ultimately character. He likened character to a skill that is acquired through practice such as learning a musical instrument. From this triage of habit, virtue and character, people come to learn and practice the four cardinal virtues of prudence, temperance, courage and justice. With these virtues acquired through habituation, Aristotle believed one achieves happiness.

Virtue brings happiness for Aristotle because when people possess character, they do the right thing at the right time in the right way. Bravery and the regulation of the appetites are examples. A person with character who does the right thing is brave (and not rash or cowardly) and moderates his appetites. The relationship between unrestrained appetites and happiness is discussed elsewhere in this book. It is habituation that brings virtue and character that brings the cardinal virtues of bravery in moderation and temperance that brings *eudemonia* or happiness. In the case of bravery, people do the right thing (being courageous and not rash or cowardly) at the right time (only when it is needed, as in war) in the right way (with intrepidness and fortitude). Habituation to this way of life is a source of happiness for Aristotle.

Achieving the right habits to be happy is easier said than done. Is Aristotle right? Can one voluntarily develop good habits to achieve virtue? Suppose an individual did not have a good upbringing and must begin from scratch; could he develop good habits? Indeed, he may have learned difficult-to-change bad habits when young that make him unhappy. This is especially important because Plato in his dialogue the *Meno* argued that virtue cannot be taught. It comes rather through recollection, wisdom and divine dispensation.

Aristotle himself admits that some people, despite intending to do the right thing cannot act according to their own choice. Some have great difficulty developing good habits. For example, someone may choose to refrain from eating chocolate cake but find themselves eating the cake contrary to their choice. Such a failure to act in a way that is consistent with one's own will is called *akrasia* in ancient Greek, which may be translated as weakness of will, incontinence or lack of self-mastery. But Aristotle argued that character is within the individual's control, or *enkrasia* in ancient Greek—the ability to do one's will. *Enkrasia* is the ability to not eat the chocolate cake because one decided not to eat it. So, the question is: Can one enkratically develop good habits in order to achieve happiness?

This author believes that it is possible with a toolbox that enables one to do so. This toolbox includes the innate human characteristics of intuition, imagination, persistence (or effort), the ability to learn, experience, skill, habit and reason. These are the characteristics that enable one to act enkratically. This is important because if one cannot voluntarily develop good habits—if people are doomed to repeat their bad habits—then according to Aristotle, they will never be happy. If one cannot stop drinking to excess, he may become an alcoholic; if one cannot stop his adulterous acts, he may divorce; if one will not work, he may be poor. These are all significant sources of unhappiness that occur because a person cannot do what he thinks he ought to do to be happy. So, one must examine these sources of enkratic action to develop good habits.

Parenthetically, it should be mentioned here that some are strangely happy being unhappy. They may relish their vices and prefer being sick, divorced or poor than enkratically developing habits that solve these sources of unhappiness. It seems that these folks are exchanging short-term pleasure for hard-to-achieve habits that bring long-term happiness, so this chapter is not for them.

Thinking intuitively helps achieve good habits because one mines the subconscious for reasons to do so. During life, people acquire a vast amount of unconscious knowledge that decisions by reason alone do not use. The results too often are poor decisions due to insufficient premises. Intuition is one tool that remedies this because one's knowledge base is unconsciously consulted, which brings to bear more information on the problem. Letting the question of why one should do something simmer for a while often enables him to intuitively gain a better reason to do it.

Imagination enables one to conceive of plausible alternatives that give rise to impulses and desires that compel him to action. On persistence, Aristotle wrote that (p) people are equipped by nature to acquire the virtues, but they achieve them only by practice. To gain a salubrious habit, one needs to persistently practice that habit. Persistence, which requires concerted effort, is a common theme in stoicism. Marcus Aurelius mentioned the need for (v) stamina and perseverance and Epictetus advised to (p) learn from the wrestling-masters. Has the boy fallen down? "Get up," they say, "and wrestle again, until you have gained strength." Others too should think in some such way as that. He emphasized the need for constant training in order not to fail, as well as habit, which he wrote (p) is a powerful influence because one must oppose one habit to another, and where impressions are most liable to make one slip, there resort to training to counter the risk. Achieving good habits requires imagination and persistence.

Human's ability to learn is an obvious source or acting enkratically to achieve good habits. Throughout life, humans constantly observe causes and consequences. If one uses his mind and good judgment, he connects the causes that lead to unhappy and happy consequences and learns to avoid the former. Those who can lead happier lives and those who cannot are doomed to forever repeat their mistakes. For the latter poor souls, happiness often remains unfulfilled.

Experience and learning enables people to avoid the bad habits of life that bring unhappiness. During life, people are constantly enlarging their experience of the world, which brings learning and a variety of benefits. People grow, mature, learn self-control and become more skillful at navigating the sources of good and bad habits. Epictetus wrote (v) that the trait of self-control involves not only strength of will but also skill; like the skill required to wrestle well.

And now to the topic of this chapter, which is the exploration of why many philosophers think habit brings happiness. In ancient times, the word habit had a different connotation, which was that it helped one achieve virtue, which collaterally brings happiness. Plato wrote that (p) virtue is created by habit and practice. Aristotle wrote that (p) moral virtue comes about as a result of habit and not nature. He emphasized that people get virtues by first exercising them and that virtue comes with practice, which eventually becomes part of one's nature and character. Echoing Plato and Aristotle, the Stoics also emphasized habit to achieve happiness. Epictetus, for example wrote that (v) if one wants to do something, make it a habit, and that habit is a powerful influence. Thus, if a person wants to be happy, he should make a habit of being virtuous in order to do the things that will make him happy. To achieve happiness habitually, do what will bring it.

The final tool in the box is reason. It is important because it accompanies every other tool. It evaluates the information acquired from intuition, it helps the brain logically imagine alternate desirable possibilities, and it helps one remain consistently persistent rather than impulsive. It also enables people to draw logical causal relations that help them learn, be experienced, and achieve skill. Reason, as Cicero wrote, enables one (v) to distinguish sequences of cause and effect, see the causes of things, become aware of consequences and link the present with the future. Reason is an organizing force that helps one judge correctly, such as whether to make a certain characteristic a habit.

Habit has a good toolbox, and Caprice does not. Habit acts enkratically, and with the use of his tools, he develops virtue and lives a happy life. Caprice acts akratically, has no toolbox and is unhappy. So, what are some of the good habits to enkratically develop that Habit has, and from what bad habits does Caprice suffer that the philosophers say to avoid? There are many, so the focus will be put on six—three good and three bad.

There are many good habits to develop to be happy, like paying attention to health, achieving an education and being honest. This book will focus on the three often mentioned by the philosophers: work, humor and persistence.

The philosophers state that work is a good habit to develop for many reasons. Voltaire wrote that it keeps people from the three great evils: vice, boredom and poverty. With work, people are too preoccupied to engage in vice, too busy to be bored and earning a living to boot. Work is fulfilling and brings reputation, success, opportunities and self-respect. Work gives purpose and something useful to do with one's life. Collectively, work supports others, whether they are customers, clients or dependents.

Historically, the laboring man never demanded to be happy or thought mortal men could be happy according to philosopher Hannah Arendt. But with human's evolution she observed in her book *The Human Condition* that this has changed, and the demand for happiness through laboring today is pervasive; without this effort, people are less contented. For Arendt, the habit of work brings happiness and contentment.

Some philosophers like Georg Hegel have wrongfully derided aspects of the value of work. In his *Phenomenology of Spirit*, Hegel criticized what he called the spiritual animal, which derisively refers to bourgeoisie professionals who focus on work and selfishly develop their own capacities. For Hegel, they are not working toward ends in themselves but rather only ends that do no good things—nor do they care about consequences. He claims, for example, that farming is an end with no satisfaction. How can this be? There exist similarities between professionals and farmers in their work that Hegel misses. A professional like a doctor heals, which is a good end, and a farmer raises crops so people can eat, which is another good end. In each case, the professional or farmer may or may not know about the consequences of their work, but in each case it is good—good health and satiation. These are eminently satisfying ends for both workers, which suggests work is a good habit to develop.

Perhaps the best viewpoint to keep on work as a habit is that it is a good one but it should be kept in perspective. It brings all the salubrious benefits described, but it can also bring unhappiness when it becomes excessive. Living in a competitive artificial work environment, losing control of destiny, and being a cog in a capitalistic machine may bring wealth but not necessarily happiness. Develop the habit of work but keep it in perspective—enjoy the other things life has to offer.

Curiously and counterintuitively, philosophers historically have argued that humor is not a habit that brings happiness. To understand this, consider the three principal theories of humor that have evolved over time. Originally, it was thought that humor and laughter expressed feelings of superiority over other people. The ancient philosophers and more recently Descartes's perspectives came from this theory. Recently, many believed humor and laughter acts like a pressure valve analogous to a pressure relief valve in a steam engine. It is the release that Freud described as a release of nervous energy. Today, most philosophers consider humor and the resulting laughter a perception of something incongruous, or something that challenges everyday mental patterns and expectations. This view was embraced by Immanuel Kant, Arthur Schopenhauer and Søren Kierkegaard.

The ancient philosophers derided the value of humor because the first explanation of it prevailed. Plato, perhaps the most influential critic of humor and laughter considered it an emotion that transgresses rationality. In the *Republic*, he admonished the Guardians to avoid laughter because it provokes violent reaction. In the *Philebus*, he described laughter as malicious, a form of scorn and delighting in evil. Aristotle agreed with Plato that laughter expresses scorn. In *Rhetoric*, he describes wit as educated insolence, and in *Nicomachean Ethics*, he describes jesting as mockery. The later Stoics followed Plato and Aristotle's views because they believed laughter diminishes self-control. Epictetus in the *Enchiridion*, for example, wrote that (p) laughter should not be loud, frequent or unrestrained.

Recent philosophers like Thomas Hobbes and René Descartes were of the same ilk. Hobbes in *Leviathan* suggested that humor comes from feeling superior, which results in laughter, and Descartes in *Passions of the Soul* expressed the view that laughter is only an expression of scorn and ridicule. Given this avalanche of criticism, is humor a good habit to develop in order to achieve happiness?

The answer is yes because there are two kinds of humor. The first is the other-depreciating and mocking kind these philosophers were responding to. The other is a combination of the release of tension and realizing incongruencies that challenge the natural mental processes, or strange and funny associations that make one laugh. When the landlord sends a letter to an overdue tenant and writes "give me a break, you are ten months overdue on your rent, I have carried you longer than your mother," people laugh. It is the latter self-depreciating, incongruent, and humble kind of humor that one should cultivate as a habit. It is a trait that brings happiness for a number of reasons.

This kind of humor relieves stress, puts problems in perspective and causes people to lighten up and be less grave. It puts issues that worry people in perspective, which diminishes the source of the worry and its importance. Humor also often resolves issues. The *Stanford Encyclopedia of Philosophy* explained that humor is a social lubricant that brings trust and redirects conflict. It, for example, redirects negative emotions like complaining, warning, criticizing, commanding or evaluating into delight that reduces negative emotions. Beyond this, it just feels good to laugh. Humor is fun and play and makes people smile and laugh like when they were kids. Both Aristotle and Thomas Aquinas described this play aspect of humor as relaxation. Humor brings levity, pleasure, entertainment and relaxation.

There is a more sophisticated form of laughter not mentioned by the philosophers that should be mentioned. It is a kind of humor that enables some to connect with others. Everyone knows down deep that everyone is egoistical, including themselves, but some through maturity come to understand that they are not the center of the world. They come to realize that they exist with other egos, so they sublimate their ego, pride and self-importance, which enables the third kind of self-depreciating humor to emerge. These others who have similarly matured appreciate the willingness to do so. They see the incongruence between what people all are—egoistical—and that they acknowledge and act in a self-depreciating way. These others know that, like them, people really do not mean to depreciate themselves, but they appreciate the willingness to do so. So people connect, and the communal laugh is one of a common acknowledgment of a reality. The humor comes from striking a realization between the way things appear and the way things are. It is a kind of a humorous laugh of consanguinity that brings happiness because people made the right kind of humor a habit. This author believes this is the best kind of humor.

Habit learned that humor brings happiness, so he made it a habit. Caprice never learned the lesson and thinks that another who depreciates himself deserves it. For Habit, this humor-habit required effort, cleverness and a certain level of intelligence to acquire. But he did it because he recognized its value. So, now Habit sees humor in everything. He laughs at the human condition, the irony in supercilious behavior and most of all humor in other people. He has come to know that people can be funny if he just looks and listens hard enough. With this, his relations with others only become more humorous and connected. He found that others repay humor with humor and, like an infection, consanguinity, laughter and happiness are the consequences.

Make humor a habit because it takes the edge off of life's problems, it is a powerful antidote to worry and depression and facilitates human relations. Humor truly is God's gift to man and a major source of happiness.

Persistence was mentioned earlier as a way to act enkratically. It is resurrected here because it is a key habit to have to be successful in life. The simple ability to never give up at some endeavor was considered an important trait by Aristotle and the Stoics Epictetus and Marcus Aurelius. With persistence, it is hard to fail, and without it, failure comes easily. It is a paradigm to see mediocre persistent successes and talented and unsteady failures. Habit worked to develop good habits, and Caprice did not.

Louis Zamperini in his book *Don't Give Up, Don't Give In* described the many challenges he faced in life. They included fighting, drinking, loss at sea and incarceration. To overcome these obstacles he had many suggestions, but the central one was to persevere in life, to never give up, to keep at it. He credited the ability to improve himself and overcome many challenges, including incarnation in a Japanese prisoner camp, to many things but persistence was one of the most important. The habit of persistence brings success, which is a source of happiness.

The Anna Karenina principle says that things can go wrong more ways than right. Similarly, because there are more bad habits than good, people are naturally inclined to develop more bad ones than good. Like humor, it takes effort to avoid bad habits. There are just too many bad habits to mention, so this book will focus on three: alcohol, drugs and the tape machine.

Alcoholism and drug addiction are habits that destroy happiness. They destroy health and mental abilities, which is fatal for happiness. At their core, they are escapes from reality. Those who find life unbearable or boring use them to achieve oblivion or aliveness. Both are escaping reality but what they are really escaping is themselves. But they will never be happy because, as Samuel Johnson wrote, when one escapes, he always ends up with the same problem, which is him. Someone may move to another country, but he only finds that his problem has followed him because the problem is him.

There are numerous definitions of alcoholism. The best is that a person is an alcoholic when alcohol interferes with his or her vital life functions. When alcohol interferes with work, relationships or health, that is alcoholism. The volume and frequency of drinking are a poor criterions for alcoholism because one person can drink ten beers and feel fine and another two and be drunk. In any case, one in twelve adults in America are alcoholics, which is a chronic source of unhappiness.

It should be pointed out that many philosophers and philosopher/writers may not be the best source of advice on alcoholism because many were alcoholics. Jean Paul Sartre, William Faulkner, Ernest Hemmingway, John Steinbeck, Hunter Thompson, Dorothy Parker and Truman Capote are just a few examples. F. Scott Fitzgerald once complained that he could never stay sober long enough to tolerate sobriety. However, they may have something to say because they knew what they were writing about.

Dr. James R. Milam and Katherine Ketcham in *Under the Influence* described the causes and consequences of alcoholism, from which a picture emerges. Alcohol abuse is an undetectable progression beginning with the problem drinker is driven to experience pleasure and avoid pain. They suffer from loneliness, depression, anger, hostility, unemployment, divorce, poverty or a generally dissatisfied life. After a few drinks they feel better, but psychological and social problems are incubating.

For Milam and Ketcham, the abusers must drink more to maintain their high and temporal happiness. With this they enter an empty place in life where many lose control of their vital life functions. They become increasingly angry, fearful and depressed. They begin to experience nausea, dizziness, tremors, loss of coordination or confused thinking. They also become agitated, irritable, moody, high-strung, tight and anxious with occasional angry emotional outbursts. Alcohol becomes a craving and begins physically damaging them with delirium tremens, convulsions, hallucinations and nutritional deficiency, which leads to loss of mental alertness and emotional instability.

Some become alcoholics due to heredity. Certainly, genes can lead to alcoholic addiction, psychological dependence and loss of control over drinking. For some, alcohol is a physiological disease they cannot control. However, for many, including those who voluntarily joined the Alcoholics Anonymous Association, it can be controlled with the philosophers' emphasis on will.

Alcoholism is an empty place bereft of hope. Milam and Ketcham describe it as a kind of temporary suicide with the only hope being oblivion. It is a place where individuals have lost self-respect and any sense of personal identity. It is a place of self-pity and isolation. Aside from its awful physical consequences, the philosophers say that when one loses inner harmony, rationality and virtue, he becomes lost in a Rabelaisian sea of meaninglessness. The result is unhappiness, so develop the habit of abstaining or controlling alcohol.

Drugs are another source of unhappiness but are more complicated than alcohol. There are many kinds of drugs with different potencies and effects. Some like marijuana create mild euphoria, some like methamphetamine waste people away and others like LSD can permanently alter the brain. Caprice for example is addicted to methamphetamines and as a result cannot hold a job, maintain his marriage and be a father. He spends his time in drug-induced degenerative comas, in altercations with others, in trouble with the law and in jail. This drug has wasted his life, and he is unhappy.

Jay Stevens in his book *Storming Heaven* described Caprice's problem, which is that drugs are necessarily a poisonous concentrated venom that is quite delicious. Stevens was describing LSD, the reasons people in Height-Ashbury in San Francisco in 1967 were taking it and the consequences. It was the 1960s heady, free, tune in, turn off, and drop out hippie time of LSD advocates like Timothy Leary, Hunter Thompson, Allan Ginsberg, Ken Kesey and Aldous Huxley.

They had many rationalizations for taking the drug. Some claimed their minds were dulled by everyday information, which was only sharpened with LSD. Others claimed they needed an occasional vacation from reality, which was really escaping life. All believed they were seeking the evasive other world, a world they could only describe with metaphors and parables but never find. Leary was escaping bourgeoisie sheep-like middle class values he distained.

With these empty reasons they developed the habit of taking drugs, and the consequences were ghastly. They lost their egos, self-worth and their minds. Many assumed they would return to normal after taking the drug, but many did not, which is a point many users did not appreciate. Many permanently damaged their brains and their lives. One young LSD user said he had come to know vividly what it is like to be mad. Their human relationships became unhappy, they became paranoid and hostile, their fragile communities began to fail and because they ignored reality, they had money problems. What they had gained from the habitual use of this drug was temporary euphoria and long-term unhappiness.

The final example of a bad habit to avoid is constantly reliving old injuries and painful experiences. People develop mind tapes that they play over and over that remind them of some past experience that brought pain, and the result is angst. They are mentally reliving unhappy, distressing and depressing incidents in their lives. They can be memories of past injustices, slights or perceived wrongs that caused distress.

Many of the memories could have come from insignificant comments by others in one's impressionable youth. A boy's mother said once that his nose was too big, his revered father said he is lazy and will never amount to anything and an authoritative figure in high school said he was not smart. So he imbeds these pejorative observations in his soul and plays them in a mind-tape over and over again. Now, as an adult, he is ashamed of his nose and thinks he is a loser and stupid. He needlessly plays these false tapes imbedded by others repeatedly, and the result is unhappiness.

The solution is to stop the habit and turn off the tape machine. Do not let the mind run wild with negative memories that endlessly repeat themselves. Rather think about the good things in life. Indeed, Albert Schweitzer once said that happiness is good health and a poor memory. Avoid destructive habits like excessive alcohol, drugs and the tape machine, cultivate Machiavelli's first kind of brain and develop good habits to be happy.

CHAPTER EIGHT

PASSION
*Do not be Sisyphus forever having to
push the rock back up the hill*

One sees the rich indolent man suffering from ennui due to lack of vigor and purpose, the seducer who must continually seduce to feel pleasure and the greedy Grinch forever trying to accumulate more money driven by passionate avarice. In each case, the only result is perpetual dissatisfaction. In philosophy, much has been written on these characters, their passions and unhappiness. Some schools have lauded the pleasure passion brings, like love, and others have derided the angst it causes, like anger. It is a smorgasbord of choices. This chapter seeks to work through a few of their thoughts and ends with David Hume and Aristotle.

Passion is natural; people would not be humans without it. Passion can be good, even salubrious. Passionate love begets a spouse, sensual passion begets children and benevolent passion sustains a family. These are some potential enduring sources of happiness. But passionate avarice begets selfishness, passionate envy engenders resentment and the loss of possessions causes anger. These are some enduring sources of unhappiness.

Passion's devil-pull is often stronger than its gifts. It is passion that inflames insatiable desire, which will be discussed in the next chapter on desire and appetites, that drives the all too common, often unhappy desires for power, wealth, prestige and sensual pleasure. Under the sway of passion, these desires can become intoxicating like a heroin addiction. Power brings legions of enemies, wealth causes insatiable envy, prestige grows corrosive jealousy and sensual pleasure leads to the perpetual pursuit of insatiable pleasure like Sisyphus forever having to push the rock up a hill. Generally, the philosophers advocate indulging, moderating, suppressing or being indifferent to passion.

Pleasure is one manifestation of passion, and those who advocate indulging passion could generally be grouped under the rubric hedonists. Hedonism is a recently coined word meant to identify the ancient Greek philosophical Cyrenaic School. It comes from the Greek word *hedone*, or pleasure. Hedonism means the pursuit of pleasure. The hedonist Cyrenaics were founded by Aristippus of Cyrene in the late fifth century BCE in Athens. They taught that pleasure is the only intrinsic good—it is the supreme and only good in life and pain is the only evil. Friendship and justice, for example, are useful only as long as they bring pleasure. Pleasure is the positive enjoyments of the sensations and in particular the physical ones, which are superior to mental pleasures.

The Cyrenaics' emphasis on the passion of pleasure alone naturally brought to light the reasons such a philosophy fails. When passion, which in this case is pleasure, is taken to an extreme, other pleasures that could bring happiness are obviated. Further, pursuing sensual pleasure alone only brings the desire for more sensual pleasure. The more pursued the more is required, and the ultimate result is unsatisfied sensual pleasure and ennui. The Playboy philosophy only works to a point. It should come as no surprise then that the Cyrenaic School died out within a century and was replaced by the Epicureans.

Greek philosopher Epicurus founded Epicureanism in the late fourth century BCE, which became a popular philosophy for life in Greece and later in early Roman times. His work was canonized in the poet-philosopher Lucretius's book *On the Nature of Things*. Epicurus envisioned a more sophisticated and realistic form of Cyrenaic pleasure in which individuals controlled their passions so to avoid becoming a slave to pleasure. In order to achieve true happiness through pleasure, the Epicureans emphasized other forms of pleasure, such as intellectual, friendship, communal associations, withdrawal from public life and retirement as well as the pleasures obtained from anticipation and memory.

Like the Cyrenaics, Epicurus identified the good with pleasure, but unlike them, he emphasized the need for the absence of bodily and mental pain—to be happy one must not only pursue positive pleasures but also diligently avoid sources of pain. In everyday life, this means one should pursue money for the pleasure it can bring but avoid making it an end due to the pain it can bring. Money alone is dead and inhuman—it has no taste. It can bring the unquenchable desire for more money and insatiable desire. Epicurus's true insight and contribution to the nature of happiness, however, came with his view that the limitation of desire through virtue promotes happiness. Pleasure as an end only engenders passionate desires, so to avoid this source of potential pain, people should adopt principles that delimit it. For Epicurus, that delimiting force is virtue. When people have virtuous principles, they concomitantly establish beliefs that limit their desires, which ultimately engenders happiness.

Limiting passion was a novel philosophic ideal that morphed into philosophies that emphasized suppressing passionate desires as a way to achieve happiness. The chief philosophy of this tack was stoicism. For the Stoics, one does not need passion to live a tranquil life.

A central tenet of Stoic philosophy is that to be happy, emotions must be controlled or eliminated. Stoic Epictetus, for example, advised to expel grief, fear, desire, envy, malice, avarice, effeminacy and intemperance. He believed those who invest their happiness in capricious passion are never satisfied. Roman stoic Seneca wrote in *Letters from a Stoic* that the passions are the greatest source of human unhappiness and thus should be eliminated. On anger, for example, he describes it as a (v) and (p) a brief insanity that one cannot tell is more hateful or ugly. For Seneca, anger is uncontrollable, harmful, unnecessary, and useless.

Unlike the Stoics, Aristotle believed a moderate amount of emotion or good temper sometimes helps. Intermediate amounts of anger, for example, can help in battle. Seneca violently disagreed. For him, anger, once unleashed, is uncontrollable and is (p) oblivious to decency, obstinate, closed to reasoning or advice, agitated on pretexts without foundation and incapable of discerning fairness or truth. The angry man, for example, will be angry with trivial transgressions and will get angrier with each new transgression with no end. As a result, he will spend his life (p) in bad temper and grief always with some ground for indignation. This is hardly a formula for happiness.

Rather than poisonous anger Seneca says that (p) happiness derives from mutual assistance, not mutual destruction, seeking help rather than doing harm and succoring others rather than flying at them. Human happiness rests upon kindness and concord, which anger only adulterates.

Seneca also wrote on grief, which is another significant passionate source of unhappiness. At one time, he was exiled to Corsica, which inconsolably grieved his mother. In his consolation, *To Helvia* (his mother), he told her that humans have the ability to mitigate unhappiness. He wrote that she must control her passion of grief by being indifferent to matters beyond her control, like his being exiled. He said people come and go, so she should prepare herself for this eventuality by distancing herself today from the inevitable loss of a loved one tomorrow. He wrote that grief can be mitigated by remaining indifferent to familial relations. With the proper use of judgments, people have the capacity to lessen the impact the passions have—in this case, the judgment of indifference.

Parenthetically, like the Stoics, later writer and philosopher Samuel Johnson wrote that passion must be conquered. He believed that in doing so, people would no longer be (p) slaves of fear, fools of hope, inflamed by anger, emasculated by tenderness or depressed by grief. Stoic suppression of passion through judgments, such as to be indifferent to loved ones, worked for stoics Seneca and Cicero (when he grieved over his daughter's death), but it is monumentally hard to do, which is probably why the philosophy died out in the second century BCE.

Nineteenth century idealist German philosopher Georg Hegel in *The Phenomenology of Spirit* had a unique perspective on human happiness or what he termed satisfaction. For him, it is not a matter of limiting passion but rather dialectically evolving out of it. In his philosophy, humankind evolves through successive inexorable states to one final state of freedom and happiness. In relation to passion and pleasure, one lower state could be characterized as Don Juan hedonism, in which pleasure is maximized. For Hegel, this stage only leads to boredom, commonness and the need for new pleasures. Thus, people evolve to the next higher state in Hegel's hierarchy to a kind of Roussean law of the heart, where what one does is what feels right. It is a state where the heart is law, and feelings tell one how to act. This, for Hegel, is a content-less state that does not tell one what to do, so people evolve to the next state, which can be described as virtue and the way of the world. In this state, the virtuous maximize their preferences and desires to achieve happiness but become disillusioned because they are faced with so many selfish virtue-less people, which makes them frustrated, hostile and alienated. So, another dead end for happiness through passion. His philosophy may help people be wary of passion, but it does not help them control it. They are just bystanders hoping for a final happy state that may or may not come. The only prescription then would be like the Stoics—fate is sealed so remain indifferent to passion.

But it gets worse with the melancholic philosopher Arthur Schopenhauer, who believed that passion only engenders resignation. In his essay *The Vanity of Existence*, he described life as a pendulum swinging backward and forward between boredom and pain. Either people are passionately striving toward something, or they have achieved it. While they are striving, they experience pain because they have not achieved their goal, but when they achieve their goal, they experience boredom because the goal has been attained. This is a similar boredom that Hegel described that leads only to more of the same. This boredom for Schopenhauer causes people to want something new and to create new goals, which swing people back to striving and pain—thus humans inevitably swing between boredom and pain.

The upshot of this endless pendulum-like process for Schopenhauer engenders a sense of worthlessness and vanity that results in the passion of angst. The angst occurs because people come to realize that the goals they are striving for are illusions—they always fade as they approach. Schopenhauer explained that if people were satisfied with existence, they would not experience boredom when their goals are achieved—and thus, no angst. The ultimate consequence of this process is resignation, which is a strange place for passion to end.

A more fruitful way to interpret Schopenhauer's theory is to view life as a project. People feel pleasure when pursuing a goal and satisfaction when it is attained. They craft projects that propel people on a mission that gives their lives happiness and purpose. Schopenhauer's angst occurs because people expect meaning in life to come from poorly established goals. If the goals they are striving for have enduring value, the passions associated with them will be good, and if they are empty, the passions will only make circumstances worse and result in boredom, angst and resignation. Achieved valueless goals have little enduring value, and an individual's passion propelled him to gloom and not happiness.

So, accept the fact that meaning and happiness in life depends on establishing the right goals. If one does so, passion will fall into its proper place without the need for indifference.

So, what does one do? Cyrenaic passion only brings ennui, Epicureanism was an improvement but not everyone is virtuous, Stoic suppression of passionate desires is problematic, Hegelianism offers no control over emotions and Schopenhauer without proper goals only brings resignation. Controlling passions is difficult, but David Hume gave one solution, to use reason, and Aristotle another, which was to use reason to moderate them. It turns out people can use reason to moderate passions in such a way to bring happiness.

David Hume believed reason is the servant of the passions—people act on passion and not cold reason. However, it turns out that they can use reason to influence passions to cause one to act in ways that bring happiness. Indeed, it is reason that tells passions to avoid Cyrenaic pleasure, use Epicurean virtue, use proper judgments and establish salubrious goals. Reason also tells people that it is unrealistic to eliminate passionate emotions entirely but rather to moderate them and avoid extremes. This is Aristotle's doctrine of the mean theory that tells people to be moderate. Passion is a two-edged sword (like Schopenhauer's pendulum), where the fore-swing brings happiness and the backswing unhappiness—moderation dampens the swings.

Consider how reason and moderation play out in the passion-driven seven deadly sins. If one is prideful, reason tells him that people either avoid him or despise him, so the moderating solution is to have self-respect. If one is envious, he feels angst, so he must develop appreciation and gratitude; with anger he only destroys the vessel, so instead, he must foster compassion, love and forgiveness;

lust is fun but insatiable, so work on abstinence and virtue; gluttony just gets one fat and sick, so learn to simply satiate hunger and thirst; passion makes greed an ugly emotion that stultifies and is ultimately meaningless, so cultivate generosity and care; and sloth is of no value whatsoever, so become industrious. To defeat the passionately driven seven deadly sins, use reason and be moderate.

So, to be happy, be wary of passion and avoid being Sisyphus forever having to push the rock back up the hill. Control passion, moderate emotions and desires through reason and focus on having the right goals to be passionate about.

CHAPTER NINE

DESIRE AND APPETITE
How pleasant it is to ask for nothing because the man who expects nothing is never disappointed

Glutton and Restraint have different habits and world views. Glutton is driven by desire, which has brought her unquenchable appetites. Her habits include over-eating, always wanting more money and unbounded sexual gratification. As a result she is overweight, shunned due to her rapacity and divorced. She is an unrestrained desire-driven pleasure seeker. Her world views both cause and accommodate her problems. She thinks the world should accommodate her appetites and all her problems are caused by others. As a result, Glutton is always anxious and unsatisfied with her life. Restraint has different habits and world views. His appetites are easily satisfied because he is not driven by desire. He stops eating when satiated, is satisfied with his financial position and enjoys sex with his wife when they are ready. Restraint is fit, trusted for his financial acumen and happily married. He is a person able to constrain his desires and appetites. His world views are the cause and natural consequence of his felicity. He expects to solve his own life problems and demands little from others. As a result, Restraint is satisfied with his life, calm and happy.

The philosophers have said much about desire and appetite. Restraint is happy because through habit and his world views, he controls his desires and appetites. Some philosophers disagree with this assertion. Thomas Hobbes, for example, believed that happiness comes from satisfying desires. For him, all human's motivations are egoistic, which means satiating desire-driven appetite is not necessarily wrong. In his twisted way, C. S. Lewis allegorized Restraint and Thomas Hobbes' positions in *The Screwtape Letters*, and in the process demonstrated the reasons excessive desire and appetite bring unhappiness.

Screwtape, the devil admonished his minion Wormwood to tempt humans, interfere with their will and emphasize change because these will bring them unhappiness. Tempting humans is their greatest danger because it initiates appetite, which is their greatest source of unhappiness. Interfering with their will enhances their appetites and brings unhappiness because they are prevented from using their will to control their appetites. Will controls appetites.

Most importantly, Screwtape advises Wormwood to foster human's natural desire for change. He wants humans to desire change, and particularly novelty, because it decreases pleasure and increases their appetites. Appetites will incite avarice, cause excessiveness, produce fashions and vogues and make them Byronic and drunk with appetitive emotion. Emphasizing change makes humans unhappy. Indeed, they begin wondering what is right and wrong, so they increasingly look to the future for answers, which keeps them in ignorance because it never answers back. Further, because the future depends on the choices they make now, they are doubly confused, which is good. In this state of emotional uncertainty, they naturally fall back on what they know, which are their appetites, which again bring them unhappiness.

This is all interesting, but many philosophers do not agree with Hobbes and agree with Screwtape's portrayal of human appetite. They think desire-driven appetites bring unhappiness. First, however, one must briefly distinguish appetites, desire and passion. Passion and desire, which were discussed in the last chapter, will be examined more in the chapters on sources of happiness (specifically *Simplicity and Nature* and *Stoicism and Epicureanism*). Appetite, desire and passion are intimately connected. Desire is to want something very strongly, like a general craving; appetites are also a strong desire or craving but for something specific like food, power or pleasure, and passion is the emotional intensity of these feelings, often in the form of love, joy, hatred or anger. Desires are broader and all-encompassing, whereas appetites are limited and specific. Appetites are a species of desire. Humans have desires for many things and appetites for only a few. For example, do not say one has the appetite to see that his children are raised well but rather the desire. Further, appetites have the ability to be satiated, whereas desire implies insatiable want. People may, for example, perpetually desire a fancier meal, but their appetite can be satiated with just food. This chapter is about what philosophers have said about desire and excessive appetites.

Most philosophers like Aristotle, St. Augustine, and St. Thomas Aquinas have pondered why desire leads to appetites and how they can be intelligently controlled. They understand that no man is rich who shakes and groans for more. They know one can never be happy wanting more. On desire and collaterally appetites, one philosopher said that if someone is not happy here, he will not be happy over there, because when he get there, it will be here. Humans naturally think the grass is greener on the other side of the fence, but it is greener only because their desire and appetites make them think it is greener. So the solution is to know oneself, know one's desires and appetites and control oneself. Know that it is desire that makes someone want a fancier car when all he really needs is reliable transportation, and it is appetite that makes one want to eat more when all he needs is satiation. People need to know when enough is enough.

Do not be a slave to desires and appetites because they will only bring unhappiness. Nature is easily satisfied, and controlling excessive wants enables people to better achieve Aristotle's definition of happiness, which (p) consists in a life well lived, in accordance with virtue and accompanied by a moderate possession of external goods.

The ancient philosophers generally taught that desire and their resulting appetites is a source of unhappiness. Plato believed that desire was the root of all unhappiness. Happiness rather comes from harmonizing reason, spirit and appetite. Aristotle was a proponent of reason, which tells one to moderate his appetite. A rational person stops eating when their hunger is satiated. The great Cynic Diogenes wondered why people become hungry for they know not what. Unhappiness comes from desiring false gods one does not need or understand. It is purported that Diogenes once asked Alexander the Great why he pursued conquest; he responded that it was in order to relax and enjoy life—to which Diogenes rejoined, "Why not just do that now?" For Diogenes, happiness resides in appreciating what one has now and not some future unknown.

The Stoics had much to say on desire and appetite. For them, like most ancient philosophers, they are the principal source of unhappiness, and controlling them is the antidote that brings happiness. There are three ways to deal with desires and appetites: indulge them, control them or eliminate them. The Stoics believed that indulging them is a mistake because they are never-fulfilling cycles that only accelerate desire. They believed they should be controlled and, if possible, eliminated. They proposed to do this in three ways: the mind should rule pleasure, it should control appetites and it is reason that accomplishes this.

Their first principle is that desire and appetite bring unhappiness, so they should be controlled by the mind. Uncontrolled Epicurean pleasure for them can never be achieved because the satisfaction of pleasure only brings the desire for more pleasure. Seneca asked if (p) desire-driven pleasure is capable of coming to an end and answered that it is not the man with too little who is poor, but rather the man who hankers for more; the latter only counts what he is yet to get and not what he already has. For Seneca, the wise man is content with himself; he is the one who is happy living in his modest house unlike those unhappily living in a fancy one. Appetite-driven gluttony, for example, only produces querulousness, impatience, uncharitableness, self-concern and unhappiness. Seneca wrote that following blind desire will never bring satisfaction, which fellow Stoic Cicero earlier presaged with his comment that he (p) does not understand the man who is happy and wants more to be happier.

The Stoics' second principle is that desire-driven avarice, ambition and luxury, which become appetites, impede happiness. This comes from Cicero's *Tusculan Disputations*. Ambition causes people to seek advantages over others, avarice makes people want more than others and luxury attenuates will. For the Stoics, each of these causes people to live outside the bounds of nature, to give into desire, and spoils people because they succumb to excess passions. When people are freed from these ailments, they will be rendered entirely happy.

On avarice, Cicero wrote (p) when money is coveted, evil circulates in the veins and vital organs, and disease and ensue, which is a sickness. When the soul is freed from avarice, it renders men completely and entirely happy. For Cicero, avarice only brings unhappiness.

For these Stoics, unguided and unrestrained ambition is a significant source of unhappiness. It is so because it is subject to fortune and thus an insatiable desire-happiness depends entirely on which way the winds of fortune blow. Stoic Marcus Aurelius wrote that (p) with ambition people become slaves to their ambitions.

Finally, on luxury, Cicero wrote that (p) love of good living is a sickness and riches, pleasures, and the acquisition of these things is disgraceful. Seneca was particularly dismayed with the advent of the ambition to live luxuriously in Rome in the first century because pleasure was indulged to the degree that the passions had become reason's master instead of servant. This leads to the Stoics' third principle, which is the importance of reason.

The Stoics' third principle is that reason controls desire and appetite and thus is a tool to bring happiness. Reason controls these three ways. The first is that rationality connects causes with consequences, which enables one to see the consequences of unbridled desire and appetite. The second is that reason tells one to adjust to the world, which means change oneself. Stoic Epictetus wrote that (p) the good life can be achieved by adjusting one's desires to the way the world is rather than trying to adjust the world to satisfy one's desires. Contemporary Stoic philosopher William Irvine echoed this sentiment when he wrote (v) the best way—indeed, perhaps the only way—to attain lasting happiness is not to change the world around humans or their place in it but to change themselves. Finally, reason tells one to want only the essentials in life because on reasoned reflection, one comes to understand that more does not necessarily make him happy. Nature is easily satisfied and when, as Seneca wrote, (p) one begins wanting things that are inessential, he hands the mind over to the body and become a slave to pleasure; he only focuses on the business of the body. Indeed, Cicero wrote that (p) when the mind recoils from reason desire, that is always greedily coveting, occurs.

To be happy, use a reasoned controlling mind to mitigate the desire-driven appetites of avarice, ambition and luxury.

Unlike the Stoics, there were many ancient schools that taught desire-driven pleasure brings happiness. Mentioned in the previous chapter on passion, the Hedonists and especially Cyrenaics blindly believed pleasure is happiness. Because their theories are thin and wrong, they will not be discussed here. However one school, the Epicureans, believed desire and pleasure bring happiness through a more sophisticated philosophy. They agreed with the Stoics that desire and appetite should be controlled, but unlike them, not eliminated. Because pleasure, they reasoned, is in part freedom from pain, then efforts should be to maximize pleasure and minimize pain. From this principle, they taught that the way to attain pleasure is to live modestly, gain knowledge of the world and limit one's desires. The Epicureans also emphasized pleasures of the mind rather than physical pleasures. They, for example, believed pleasure comes more from with whom a person eats rather than what is eaten. Following this regimen in their view brings tranquility, or what they called *ataraxia* or a state of freedom from fear and absence of bodily pain.

Epicurus, the founder of Epicureanism, distinguished three kinds of desire-driven appetites. The first natural and necessary appetites are eating, drinking and sleeping. These are natural and easy to satisfy. The second natural but not necessary appetite includes sensual pleasure. For Epicurus, these are not necessary for satisfaction and can be mastered. The third are those appetites that are not natural or necessary, so they must be rejected completely. Few would disagree with his first category, fulfilling natural and grounded desires, certainly brings satisfaction. The Stoics might call these natural bodily functions rather than appetites. Epicurus's second appetite runs afoul of the Stoics because they believed desire once unleashed is very difficult to control. When men commence desiring wealth, power, prestige and sensual pleasure, they are set on a path that is exceedingly difficult to stop. They are like becoming addicted to heroin. For the Stoics, the best solution is to not to develop the addiction or attain the desire. Epicurus's third appetite is straightforward but also difficult to surmount. Unnatural and unnecessary appetites achieve nothing. Desiring exotic food from a distant land in order to be happy is pointless. Resisting them once the desire has been ensconced is also problematic for the Stoics because they too often defy dismissal through individual effort and reason. The best solution is to avoid desire altogether. Indeed, Voltaire believed that there is pleasure in having no pleasure. The problem with this for the Epicureans, however, is that desire is natural.

Ancient Roman philosopher Boethius also advises to avoid desire and the appetites it engenders. In his *Consolation of Philosophy* he wrote (p) that desire and the pleasures fill one with anxiety, are bereft of fulfillment and full of remorse. When people desire wealth, they think it will bring happiness, but what they find is it does not. What they find is that one never has enough of what he desires, the desired ends constantly fluctuate and change, chances of achieving them are uncertain and if one does succeed he lives in constant fear of losing what he has gained. People only achieve a state of always wanting something they do not have and not having enough of what they do have all of, which brings illness, pain, anxiety and even bitterness when fortune thwarts desires.

On the desire for power, Boethius wrote that one cannot have power over anyone with a free mind and cited Zeno, who once bit off his tongue and threw it at a tyrant to prove the point. With power one can suffer, because what he is capable of inflicting on others, they can inflict on him. Indeed, power only brings danger to those who possess it. Kings, for example, do not live free from worry, require bodyguards and are sometimes terrorized by their subjects. The more power they gain the more enemies they acquire and the more danger they face.

Because power often brings wickedness and high office has no beauty or worth of its own, power itself does not make a man worthy of respect. Indeed, for Boethius, those with it only become more despised. Further, because a king's power depends on others who serve him, he is never master of himself, which makes him a prisoner in the chains of the lust that engenders power.

For Boethius, to achieve happiness, avoid desire and seek a condition of self-sufficiency with no wants. With this, people live serene lives and smile at the raging storm. True happiness comes from being self-sufficient, having strength, being worthy of respect and just being joyful.

A persistent theme in writer and philosopher Samuel Johnson's *The Vanity of Human Wishes* is that wishful thinking is an illusion because desire distorts reality, which brings false expectations. He famously wrote that (p) no man can, at the same time, fill his cup from the source and the mouth of the Nile. Put another way (v) no man can taste the fruits of autumn while he is delighting his scent with the flowers of the spring. For Johnson, one cannot have everything desire demands because nature's gifts are conditional. When someone gets one desired goal, he inexorably loses another. One may achieve wealth but lose human relations or may gain power but lose security. As Johnson put it, (v) nature sets her gifts on the right and on the left. This means nature's gifts carry a price. Further, the closer one gets to his desired goal the less he desires it because his reason for wanting it fades. This only causes him to naturally start looking for another desire to fulfill. This only causes a vicious unhappy cycle; when people attain their desired goals, their reasons for wanting them fade, and when they want something and do not get it, their unhappiness burns.

Johnson's solution is (p) to attain virtue, which brings quietness of conscience, the prospect of a happier state and the ability to endure calamity. Indeed, such a person living well cannot be despised.

With few exceptions the philosophers so far in this chapter have described desire and appetite as sources of unhappiness. The theme continues with Baudelaire, who believed desire is a vicious unhappy cycle that feeds on itself. Desire causes unhappiness, which people try to satisfy only by desiring more. Thus, (v) life is a hospital where every patient is obsessed with the desire of changing beds. One would like to suffer opposite the stove, another is sure he would get well beside the window. Desire only breeds more desire, so the solution for Alexander Pope is to stop desiring. He wrote that (v) blessed is the man who expects nothing, for he shall never be disappointed. For Pope, temptation must be resisted because man's felicity depends on his ignorance of things and circumstances that could be desired. Thomas Mann wrote that (v) desire is born of defective knowledge, Henry David Thoreau that (v) a man is rich in proportion to the things he can afford to let alone and Bertrand Russell that happiness comes from letting go of desires through individual power.

Gregg Easterbrook in *The Progress Paradox: How Life Gets Better While People Feel Worse* wrote that unhappiness comes from desire. People want many things they do not have, and it is the gap between having and wanting that is the essence of unhappiness. With this gap, people constantly think their lives can be better, which itself is a source of negative feelings and unhappiness.

Poignantly, much of this line of Western philosophers thinking on desire and appetite is similar to some eastern religions like Buddhism. Daisetsu Suzuki, a Japanese author of books on Buddhism, believed that Buddahood allows a man to have a view in mind with no desires or external objects to defile him. With him is the sense of Zen, which is the ability to see the nature of one's own being that enables him to overcome desire and escape suffering. For Suzuki, these lead to enlightenment and the elimination of desire. The Eastern religions tend to emphasize that desire is surmounted through intuition, whereas Western philosophers emphasize reason and intellect. For this author, it really does not matter which works, only that one works in order to limit desire and appetite in order to achieve felicity.

A more sophisticated Western rational view of desire has been offered by contemporary philosopher Harry G. Frankfurt in *Freedom of the Will and the Concept of a Person*. Frankfurt assumes some desires are good and others bad and asks the question of whether people can control the bad desires. He answers it with first- and second-order desires, volitions and wantonness. His first order-desires are simply the desire to do one thing or another, which means people may have some bad desires. His second-order desire is the desire to have the right desire, which he believed is a uniquely human trait due to reflective self-evaluation. The essential difference between humans and other animals is the ability to do one's own will and make decisions based on prior deliberative thought and thus form second-order desires.

Some humans with second-order desires develop the desire to desire their will, which Frankfurt calls volition. Volition is essential to being a person and without it and second-order desires, people are wonton, or like animals not caring which of their inclinations are strongest, hence his view that the essence of a human being (v) lies not in reason but in the will. It is interesting to speculate how close Frankfurt's will is to Suzuki's intuition, but that is another book.

To demonstrate his levels of desire and volition, Frankfurt uses a drug addict. The addict (p) who does not care if he takes drugs is engaged in a first-order desire, to take drugs, and is wanton because he follows his first-order desire without concern. He is like an animal acting with no rational direction, doing only what his desires demand. He lacks reflective self-evaluation and remains mindlessly indifferent to evaluating his own motives and desires. The unwilling addict is different because he lives a conflicted life taking drugs but not wanting to. He has the first-order desire to take drugs, but he has also formed a second-order desire not to take drugs. He both wants and does not want to take drugs. If he can do his second-order volition, he will stop taking drugs, and his second-order desire will prevail. If he cannot, unlike the wanton addict, he will experience internal discord and struggle because he is doing something he does not want to do. For Frankfurt, it is precisely this internal struggle that makes people human because people are struggling against their own desires, whether they are drugs, wealth, prestige, or sensual pleasure.

So, what does all have to do with human happiness? It means that some can be happy and others cannot. Those incapable of second-order desires and volitions are wonton and thus (p) helpless bystanders to the forces that move them. Only those with second-order desires and volition can achieve happiness. In the introduction to this book, it was mentioned that some may not be able to achieve happiness through their will, which is a point Frankfurt explains, Hobbes touches on and Suzuki does not address.

To elucidate the relationship between desire, appetites and happiness, consider this mind experiment. Imagine that one suffered some rare unknown genetic mutation when conceived that caused him to live 300 years. He was born in 1950 and lived to 2250 and died at the ripe old age of 300. He would have watched his parents, siblings, wife, children, grandchildren and great grandchildren die as well as all his friends and relatives. Now consider that he had 300 years to satisfy every desire and appetite to their utmost. He could accumulate unparalleled knowledge, unrivaled wealth, incredible prestige and honors, incredible power, matchless fame and experience endless sensual pleasure. Indeed, learning a little every day, investing a few dollars regularly and learning how to seduce the opposite sex could fulfill every desire to have knowledge, be rich and be completely sexually satisfied. Every nook and cranny, every aspect, every one of his desires could be satisfied beyond imagination. But would he then be happy in the future?

It is unlikely because his time would be gone and it would just be more of the same. His time had passed and everyone he loved is dead. He would be lost and unknown in a time not of his own. He would be a stranger. He satisfied his natural desires during his time and now he is alone. He would be living like an alien in a strange world with just more desires and appetites. It would be a world of others in which he is a desire-thing with no real meaning or purpose. Further, his desires would just be more of the same and once he had fulfilled his desires, new ones would arise, and the endless desire-cycle that the philosophers predicted would occur begins anew.

With such longevity, he could also develop new unnatural and unnecessary desires because the natural and necessary ones no longer satisfy him. He would then fall into Epicurus's trap desiring what he does not need. And to make matters worse, after 300 years, his desires would wear out because he got too much of what he no longer desired.

This thought experiment demonstrates the vanity of endlessly pursuing desires and appetites. Happiness comes from living now with the people of this age fulfilling natural and necessary desires and appetites. One must appreciate what he has now and not what he thinks he wants.

Humans need little to be happy. Many spend their lives desiring what they do not need. Many Americans today, for example, believe happiness comes from material possessions, more prestige or more sensual pleasure, but the opposite is true—true happiness comes from having no needs and being satisfied. There is an old proverb that says a man cannot lose what he never had. If one does not desire something he does not have, then he cannot feel a loss without it. With desire, people are always facing the unhappy circumstances of where they are or what they have and where they want to be and lack.

The philosophers like Boethius and Seneca are right—endlessly satisfying desire and appetite does not bring happiness. To be happy, one must satisfy the right ones only, and appreciate what he has.

CHAPTER TEN

ESCAPE BOREDOM AND PAIN
Avoid the pendulum and live the Earth life

Art is a young man living at home addicted to the excitement of computer games. His upper class upbringing in the city has been comfortable, he views life with detachment, his desires are unformed, he is not ambitious and he has no life goals. His life is plain. His life consists of working as a menial warehouseman during the day and playing computer games at night. But Art feels empty. He finds himself in a vicious cycle of unhappiness. He plays his games because they are exciting—they transport him from his common everyday life, but after a while the games just become more of the same, so he quits. But when he stops playing them he becomes bored and listless, which depresses him. He finds the boredom intolerable, so he quickly starts playing his games again, which resurrects his excitement. But then the cycle begins again; his excitement leads to a surfeit of pleasure that cannot be increased followed by ennui, so he quits, which only leads to listlessness and boredom, which incites him to return to the excitement of his games. Art is not happy.

Many philosophers have described this inexorable interplay between boredom and pain that brings inescapable unhappiness. This chapter is about what those philosophers have said and how to escape this vicious cycle in order to achieve happiness.

This cycle was briefly discussed earlier in chapter eight on the passions and is resurrected here in more detail. The melancholy philosopher Arthur Schopenhauer is the architect of this paradigm, which he described in his essay *The Vanity of Existence*. In that chapter, human life was described like (p) a pendulum swinging backward and forward between boredom and pain. Either one is striving toward something, or he has achieved it. While he is striving, he experiences pain because he has not achieved his goal. When he achieves the goal, he experiences boredom because the goal has been attained. The boredom causes him to want something new and to create new goals, which swings him back to pain; hence, the swinging between boredom and pain.

For many philosophers like Schopenhauer, a great irony in human nature is that when man achieves something he desires, he is not satisfied. He feels a sense of worthlessness and vanity. He realizes that the goal he has striven after is an illusion that fades when reached. From this, Schopenhauer makes the interesting observation that because human life is not satisfied with existence, it must be a mistake. If humans were satisfied with existence, they would not experience boredom when their goals are achieved.

Schopenhauer's theory has a little truth and a lot of falsity. It is true that people do feel pleasure when striving after a goal, and it is also true that when they achieve it they are often dissatisfied. However, this assumes that humans are animals unable to transcend nature with reason. Reason teaches that the striving is just excitement, which is enjoyable like Art's games—but that is all. It could teach that games are not the end or purpose of life but only entertainment. It could reveal that excitement is an unusual human emotion and most happy human lives are lived in quietude. It could show that this human-created game is just an unreal cyberspace transitory event with no inherent meaning. Finally, it could divulge that there is no ultimate purpose to life, as the extentialists say, so meaningful purposes that transcend computer games must be created. The feeling of boredom after playing the game comes from expecting more from it than it is capable of offering.

The need for excitement comes from unrestrained desire. In the last chapter, Samuel Johnson was quoted as saying that desire distorts reality and brings false expectations. When one achieves one desired goal, the desire for it fades and he becomes bored, so he immediately starts pursuing another desired goal. Johnson's vanity of human wishes explains Schopenhauer's vicious cycle of boredom and pain. The only difference in Art's case is that he continually pursued the same goal, playing computer games in order to escape his boredom.

Philosopher Georg Hegel also believed boredom causes unhappiness but added that only humans experience boredom. His reasons for this derive from his historic dialectic and the very nature of pleasure. In the historic evolution of humans, Hegel envisioned a master/slave stage in which the slaves are deprived of freedom. In order to escape this condition, Stoic philosophy was invented, which transcended this worldly limitation and offered freedom from all conditions of existence. Indeed, Epictetus, a leading Roman Stoic had been a slave. The slaves like Epictetus adopted this philosophy and thus became happier. However, according to Hegel, the slaves eventually abandoned stoicism because they became bored. They became so because, even though the philosophy freed them in a way, it deprived them of action. Stoic philosophy for Hegel was invented to justify slave's inaction—it inclined them to inaction. For Hegel, this was unacceptable because his historic dialectic could not advance; the slave does not fight the master, he only becomes bored. Ultimately, the slave falls into brutishness and decay and becomes a skeptic/nihilist. This would not do for Hegel, hence the reason for the eventual abandonment of Stoic philosophy.

Hegel's second reason for human boredom, which is similar to Schopenhauer's, is due to human's propensity to pursue pleasure. In another of his dialectical stages he explains that man enters a hedonistic phase in which he endeavors to maximize his pleasure over pain. However, he finds this unsatisfying because he finds himself continually seeking the same thing, which becomes just more of the same. The predictable result is that he becomes bored with the commonness of it all. To escape his new-found enemy, boredom, he seeks new pleasures, which only return him to his original state of requiring more unsatisfying pleasure. The irony Hegel is explaining is the exciting pursuit of pleasure only dulls pleasure, hence the inexorable consequence of boredom.

Schopenhauer, Johnson and Hegel describe Art's cycle of boredom and pain, but Bertrand Russell filled in the blanks. Like Hegel, Russell in his *The Conquest of Happiness* also believed humans are unique in experiencing boredom. Russell wrote that many of the sins of mankind, such as wars, pogroms, prosecutions and quarrels with neighbors, are due to human's desire to escape boredom. For Russell, boredom causes unhappiness, and efforts to escape it are natural.

Russell cites three reasons humans become bored, which are excitement, competition and desire. Russell believed too much excitement brings a (p) life of distractions and dissipations and causes thoughts to always be directed toward the next pleasure rather than distant achievement. Too much excitement is a deep-seated human over-cultivation of the will at the expense of the senses and intellect. Gambling, ubiquitous iPhones and Art's computer games are instant pleasures, but when the pleasure ceases people feel (p) dusty, dissatisfied and hungry for they know not what. A life full of excitement is exhausting, requiring stronger stimuli to achieve pleasure, which eventually brings ennui and boredom. For Russell, boredom is not necessarily evil, but its consequences are. Boredom brings morbid cravings and exhaustion, which humans cannot stand for long, which propels them to seek excitement—hence Schopenhauer's unhappy cycle repeats itself.

Russell believed the reason people experience boredom is because humans have detached themselves from the slow processes of nature. He called it the rhythms of Earth life. Eons of evolution have adapted humans to nature and her natural cycles. These cycles do not produce excitement or joy but are profoundly satisfying. They are the instinctual pleasures that connect people with the life of Earth. Fast living, fast time and technology have detached people from the life of Earth, which has brought the bastard boredom.

Russell used sex without love as an example. Today, humans pursue sexual intercourse to bring them orgasmic pleasure. But sexual intercourse alone is ultimately unsatisfying because it just becomes Epicurus's more of the same. It is an experience that only gives momentary pleasure, but then fatigue, disgust and a hollow feeling follows. For Russell, love is part of life on Earth, and sex without love is eventually boring and never satisfying.

Russell believed competition brings boredom. Competition can be exciting, but in excess, it produces nervous fatigue that only results in the desire to escape, and the result is leisure. Leisure, although relaxing, is boring, so some seek competition, and the Schopenhauer's cycle begins anew. How human desire initiates the cycle of boredom and pain is more obvious. Desire brings excitement, but excessive desire brings, again, more of the same. The result is ennui and boredom. This boredom, which is a thwarted desire for events, becomes intolerable so to escape it people again pursue their desires for excitement, and again Schopenhauer's cycle repeats itself.

Russell wrote that some people are particularly susceptible to this cycle and thus unhappy. He mentioned urban dwellers, the rich and those who rise in the social scale. Urban populations are bombarded daily by sources of excitement, which detaches them from the life of Earth. He described their lives like a dusty and thirsty pilgrimage in the desert. The rich and particularly those in the city have innumerable choices how to live their lives, but they are mere distractions. They pursue their lively entertainments but feel empty. For Russell what they are really endeavoring to escape their fear of boredom. Those with new social status are overwhelmed with new intense entertainments, which cause them to expect more. They begin desiring new, previously unknown excitements and new places. Art is an example of the upper class wealthy city dweller Russell described, whose excitement is computer gaming that only leads him to boredom and pain.

There are many ways to escape Schopenhauer's cycle, the first of which is to escape desire. What they have in common are ways to relieve the need for excitement and endure boredom.

This may sound odd, but escaping desire in a way means to develop the capacity to endure boredom. Indeed, Russell considered the ability to endure boredom an essential ingredient of happiness. Boredom can become relaxation, quietude and peace. Why not consider boredom these? Indeed, Russell advocated living in Earth time rather than excitement. He wrote that few great men's lives have been exciting and that most live the quiet life. Henry David Thoreau living on Walden Pond living the quiet and simple Earth life was far happier than the rich urban dweller like Art.

Other ways include putting competition in perspective and philosophy. People should compete but not make it an end in itself. Competition brings out the best in products but too often the worst in man. Many philosophies of life include ways to deal with the sources of excitement and boredom. Stoic philosophy, for example, gives ways to limit desire, and Epicureanism offers alternate sources of pleasure. Both philosophies mitigate pleasure and the need for excitement as well as limit the sources of pain and the occurrence of boredom.

Two ways to limit boredom and pain, which have been described throughout this book, are to have the right goals and develop meaning and purpose in life. Playing computer games to pass time is not an enduring life goal. With this goal, Art only achieves temporary excitement and distraction and not anything permanent or meaningful. He is not striving for some worthy life goal. The pursuit of wealth, for example, could be the goal to support a family and achieve financial security or avarice. The former is an enduring and worthy goal, and the latter a treadmill that only leads to more of the same emptiness and eventually boredom. Excitement and boredom are free-floating aimless states that have no direction, so developing directed, meaningful purpose in life is another way to avoid them.

This precipitates an oft-discussed issue in philosophy, which is whether life has any ultimate purpose. The existentialists, for example, believed there is none, which means that the real lesson from Schopenhauer's theory is that people must accept the fact that meaning in life is created by mankind. If people want to avoid boredom and pain and wish to achieve satisfaction, they must be satisfied with what meaning they can create in life and cannot expect if from somewhere else, like from one of Art's computer games.

Finally, engaging reason mitigates boredom and pain in a variety of ways. With reason, people connect causes with consequences, so the sources of pain become conspicuous. This helps them find solutions that help them avoid Schopenhauer's cycle. Using a reasoning brain also, as Russell pointed out, occupies one's mental faculties. One uses his mind and thinks, which is an active process and not the passive one in the case of excitement and boredom.

Philosophers Schopenhauer, Johnson, Hegel and Russell have explained a source of human unhappiness. The cycle of boredom and pain driven by excitement, competition and desire must be transcended in order to achieve happiness. In the introduction, it was asserted that happiness requires effort, and some solutions that require effort have been offered, including escaping desire, living simply, limiting competition, becoming a philosopher, having the right goals and purpose in life, and using reason. Do not be Art, avoid the pendulum and be happy.

Chapter Eleven

DEATH
Do not Be Denial, Folly, Neurotic, Hermit or Forceful

It is purported that dying atheist W. C. Fields was once caught reading a Bible and when asked why, he said he was looking for a loophole. A common fear among all humans is the thought that their short lives meet empty eternity. Knowing that people die and become nothing causes great fear, angst and unhappiness in people. Unlike the other animals, God played a cruel hoax on humans—he gave them unique knowledge that they die. Ernest Becker once wrote that man's terrible burden is to know he dies. Other animals without a human brain are unaware they die, which brings a kind of unreflective contentedness. Humans do not have this luxury.

In response to the fear of death, philosophy says that in order to be happy, people must overcome knowledge and fear of it—they must accept it. Indeed, philosopher Martin Heidegger once wrote that death is a necessary condition of life, which means that to admit that people are human beings that die is healing because it enables them to live a stronger and more vivacious life unencumbered by the fear of death. For many, this is a tall order.

It is this tall order that has particularly interested philosophers, as this chapter reveals. Its mystery, finiteness and metaphysical implications have attracted their attention for centuries. Albert Camus once wrote that the only serious philosophic problem is whether to commit suicide. Ancient philosopher Epictetus constantly reminded people that death and disease will overtake them whatever they are doing, and Roman stoic philosopher Cicero believed that the best thing for men is to not to be born at all; if they are, the next best thing is to die as soon as possible. For Cicero, the whole life of the philosopher is preparation for death. This chapter is about these philosophers' thoughts and how they can help man deal with death and live happier lives.

There are two parts to this chapter. The first part explains why people fear death, and the second offers reasons why they should not.

Most intuitively know the first part but are unaware of the second. It should be noted that Roman poet and philosopher Lucretius, who wrote extensively on death in his book *The Nature of Things*, is quoted from that book throughout this chapter.

Above all, humans fear the unknown. They fear that which they cannot know or comprehend. How does one comprehend death? No one who has died in human history has ever revealed what really happens after a person's last breath. Death is the great impenetrable unknown. Certainly, people all live with unknowns, such as what the future holds, but death is final—it has no future. Too often this fear of the unknown death incites imaginations to create solutions such as afterlives, heaven and reincarnation. Indeed, Søren Kierkegaard in *Three Discourses on Imagined Occasions* wrote that death is not a monster except for in imagination. Things people cannot understand incite fear, which their imagination magnifies beyond proportion. Such is the case of death.

Many fear the pain from illness that accompanies dying. This is certainly a real fear due to a physical cause—this is a fear not created by the mind or imagination. The lung cancer patient enduring suffocation, the dying pedestrian hit by a car feeling multiple stings and pangs, and the heart attack victim with the feeling of an elephant on their chest are real physical sources of unhappiness. Not much can be said to ameliorate this fear other than not all deaths involve pain, such as a dying person in a coma, and thanks to modern medicine, there exists today a variety of analgesics that lessen or eliminate pain. Further, many societies today, such as the state of Oregon, allow those who know they are going to die the option to commit suicide—hence avoiding the pain of death.

To become nothing is a fearsome thought. The time when, as Turgenev wrote, the brain hands in its resignation, the body ceases to function and one dies and becomes a corpse is hard for one to comprehend. Ernest Nagel in *What Does It All Mean?* explained that no one can conceive of their own nonexistence. It is like trying to describe what it is like to be unconscious, but one cannot. People simply cannot conceive what is like to be annihilated. This is a fear humans hold, which Epictetus wrote is the source of all human evils—the fear of death and nothingness.

But why is being nothing such a terrible thing? It is neither pleasant nor unpleasant because people cannot experience it. And why worry, because people have no control over whether it happens. Spinoza wrote that a free man does not think of death rather meditates on life. So the solution is to focus on life and accept nothingness.

Some lament the end of their experience of living. They are accustomed to life and naturally want to preserve it. People feel remorseful about losing experience in two ways; the loss of experience for themselves, and the loss of experience from others. When people think about losing their experience, they really fear the loss of themselves and their loss of experience. They are, in effect, saying goodbye to themselves and mourning the loss of the self. This often translates into the desire to experience sensation in death in order to make one survive. But this is a waste of time, because it is impossible to survive death.

Losing experience from others, on the other hand, is the fear of losing loved ones and friends. People lament leaving other people. They are sad at having to say goodbye to their wives, children and old friends. They also mourn not knowing what will happen to them. One mother who had spent a lifetime caring for children lamented death because she would no longer know their future lives and fates.

Philosophers and literary figures have described the angst due to the fear of death, its consequences and the various strategies people use to escape it. Unfortunately, the strategies they describe invariably fail. Two such thinkers are Ernest Becker and Søren Kierkegaard.

Becker, in his profound book *The Denial of Death*, described how death pervades thoughts and life experiences. He described death as man's peculiar and quietest anxiety. He described it as a human paradox in which people are out of nature due to their mind but helplessly in it due to their body—the splendidly unique mind is helplessly aware that the body that supports it will someday go into the ground to rot. With this realization, the mind creates strategies to overcome the fear of a rotting body.

Some endeavor to ignore or simply forget that they die and rot, but it seems impossible for them to ignore what they know. Others endeavor to deny their grotesque fate, but the cost is pretending not to be mad. Some escape into Epicurean pleasure but find pleasure insatiable. The industrious retreat into work to keep them from thinking about death and going mad, but their lives are made less full, and when not working, the thought of death remains. Finally, many escape into illusion to avoid the fear of death and remain happy and well adjusted. They use illusion because they cannot live with the truism that people die. Ironically, this may be the common collective strategy—those with the purest illusions are called normal and those with no illusions are called neurotic. Indeed, it has been said that illusions are necessary for normal life—if people could read others' thoughts, they would have no friends. But illusions are in constant tension with reality and ultimately break down. All these strategies fail, so Kierkegaard's solutions must be explored.

Kierkegaard was a philosopher who also believed death is man's greatest anxiety. He wrote that people are given consciousness of the terror of their own death and decay, which is a dread from which they cannot flee. To cope with this terror, people develop strategies that lead them to either three types of inauthentic or two types of authentic men.

The first of the three inauthentic men is Mr. Denial, who blocks off perceptions of reality. He artificially limits perception in order to eliminate sources that remind him of his inevitable death. This kind of strategy only results in character defenses and armor. He lives with automatic styles and uncritical living that obviates his own uniqueness. He does not belong to himself and is not his own person. He is confined to culture and a slave to it. For Kierkegaard, he is tranquilized into the trivial.

The second strategy comes from Mr. Folly, who has too much possibility, which only results in madness. He is a man beaten by the world due to his knowledge of his impending death. He is bound by a finite body, which limits his freedom. To escape madness, he endeavors to live a lie, but this flaunts reality that only results in a breakdown of character. Too much possibility brings only depressive psychosis and a blinding of alternative ways of life and freedom from a network of obligations. So, he forgets himself and embeds himself in others, which only leads to slavery, which he believes is safe and meaningful. This strategy for Kierkegaard literally leads to one who has died to live but must remain physically in this world.

The third is Mrs. Neurotic. This is how most people escape the fear of death—by becoming neurotic. They are people who avoid extremes and follow a middle course. Kierkegaard called this philistinism. These people figure out how to live safely within the probabilities of a given set of social rules. They tranquilize themselves with the trivial.

The fourth and fifth stratagems are used by authentic persons. The fourth shall be called Mr. Hermit. He has contempt for immediacy, tries to cultivate his interiority, bases his pride on something deeper and creates a distance between himself and the average man. Kierkegaard calls this man an introvert. He enjoys solitude and withdraws periodically to reflect and nurse ideas on what might be. He holds himself somewhat apart from the world but not completely. He prides himself on a vaguely felt superiority.

The fifth and final strategy is used by Mrs. Forceful, who asserts herself in order to escape the fear of death. She tries to be God, self-created and master of her fate. She plunges into life with a restless spirits, which often manifests itself in wonton sensuality and perhaps debauchery. She sometimes becomes demonic in her revolt against existence.

These characterizations of people and their various strategies by Becker and Kierkegaard to avoid the fear of death only result in neurosis, illusion, debauchery, madness, isolation and pride. They all fail because their strategies fail, and in the end Denial, Folly, Neurotic, Hermit and Forceful still fear death.

There remains one final solution to avoid demise, which is religion. For many, the thought of an afterlife truly is the balm for their fear of death. Adopting a faith in an afterlife brings them relief from angst. This may be a stratagem that works for some, but it does not work for those without faith. And even those with faith often live in fear of losing their illusion and returning to reality.

It seems none of these strategies to avoid the fear of death work—they are all paladins. So, one must look at life from a different reasoned and practical perspective, or that of some philosophers. Their solutions are to be realistic, face death and accept it.

The natural question is: why consider these philosophers' solutions? If one commits suicide, the question evaporates. But then he is left in a bind because if he fears death he fears committing suicide. Indeed, as was mentioned in the introduction, philosopher Albert Camus once wrote that suicide is the only real philosophic problem. The ancient stoics, for example, advised suicide as a solution for unhappiness, and stoic philosopher Seneca wrote that freedom is always near—just kill yourself.

To further complicate the introduction to the philosophers' solutions for not fearing death, consider ancient presocratic philosopher Thales' view. Thales held that there is no difference between life and death. For him, it is the same thing to be living and dead, the former aspect becomes the latter, and the latter becomes the former. He was asked then why he did not kill himself, to which he predictably answered, "Because there is no difference." So, it seems that it does not matter that one dies because one will die. It seems that it does not matter that one dies and it does not matter that it does not matter. Indeed, Anna Akhmatova in her *Requiem* wrote that death will come in any case—so why not now?

So, one arrives at an ostensible state of ambivalence, where it does not matter whether one lives or dies, in which suicide becomes a viable alternative. So why then do more people not commit suicide, get life over with and stop fearing death? They do not because they want to live, which is the point of all this. It is the desire to live that is the source of the fear of death. So, from this perspective consider the philosophers' rational reasons why not to fear it. One may discover that the specter of death is not so bad after all. Indeed, Gustave Flaubert wrote that death holds no terrors for a philosopher.

The first thing to consider is whether life itself is so great. If it is not so great, then why lament leaving it? Life is a bitch on three levels. The first level is earthly—the body. Think of it: Bodies must be fed, kept warm, eliminated, cleaned, medicated, slept, sexually satisfied, groomed and exercised to name a few needs. People live in fear of their bodies contracting illness, facing pain or being emotionally disturbed. Bodies are a source of ongoing trouble and angst in life. The second level is social. During lives of drudgery, people quarrel with others, fight with their spouses, divorce, endure work, face bills, struggle with debt, face disapprobation from others, and sometimes are fined or jailed, endure poverty, are robbed, are spurned and suffer jealousy—the list is endless. Jean-Paul Sartre once wrote that hell is other human beings. If this is not enough, there is a third ontological level consisting of circumstances beyond one's control, such as death in war, pestilence, earthquakes, fire, typhoons and carnivorous animals. Many bad things can and do happen to people that are totally beyond their control. Knowing all this, one must ask: Why life is so great? There are far more sources of unhappiness than happiness in life, so why cherish it? Happiness indeed is a very fragile thing.

Philosophers and writers have considered life's difficulties. Lucretius believed people should not fear death because when they no longer exist, nothing can happen to them. For Lucretius, thanks to death, people become free from mental anguish and fear and find an end to their troubles. In death, they no longer endure pain, have to provide food for their bodies or, it must be added, pay bills. In death, people no longer miss their selves or lives because they are dead. They are freed from that Sisyphean life of forever having to roll the stone back up the mountain. Indeed, Lucretius asks what is so bitter about sleep and repose.

Shakespeare famously asked in *Hamlet* whether it is better to live or die—or to be or not to be. Hamlet was facing a plethora of troublesome life issues, like most people. He, like others, sometimes found himself slowly dying under the fist of fortune. Like Hamlet, most face the question whether it is better to endure fortunes blows or just die. Life for many is full of trouble. So why not die and avoid the troubles? Mark Twain often said that he envied the dead. His view was that living is full of troubles that the dead do not suffer, which is a reason for envy.

Turgenev and Plato took these thinkers thoughts to their logical conclusions. Turgenev in *Fathers and Sons* wrote (v) the noonday blaze dies away and is succeeded by the evening and then the night; and returning there, in peaceful retreat, the tormented and weary find their sweetest sleep. Death may indeed be a sweet sleep at the end of life's struggles, disappointments and tribulations. Plato in the *Timaeus* wrote that (p) his soul will be loosened from the bonds and able to fly away with joy when he dies. For Plato, death is freedom from everyday cares and burdens—it is a pleasure and not a pain.

So, if one agrees with these philosophers' views that death is a happy ending to a life of trouble, he must consider Marcus Aurelius' thoughts that (p) one should pass through this tiny fragment of time and then leave it gladly and that human life is mere smoke and nothing—why then the stress over dying?

Plato once wrote that desire causes unhappiness. Perpetually desiring what one does not have only brings dissatisfaction and a vague sense of empty yearning. What better way to eliminate yearnings than death? As Cicero wrote, (p) happiness comes when people have left their bodies behind and are free from all desires and envies-the burdens of care are relaxed. Desire demands a reward and, as Lucretius said, people think death is awful because it takes away the prizes of life, but on the other hand it also takes away the desire for these prizes. Indeed, as Seneca pointed out, how nice it is to have outworn one's desires. Death is the ultimate way out from unhappiness due to desire. It is, as Marcus Aurelius wrote, a relief from one's reaction to the sense, impulse, the analytical mind and the flesh.

Consider a thought experiment. Desires presuppose one cares about something. Put another way, if one did not care to live, then he would have no desire to live. If he had no desire to live, then he would not fear death. From the perspective of living a healthy life, he knows someday he will become feeble and die, so why not think of that time of infirmity now? Doing so would make death not so bad because he would be finally freed from his desires and cares. Why not embrace its salubrious benefits now rather than wait for them to come in the future? Cicero once wrote (p) how delightful should the journey of life prove that when it closes it leaves no further cares or anxieties for the future.

Earlier in this chapter, it was asserted that human's fear of the unknown is a source of the fear of death. Certainly, what happens after one dies is unknown, but that one dies is known. Everyone dies. Epictetus wrote that it makes no difference how one dies because he must, and Shakespeare poetically described life as short blips in time round with sleep. Indeed, death is the norm and living is the exception, so it must be natural to die and become dead forever. Actor Guy Langland in the movie *The Misfits* said that everyone has to die sometime, so dying is as natural as living.

The point of this is that death is natural—it is normal. So, the philosophers would ask: Why fear something that is natural and normal? Eating, sleeping and sex are natural and normal, and people do not fear them, so why fear death? Epictetus said that sensible corn would not want to be reaped, but sensible or not, corn naturally dies, so why should sensible man curse natural death? As adults, people should accept death as a function of nature—only children according to Marcus Aurelius fear nature's functions. People are, he continued, simply awaiting death as one of the functions of nature. Bodies, Epictetus says, are not one's own rather are nature's corpses.

Many philosophers discuss the cycle of life: birth, living and death. For them, it is a timeless cycle that people should accept rather than fear. People should be grateful that they have the opportunity to experience the cycle, enjoy its benefits and then gratefully pass on. Lucretius wrote (p) that people grow up, enjoy the prizes of life and yield to their years—it must happen this way because old things always yield to new things. People must perish so future generations may grow, who in turn will follow. Life is a possession of no one, but on loan to all.

Cicero put it more bluntly when he wrote (v): die when nature says—those were the terms of the loan. Virgil put it more poetically in the *Aeneid* when he wrote (p): I have lived and completed now the course that Fortune long ago allotted me. The cycle of life ought not to be feared because, as Epictetus pointed out, people are restored again to the material whence they came.

So, this thought on the cycles of life can be concluded with Seneca, who believed that people should not be disturbed by death because it is (v) unnatural to hope for one more day. Indeed, if one thinks about it, death is like long, calming sleep after a very strenuous day.

Another question the philosophers would ask is: why would one want to live forever? Eternal life could be hell if one thinks about it. A person would end up doing the same things over and over and life would be dull and boring. For Marcus Aurelius, it would be just more of the same, and life would become wearisome and tiring. He wrote that (v) that it makes no difference if one lives a thousand years because he will see the same things. This same thought was reiterated by contemporary philosopher Thomas Nagel, who thought that death should be something to be afraid of only if one survives it. If one survived it he would be immortal and forever live a life of dull repetition.

One of this author's favorite thoughts along these lines comes from Friedrich Nietzsche, who believed that everyone should die at the right time. This means each person has an allotted time to live, a time of his or her own, to be a child, develop friends, marry, have families, become grandparents and then die. It is a special time, and when it is over, one should die, which happens at the right time. If a person lived before or beyond this time, he would be an outsider, a stranger in others' time. His parents, childhood friends, spouse, children, grandchildren or even descendants would not be there. The point is for one to appreciate his unique time alive and accept death when it comes.

Another of this author's favorite philosophic reasons not to fear death is that a person was nothing before they were born and do not fear that, so why should they fear returning to that state when they die? Ancient philosopher Seneca wrote that in death it will be the same for one as before birth, and Lucretius asked (p) if the vast amount of time before is nothing, why be distressed to return to it? Indeed, he wrote that people were nothing before they were born and do not fear that, so why should they fear becoming nothing again after they die—it is the same. Contemporary philosopher

Thomas Nagel echoed the same theme when he asked why it is hard for some to accept a world without them. He asked, (p) when one accepts the fact that there was a time before he was born and did not exist, why should he be so disturbed at the prospect of a similar time after death? The world was without him then and it will just return to being without him again. It is the same, so it should not matter.

Philosophers like Marcus Aurelius say that departing from the world of men is nothing to fear. Why fear being dead if it is a place where one feels no misery? Lucretius wrote that (v) a person who does not exist cannot be miserable. Indeed, misery becomes irrelevant because if a person is dead, it does not even matter that he was born. Contemporary philosopher Charles Hartshorne wrote that (v) only dead people have fully definite careers. In death, there are no more failures and disappointments. Like Lucretius, Hartshorne is echoing Aurelius's admonition that death should not be feared because in it one cannot be miserable.

For Lucretius, death should erase misery because nothing matters. In death, it would make no difference to someone who he was before, it would not matter that he was born and he would remember nothing. Humans fear misery because it makes them unhappy, but death eliminates misery so it should be embraced rather than feared.

The question can be posed—who fears death? As it turns out, death is usually feared most by those furthest from it. For them it is like a malevolent kind of unknown stranger ushering them into a house of doom. Ironically, as one grows closer to it, death becomes more like an old friend welcoming him home. In many ways, it is feared at a distance, but a friend close up. Ultimately, death is, as Michel de Montaigne wrote, just the moment when dying begins. It is just a moment and nothing before or after that moment. So why do people have so such dread of the moment of dying? And why attach so much importance to the periods before and after that moment? If death is just a moment, why contaminate life before that moment with the dread of it? Indeed, according to Lucretius, it is not the prospect of death, emptiness and nothingness that humans dread but rather fear of chance in life.

A common theme to assuage the fear of death among philosophers is to remain indifferent to it. Seneca, for example reasoned that because people cannot control that which is outside their choice, such as death, they should remain indifferent to it. He wrote that (p) a man is a fool who wishes to have lived a thousand years ago, and similarly the one who wishes he could live another thousand years. They are the same—one did not exist and will not exist; neither period should concern him. For the stoics like Seneca, happiness and freedom lie within the field of choice, and unhappy servility derives from matters of inevitability, like death. Their solution is to remain indifferent to fate.

A similar view was espoused by French existentialist philosopher Simone de Beauvoir. She wrote: (v) My death interrupts my life only when I die, and that is only from the point of view of others. Death does not exist for me while I am alive; my project goes right through it without meeting any obstacles. The full impetus of my transcendence runs into no barriers; it alone determines when it shall run down, like the sea, which strikes against a smooth shore and stops at a certain point, to go no further. So, acknowledge and accept death and remain indifferent to it. Do not let its specter contaminate one's project and one's only time to exist.

The ancient philosophic school of stoicism is quoted throughout this chapter because its philosophers pondered at length the fear of death. Their views are many, so for brevity four common themes espoused by Cicero, Seneca, Epictetus and Marcus Aurelius on death and how to think about it will be presented. They are that old age is pleasant, that death enables people to escape their troubles, that one should be grateful for the life he had and that one should accept death.

For the stoics, old age is a pleasant time of life that all should enjoy. Seneca compared it with the experience of childhood when he wrote that (v) at either end of life there is deep tranquility. His wonderful metaphor is that people should (p) cherish and enjoy old age because fruit tastes most delicious when the season is ending. Cicero also lauded old age because in it people can happily exit life. He wrote that (p) ripeness, or old age, is so pleasant because the closer one comes to death the more he seem to come within sight of land, coming at long last into harbor after a far voyage. The end of life's voyage makes one ripe for death. For Cicero, old age is like the last act of a play in which, if one has had his fill of the play, he ought to make his exit.

The consolation of death that enables people to escape their cares and desires discussed earlier is the second theme of the stoics. Cicero wrote that (p) in death one escapes the shackles of the body and the chains of life. With death, life's duties have been discharged, and in it there is no anxiety for the future. For Cicero, when people depart from life, they should joyfully and thankfully consider that they are being set free from prison. For Seneca (pe) when man has learned how to die, he has learned how not to be a slave to life, particularly from political powers. For Epictetus, death enables one to escape life's troubles, which makes it (v) every man's heaven and refuge.

My favorite reason not to fear old age and death is that one should be grateful that he has had the opportunity to live so long. Think of all the people who have died young in childhood or from disease, famine and war that never had the chance to grow old. In many ways, old age and impending death is a blessing that few experience. Indeed, prior to modern times, people died early—often in their forties or fifties. People should be grateful that they can grow old because not everyone has the opportunity. Epictetus wrote that (v) people should say when they die that they are thankful for the time they got to use and are content with the time they had, and Cicero added that one should (pe) be grateful for the life he had and die with a song of rapture for the life he has lived. Marcus Aurelius put it simply with the idea that (p) one should be content with his allocation of time. The fear of death is dampened when one considers what he has had rather than what he will lose.

The final stoic theme that has been repeated throughout this chapter is to accept death. Seneca wrote (v) do not fret about death before your eyes because it is unnatural to hope for one more day—every journey has its end. Cicero thought that death is sleep, there is no loss and should thus be met calmly. Epictetus said that the world will not be turned upside down when one dies, and Marcus Aurelius concluded with the thought that one will die and shortly after not even his name will be left. Accepting inevitable death brings peace of mind and ultimately happiness.

Given the thought that death is a necessary condition of life, this chapter will conclude with three ideas that ameliorate the finality of the condition. The first wonderful sentiment comes from Lucretius who wrote that (p) one should depart like a banqueter who is sated with life, and embrace untroubled quiet with calm of mind, having had a grand time and being grateful to be invited to the party. What one has enjoyed is over, it is hateful to seek more, which itself would eventually perish. The second comes from Cicero who sprightly said when death looks a man in the face, the only thing he can do is smile back. So, smile back at death. The final thought comes from an old proverb, which is to remember that everyone only dies once. Even if one fears death, at least he only has to do it once.

Chapter Twelve

PRIDE AND ENVY
*Remember each person dies
and probably has average abilities*

Jim is a closet egomaniac. He thinks he is better than others and everything that happens in the universe happens to him. His demeanor is naturally arrogant. In conversations, Jim invariably talks about himself, and if the conversation drifts away from him, he always brings it back. Every sentence is imbued with "I"—I am this, I did this and I have this. People feel weakened around Jim as if their life blood has been sucked from them. They usually feel like they are not in the room. Louis is less concerned with himself and more concerned with comparing himself to his neighbor. Looking at his neighbor's better house and fancier car makes Louis angry. He always asks himself, "Why should my neighbor have those nice things and not me?" He always thinks that he deserves them. In conversations, he constantly demeans others. Louis has a sharp, volatile, unpredictable, sometimes irrational edgy personality that is prone to outbursts of anger. Jim and Louis are unhappy and not sure why.

Pride and envy are sources of unhappiness. In Jim and Louis's cases, it is because people do not like them and avoid them. Jim makes people feel unimportant, and waspish Louis irritates them. There are a number of reasons pride and envy are among the seven deadly sins, but one is because they make those that possess them miserable and unhappy. Blaise Pascal wrote that (p) all men seek happiness, even those that hang themselves, but some seek happiness in pride. Some inflate their self worth in order to imagine themselves important. William Shakespeare in *Julius Caesar* described envy as that (v) lean and hungry look. It is a look that reveals anger and revenge. So, this chapter will examine what the philosophers say about pride and envy, why they bring unhappiness and how to avoid them.

Pride is a recurring topic in philosophy. People all know the proverb pride goes before the fall and many have read Alexander Pope's poem on pride in *An Essay on Criticism* (v);

> Of all the causes which conspire to blind,
> Man's erring judgment, and misguide the mind,
> What the weak head and strongest bias rules,
> Is pride, that never-ending vice of fools.

The question is what pride is. Is it, for example vanity, self-esteem or hubris? Aristotle believed pride is different than hubris. He considered it (SEP) a virtue and necessary for a noble and good character. Some worthy individuals are entitled to feel pride, which he calls rightful pride. In this case it is not vanity, or excessive pride. Those who think themselves worthy of little are temperate and not proud. Hubris or excessive pride manifest in arrogance is due to gratification that naïve men feel because they believe that by ill-treating others they make themselves superior. Hubris brings shame for Aristotle. Self-esteem is a kind of pride in which one feels worthy, confident and self-respectful. The question of pride then deals with how it manifests itself. In, hubris it is a vice, whereas in rightfully honoring oneself, as in self-esteem, it is a virtue. Indeed, the edgy actor Rod Steiger once said that if one did not think he was special, he would never get up in the morning.

Pride as hubris is a vice because it hurts the prideful. They may be looking for praise or adoration in order to be happy, but in reality they are not because people despise them. David Hume in *A Treatise on Human Nature* wrote that (v) excessive pride or overweening conceit of ourselves is always esteemed vicious and is universally hated. Benjamin Franklin wrote in *Poor Richard's Almanac* that (v) pride that dines on vanity sups on contempt. If people are vain and arrogant they will be held in contempt. Such hubris is deadly; it ruins relationships, warps opinion, causes war and robs it victim of happiness.

Pride originates when people excessively focus on themselves. C. S. Lewis in the *Screwtape Letters* has Screwtape advise Wormwood to keep humans focused on themselves because it will engender cynicism, gloom and cruelty. Self-love will keep humans focused on what is in their favor and keep them from loving their neighbor. The enemy according to Screwtape perpetuates a lie, which is that one can love another, when in reality it is impossible to love another. Vanity is the solution for unhappiness. With it, people become cynical, gloomy and cruel, and they separate themselves from others' affections.

For the philosophers, to be happy, one must avoid excessive pride and not be self-absorbed or preoccupied with oneself. Bertrand Russell wrote that (p) vanity seeking love has no genuine interest in the other, so no real satisfaction or love is obtained from them. The vain are not of interest to others because a man who is only interested in himself is not admirable. For Russell, admiration comes from being other-regarding. Alexander Pope stated that it is presumptive for a person to think the universe revolves around him and La Rochefoucauld that (v) the vast pleasure people get from talking about themselves should warn them that they are giving almost no pleasure to those who are listening.

Boethius, who has been quoted often in this book, in *The Consolation of Philosophy* says that (p) due to vanity, people may seek glory and fame ,but ultimately they will be forgotten. There have been many famous men in history, but they are now unknown. Compared with eternity, fame is nothing. Fame is just from common gossip of the people, and people have many wrong opinions. Popularity's acquisition is fortuitous, and its retention continuously uncertain. For Boethius, those who have fame have nothing.

Happiness cannot be measured by pride-driven popularity derived from other people's feelings but rather by the true voice of one's own experience. So, for Russell, Pope, La Rochefoucauld and Boethius, people must avoid prideful vanity, focus outward and humble themselves because some day they will be forgotten.

Two pejorative consequences of vanity are boredom and isolation. Bertrand Russell wrote that (v) vanity kills pleasure and leads to listlessness and boredom. Those who are self-absorbed lead inert lives of inactivity and unhappiness. He also believed that egoistic pride isolates people from others. No satisfaction comes from an over-cultivation of one element of human nature, in this case pride over others. For Russell, to be happy, people should focus on external objects because it leads to activity and connectivity with others. It brings friends, which bring pleasure and happiness.

Philosophers have emphasized the importance of good judgment as an antidote for vanity. Seneca believed that to be happy, people must use proper judgments of impressions because it will result in the holding of right beliefs and attitudes. Vanity is a wrongful attitude because, as Seneca pointed out, (v) no one cannot lead a happy life when one thinks only of himself and turns others to one's purposes. Seneca wrote in his *Letters from a Stoic* that (v) sadness will cease as soon as one takes his eyes off of himself.

David Hume in *A Treatise of Human Nature* took Seneca's observation to the next level when he observed that proper judgments also include judgment of one's own abilities. Few resent the talented individual with quiet pride, and everyone resents the untalented vain individual. Pretense is almost universally despised by people. Hume wrote that (v) nothing is more disagreeable than a man's over-weaning conceit of himself and that (p) the impertinent and almost universal propensity of men to over-value themselves has given people such prejudice against self-applause that they are apt to condemn it whenever they meet with it. Indeed, La Rochefoucauld wrote in his *Maximes* that (v) pride exists equally in all men; the only difference lies in what ways they manifest it.

To be happy, put a fence around pride and look outwards. If one lacks this ability because he feels a lack of self-esteem, remember Eleanor Roosevelt's comment: (v) nobody can make you feel inferior without your consent.

Now it is time to look at what the philosophers say about one manifestation of pride, vanity and hubris, which is envy.

The philosophers have different views on the nature of envy but agree that it is a source of great unhappiness. Aristotle in *Rhetoric* wrote that envy is the pain at the good fortune of others. Adam Smith in *The Theory of Moral Sentiments* wrote that envy is that passion which views with malignant dislike the superiority of those who are really entitled to all the superiority they possess. Freud believed that the concern for justice is the product of envy, which leads to the concern for equal treatment, and Nietzsche considered envy the consequence of egalitarian ideals and slave morality. Generally, envy is a two-party relationship, where pain is felt by a person when he thinks he should have what another has.

Philosophers (SEP) universally consider envy unreasonable, irrational, imprudent, vicious and wrong to feel. They think envy is an emotion, a form of distress experienced by a subject because he does not possess the goods a rival has and desires them. One reason envy is seldom advisable is because it harms the one who feels it. Envy is a form of pain. It is a subjective sense in which well-being, self-worth and self-respect are diminished. This is not a formula for happiness.

Envy, resentment and jealousy are different. Some philosophers think the envy previously described is really resentment. However, resentment is not envy per se but rather the aggrieved feeling caused by envy—it is a consequence and not a cause. Jealousy is a cause and thus akin to envy but different. Jealousy (SEP) involves three parties: the subject, rival and beloved. The jealous person is concerned with the beloved and fears losing their affection. Losing affection in jealousy is different than desiring what another has. Jealousy deals with the fear of loss, and envy with the desire for gain. In either case, the consequence is unhappiness to the jealous or envious person. It is interesting to note that not all philosophers agree with this conclusion. John Rawls, for example, in *A Theory of Justice* wrote that (SEP) for those suffering hurt, envious feelings are not irrational because they gain some satisfaction from their rancor, which makes them better off.

Certainly, some may feel a pleasurable sense of satisfaction in feeling angry for their suffering, but in the end envy is a painful emotion. Perpetually looking for injustices to oneself only makes that person a victim, which perpetuates unhappiness. Such a view offers no solutions to pain; it only increases it. Samuel Johnson in *The History of Rasselas, Prince of Abissinia* wrote that (p) families are torn with envy, children rival with parents, benefits are allayed by reproaches and gratitude debased by envy. Such envious circumstances only bring greater unhappiness.

People are also ashamed of their envy. La Rochefoucauld wrote in his *Maximes* that (v) one can often be vain of his passions, even the guiltiest ones; but envy is so sneaking and shameful that he never dare confess it. One feels ashamed about exposing his envies because they expose his deepest weaknesses and what he lacks, which challenges his self-esteem, vexes his pride and makes him feel inferior. These are the fearful consequences of envy and why people hide it. They are collaterally the reasons envy brings unhappiness.

Many philosophers believe the source of envy is competition and its inevitable companion comparison. The next chapter on competition will explore why Bertrand Russell believed competition brings unhappiness. Competition leads to the need to control others in order to succeed, and if one fails he feels frustration and anger. The natural consequence then is to feel envy. Envy is very much a consequence of excessive competition.

Comparing oneself to others is the other source of envy. David Hume in *A Treatise of Human Nature* wrote that (p) overweening conceit (pride) is vicious, causes uneasiness in all men and presents a person at every moment with a disagreeable comparison. He observed that (p) those who have an ill-grounded conceit of themselves are forever making comparisons and have no other method of supporting their vanity, whereas a man of sense and merit is pleased with himself, independent of all foreign considerations; but a fool must always find some person that is more foolish in order to keep himself in good humor. So pride causes others to dislike someone, which causes unhappiness, which is increased when pride also brings comparison, making the untalented man a fool who is further despised, only increasing his unhappiness. For Hume, unwarranted comparison only brings unhappiness.

Immanuel Kant in *The Metaphysics of Morals* wrote that (SEP) the standard people use to see how well off they are is not the intrinsic worth of their own well-being but how it compares with that of others and it aims, at least in terms of one's wishes, at destroying others' good fortune. This is envy derived from comparison, and the only consequence if one fails at destroying another's good fortune is unhappiness.

Envy is the cancer of happiness. The envious inherently consider themselves victims and perpetually blame others for their problems. Nothing good comes from it, so one must keep competition in perspective, focus on his strengths and work to improve himself.

It was mentioned that pride enhances envy. The more proud people are, the more they feel the pangs of envy. When pride is violated, they feel more envy, are inclined to be isolative, and become self-absorbed, self-centered and detached from reality. The consequences are a smorgasbord of maladies including fear, a sense of sinfulness, self-pity, self-admiration and envy. Perhaps the worst is that sanctimonious feeling of having been treated unjustly.

Some philosophers believe envy-inspired feelings of injustice are a significant source of individuals' political philosophies. The envious cannot brook meritocracies like capitalism that diminish equality. They naturally embrace egalitarian, leveling philosophies like socialism because they emphasize equality. Envy causes pain when another has more, which translates into a perceived injustice. The result is an egalitarian form of social justice that ironically often does not treat all equally. The social justice of the envious ignores desert, which causes them to champion equality and diminish freedom.

This lead to the point that not all envy is justified. Envy unwarrantedly directed at something like fear can be unfittingly felt at something that is not dangerous. Why be envious of someone who has wealth but stole it? They gained advantage unfairly and immorally and are thus not fit for envy. This is a point that reveals the truism that the envious secretly admire those that gain through moral merit.

For one philosopher, the philosophers themselves are not exempt from envy. La Rochefoucauld wrote that (p) scorn for wealth among philosophers is at bottom a desire to avenge themselves against fate by despising the very things of which she deprived them. It is a strategic way of avoiding the humiliations of poverty, a roundabout way of gaining an esteem they could not get through wealth. It appears philosophers do not always exempt themselves from their own theories.

The point of all this is that envy-driven philosophies lead to anger and unhappiness. The envious man rages at his fellow man, is perpetually angry and wallows in self-righteous indignation. Envy does not bring happiness. To be happy, it is far better to transcend one's personal feelings and build oneself up rather than forever trying to tear another down. One must do what he can with what he has, be industrious, start a business and get rich. This is a far better formula for happiness.

Remember that there will always be someone more successful, so avoid the pangs of envy. Iris Murdoch wrote that (p) crippling envy can be a terrible disability, and to overcome it is a prerequisite of success. Envy is a weed that should not be watered.

Jim focused excessively on himself and was prideful, and Louis focused excessively on others and was envious, and both were reviled and unhappy. Their weaknesses only worked to destroy the vessel, so to be happy, avoid their maladies of pride and envy.

Chapter Thirteen

COMPETITION
Compete but do not make life a contest

Michael enjoys competing in sports. He loved winning but viewed the contest as a game. In life he is interested in challenges because they enable him exercise his talents and to try and improve himself. In the process, he found that he gained not only confidence but the respect of others for his achievements. He enjoys life and views it more as a journey that blends competition and cooperation. Vince is different. He views life as an ongoing intense contest of winners and losers. He cannot brook the idea of being less to anyone and thus views people as potential enemies and something to overcome and subdue at all costs. Michael is a balanced person enjoying competition and people, and Vince is always guarded, wary, combative and intensely competitive. These individuals respective sense of competition has much to do with their happiness.

Philosophers have explored the relationship between happiness and competition, and their thoughts are varied. Three such philosophers with different views are Adam Smith, Jean-Jacque Rousseau and Baruch Spinoza. Smith in *The Wealth of Nations* wrote that (p) the drive of individual self-interest in an environment of similarly motivated individuals will result in competition, which will result in the provision of those goods that society wants, in the quantities society desires at the prices society is prepared to pay. For Smith, competition is good because it results in abundance, which is one source of happiness. At the other extreme, Rousseau in his *Discourse on the Origin or Inequality* wrote how the desire for reputation, honors and advancement excites and multiplies human passion, which creates competition, rivalry and enmity among men. For Rousseau, competition is evil because it brings discord, which is a source of unhappiness. Similar to Rousseau is Spinoza, who believed man is essentially uncompetitive. For him happiness derives from peacefulness, respect and promoting the happiness of others. So who is right?

It seems there is a little truth and falsity in all these assertions. Competition can be all these things and none of them. It can bring wealth, it can bring earned respect, it can inflame passion and promote cooperation and it can bring divisiveness. Depending on the nature of the competition, it can also bring salubrious happiness or painful depression. The important thing is to discern the different forms of competition and put them in perspective.

Most philosophers have focused on the negative aspects of competition because it is a significant source of human unhappiness. Most of their views center on economics, and in particular the relative merits of capitalism and socialism. Marx, Lenin and Fourier were socialists who derided the tyranny of capitalistic competition. For them, competition only brings winners and losers. This issue is beyond the scope of this book, but it can be said that capitalism does entail competition, history shows that competition brings wealth and socialists could be Ayn Rand's men of blood and rust. Given all this, one can acknowledge that competition is real—humans are naturally competitive due to instinct and limited resources. First, this chapter will describe some of competition's benefits and then delve into its forms that the philosophers say should be avoided.

Political philosopher Adam Smith believed competition brought wealth that acted as an automatic regulator for market forces. Ayn Rand in *Atlas Shrugged* wrote that motive power is the heart of everything. It is motive power that is the engine of competition. Thomas Hobbes believed that in nature the life of man is solitary, poor, nasty, brutish and short. In such a state, it is only natural that man would be competitive in order to survive. For Hobbes this is a source of his social contract ethical theory that drives humans to cooperate and live in peace.

Ancient philosopher Heraclitus of Ephesus criticized his fellow citizens for their lack of respect for talent and the competitive spirit. The citizens of Ephesus had exiled a certain Hermodorus because he was worthier than others. Heraclitus wrote that (p) he would have them all go hang themselves for banishing Hermodorus, the best man among them, and believing that no one shall excel, and if he does let him do it elsewhere among others. Cicero echoed

Heraclitus's criticism, exclaiming how wrong it is to not allow the best to lead. In each case, competition is a source of some form of happiness, whether it is wealth, moral cooperation or exceptional achievement.

If people are industrious and competitive, they usually get what they want, whether it is money, possession, a spouse, a promotion or a nice home. These are successes that are a great source of happiness. Rather than waiting for a handout, being competitive is a way to earn desired things. It also is a source of recognition. To be competitive in a sport means to use abilities and will to train and think how to be the best. Competition creates better athletes, and those that win gain recognition and with it self-esteem. When people compete and succeed, their sense of self worth is enhanced. How can it possibly be wrong to be the best at something, to be the best one can be or try and be a better version of oneself?

Competition is also energizing. One can live their life as Mill's satisfied and underachieving pig or as a dissatisfied striving successful Socrates. Competition galvanizes energy and talents and focuses one in a single-minded way to achieve some goal. Competition also enhances certain virtues like industry and bravery. It compels people to work hard and have courage. Finally, competition fuels innovation. It was in part the spark that caused the Wright Brothers to fly, Henry Ford to build a better and less expensive Model T, Robert Watson to invent a steam engine that propels ships faster than sails and Sarnoff to turn black and white television into color. It is clear that certain forms of competition bring success, fulfillment and happiness but now turn attention to the kinds of competition philosophers deride.

Famous football coach Vince Lombardi said winning is not everything, it is the only thing, and losing is a sin; it is just a way to live with oneself—a way to live with defeat. Such thinking brought the Green Bay Packers football team success, but for many, it is a form of bad competition. For some philosophers, bad competition locks people in a treadmill, causes fatigue from overwork, brings worry and indecision, makes people too concentrated and anxious to be happy and only results in a one hundred yard dash to the grave. There are many forms of bad competition, of which the first is excess completion.

Previously mentioned David Sarnoff was the head of RCA Corporation. He competed intensely with his rival William S. Paley to develop radio, television and color television. He won, but he concluded that competition brings out the best in products and the worst in man. Many philosophers dislike excess competition because it pits one against another, brings out some of the worst human characteristics, is based on self-interest and does not promote the social weal. They believe that it is a mistake to take competition to its extremes.

There are many sources of excess competition including avarice, desire and misguided beliefs. Some, like Rousseau, blame the socialization process itself. He believed that humans in their original state were good and naturally cooperative, which the process of civilization debauched into inequality and competition. Early French socialist François Fourier imagined a society founded on the emancipation of the passions that would liberate humans from savage competition and ceaseless toil. Whatever the source, excess competition does bring a fallout of problems, including unhappiness.

Many mental and physical maladies come from living in demanding, pressure-filled environments of excess competition. When a society values productivity, money, aggression, competitiveness, status and power, undue competition naturally ensues. Individual aspirations and needs become sublimated, and humans too often become rats navigating the corridors of some contrived competitive maze. Under oppressive competition, lives often become one of obligation and duty, during which many lose what they need to be happy. It seems that many diseases are a consequence of excess competition, such as heart disease, alcoholism, anxiety, depression and ulcers. It is strange to think many modern maladies are largely culturally created due to excessive competition.

Another form of bad competition that engenders unhappiness is artificial competition. The Beeswax Company competes with the Wax from Bees Company to sell beeswax. Natural competition is when the rivals pitch their story to buyers for their product emphasizing the reasons they make superior beeswax. But Wax from Bees is losing the contest because their product is inferior, so its president decides to create a sales force within the company who are rewarded by beating the other in-company salespeople and not the Beeswax Company. The result is a hyper-induced frenzy of aggression to sell Wax from Bees beeswax. This is artificial competition, and the winner in this scenario may well be Wax from Bees, but the loser is the individual human caught in an unreal, contrived, pressure-filled environment. The individual is no longer a member of a cooperating team but rather one against all, and the result is loneliness, desperation and panic for the many losers.

Artificial competition makes humans insignificant cogs in a machine with unconcerned engineer-masters driving their pace and existence. Competitive pressure makes life for many miserable—something to endure and not enjoy. It was not competition per se that Rousseau and Fourier disparaged but rather the excessive and artificial forms of competition that cause unhappiness.

Human desire is discussed in this chapter and throughout this book and is briefly resurrected here because it is a significant source of excessive competition. Many philosophers believe that unrestrained, wrongful desires bring undue competition, and with it, unhappiness. With excessive desire, people become prone to anything that will satisfy it. When they face obstacles that thwart their desires, they intensify their competitive efforts to prevail, and the consequences too often is an artificial world detached from what human nature requires for happiness.

The pursuit of wealth that segues into avarice is one significant example or unrestrained desire. Boethius wrote that the desire for riches creates a want of its own, and once it is won, it never leaves people free. The single-minded competitive pursuit of money does not bring enduring happiness because money never satisfies, it is hard and it is unemotional. One is not warmed by something inert and dead. James Buchan in his book *Frozen Desire* describes money as frozen desire. Satisfying simple natural desires with money is not itself ruinous, but the unrelenting pursuit of money magnifies desires. With it, many find themselves on a treadmill always thinking they need more money to be happy. They come to measure their happiness not by what they have but rather in relation to another who has more. Even if they succeed in getting more than another, they still are not satisfied because someone always has more than them. The consequence of this avaricious cycle is a competitiveness that brings an anxious kind of empty fulfillment that cannot be described as happiness.

Bertrand Russell in his book *The Conquest of Happiness* described another reason competition brings unhappiness. He wrote that (v) viewing life as a contest, a competition, leads to an undue cultivation of the will at the expense of the senses and the intellect. There is more to life than the success competition sometimes brings. Excessive will derived from competition also leads to a need to control others in order to guarantee the outcomes desired. But endeavoring to control others is a significant source of unhappiness because others resent being controlled. They usually respond in resentful passage-aggressive ways that only lead to the controller's frustration and anger. The controllers incrementally find themselves further isolated from the affection of others, alone and unhappy.

When the will dominates life, the simple pleasures of just living are often lost. When life becomes a contest, people lose spontaneity and zest for life. They end up intricately planning their lives rather than living them as they unfold. Hyper-will overwhelms and numbs the sensitive receptors that allow one to appreciate the finer things in life. In order to appreciate art, music, and literature, for example, certain senses must be cultivated. If one wishes to understand philosophy, he must be open to alternate possibilities that the will alone may discourage. Will may tell one to be industrious, which causes one to forget the value of leisure. Competition alone makes one monodimensional and unbalanced.

Russell believed that when people focus excessively on work, they lose their perspectives on life. The result is fatigue, nervous strain and the inability to be interested in matters unrelated to work. The ultimate consequence is unhappiness. An excessive competitive work ethic fosters a myopic mind-set with its emphasis only on work and success. People become so absorbed in their own small pursuits they lose their perspectives on life. Certainly, work is essential for well-being, but when it is overemphasized, people lose the sheer enjoyment of living.

Finally, when people exceed in competitive struggle, the good self-esteem it engenders too often segues into pride. An inflated sense of self-worth is often the result, in which an individual comes to think he is better than others. This consequence of competition is a major source of unhappiness because as people become arrogant they collaterally become detached from others and their regard and affections. They become a kind of emperor with no clothes, where they think they are great while others think them asses.

To be happy it is better to adopt Michael's rather than Vincent's attitude toward competition. Life is more than competition and, as Thoreau believed, one should not live it with unnecessary worries because they only lead to a life of quiet desperation. Instead, one should dance to a different drummer, simplify his life and put the tyrant competition in its proper place.

Like death, competition naturally exists, but the message from the philosophers is to keep it in perspective to be happy. One must moderate competitive instincts, not let will alone run his life, put less emphasis on material things and money, have moderate desires for the right things, have self-esteem and avoid pride.

A well-rounded life requires that people keep their competitive spirit in check—championships alone do not bring happiness. It is better to experience all aspects of life by balancing willfulness with the need to cultivate the senses and intellect. Do not succumb to the siren call of injurious excess and artificial competition.

Aristotle's doctrine of the mean says to avoid extremes and live a balanced life. Life should be expansive, it should be full and it should include a variety of activities and interests to be healthy. Life is not a contest; one never regrets loving too much in life, and nature truly is easily satisfied. Focus on the simple things to live a long and happy life—do not make things complicated. One must appreciate what he has and be less competitive.

Chapter Fourteen

FEAR AND TREMBLING
Do not live in fear and trembling

Believe has a schizophrenic relationship with her faith. On one hand, the ideas of an afterlife, a caring, all powerful God and singing and prayer make her feel happy. She is particularly drawn to miracles and the good they bring. On the other hand, the thought of going to hell, a vengeful God that punishes nonbelievers and being ridiculed by others for her beliefs makes her feel unhappy. She secretly harbors the concern that miracles may not be true because they rarely happen and is especially worried that she might lose her faith and with it the happiness it brings. The conflicts Believe endures demonstrate the issue of faith and happiness. She is happy and not happy with her faith, which is a circumstance that belies unencumbered happiness through faith.

The topic in this chapter is whether faith can bring happiness. The philosophers are generally split on this issue with ancient philosophers arguing it does and recent philosophers that it does not. But first, a brief description of kinds of faith beginning from the most primitive to the more advanced. Superstition permeates most primitive societies due to ignorance and fear. The very word implies fear of unknown things. Cicero correctly observed that there is a distinction between religion and superstition. Spirituality is a mixture of magical superstition and faith. It tends to branch off into a variety of imagined mystical beliefs and unusual experiences. When superstition moves beyond fear, hope and faith are the consequence. Faith is a rationally unsupported commitment to a belief. To have it, one must make a Kierkegaardian leap and assume something to be true. Some thinkers have criticized this leap of faith including Annie Dillard, who in her book *Pilgrim at Tinker Creek* asked, if the faithful belief that people do not go to hell because they are ignorant of God and sin, then why do the priests talk about them. Religions like Christianity, Catholicism and Protestantism are the organized and ritualized expressions of superstition, spirituality and faith. The important point to note is that religion would not exist without faith. This is important because this chapter discusses faith and happiness and faith is often expressed in various religious beliefs. Believe's conflicts that affect her happiness involve both faith and religion.

Because this chapter is about faith and happiness, the nature of faith must be discussed in more detail. Faith is a feeling that manifests itself in an emotional urge that arises from human's desire to be happy. Individuals seek pleasure and avoid pain in order to be happy in many different personal and esoteric ways. Faith is some people's response to those sources of pain when they do not understand them. Humans mine their imagination for solutions and find ideas that make them happy, which become feelings manifest in faith.

At its essence, faith is the beliefs one has adopted to feel good and be happy. Indeed, nobody says that their faithful beliefs make them feel awful or miserable—rather they universally cite the happy state their faith brings. Faith is the attitudes and beliefs people adopt to make themselves feel good. Even masochists' beliefs that intend harm and unhappiness in some twisted way make them happy. In some ways faith is like trying to set aside a pain that comes back and bites. Believe adopted some religious beliefs that made her happy, so faith indeed brought her happiness. Unfortunately, her faith's baggage included some things that made her unhappy. So which is it? Does faith bring happiness or not? Mentioned previously, the philosophers are divided on this question so the ones who do not think it brings happiness will be discussed first.

Jonathan Swift wrote that some have just enough religion to hate and some not enough to love. For him, if one is religious, he is unhappy either way—being religious gives only enough to hate which brings unhappiness, and being religious brings not enough to love, which is a source of unhappiness. Religious faith does not bring happiness for Swift. Friedrich Nietzsche was particularly disdainful of faith and its ability to bring happiness. He wrote that priests, in order to support their superiority, invoke a kind of faith for asses and the inept. For him, priestly Christianity is a dogmatic faith that only leads to unhappiness. Karl Marx derided a variety of sources that he believed bring unhappiness. For him, unhappiness derives socially from class, politically from capitalism and most famously from religion, which he described as the opiate of the masses. For socialist Marx, religion is a tool used to control humans' minds and daily lives in a way that oppresses and causes materialistic misery.

Bertrand Russell had some thoughtful reasons that questioned faith's ability to bring happiness. He observed first that faith too often limits the minds of the young, which causes fanaticism, intolerance and group hostility. Such nascent minds are less inclined to cooperation and the open-mindedness so urgently needed to thrive and be happy in life. Second, to be happy, Russell believed one must set emotions and faith aside and coldly evaluate himself. This is the ancient injunction to know thyself, which Russell believes solves the problems people face that bring unhappiness. This means for Russell and the ancients that happiness originates from within. For Russell, it is cold introspective reason that solves problems and not faith because it ignores reason.

From an alternative discipline, French archaeologist Salomon Reinach wrote that religion is a body of scruples that impedes the free exercise of one's faculties. It would seem that when faith and religion limit their faculties, people become less able to solve the real problems that make them unhappy. In the chapter on health, this important relationship between the need for healthy facilities and happiness will be discussed. People need unimpeded healthy bodies and minds to wrestle with the many sources of unhappiness that life throws their way.

Mark Twain surprisingly invoked the role doubt plays in faith and its potential for unhappiness. He wrote that faith is (v) just wanting to believe what you know ain't true. This ostensibly humorous quip is profound because it reveals a deep source of religious unhappiness—the fear of losing faith and the happy illusions it brings. Down deep, when people assume some idea and they always know they just assumed it, this brings wariness and the collateral dark fear of doubt. Twain was right; living with doubt is a major source of unhappiness for those with faith. Indeed, American theologian Reinhold Niebuhr wrote that (v) frantic orthodoxy is never rooted in faith but in doubt.

The two greatest thinker-philosophers arguing against faith bringing happiness are Sigmund Freud and David Hume.

Famous psychologist Freud did not believe faith in the form of religion brings happiness. In his *Civilization and its Discontents*, he described religion is a consequence of infantile helplessness. Life is hard, and religion is a palliative measure to fulfill one's wishes and desires in order to be happy. For Freud, religion is an irrational oceanic illusion that people created in order to make themselves happy. Faith itself is a kind of mass delusion that distorts the real world, depresses the value of life and prohibits other ways to happiness.

For Freud, the origins of unhappiness derive from civilization. Indeed, he wrote that humans are constitutionally incapable of happiness due to civilization. Civilization makes earth serviceable, protects against nature, and brings beauty, cleanliness and order. But civilization naturally restricts the individual and brings an eternal struggle between the claims of the individual and the group. It is civilization's and the group's sublimation of individuals' instincts that structurally eliminates human happiness. For Freud, civilization restricts human's aggressive instincts and turns them inward, creating a conscience and sense of guilt. Guilt is particularly troublesome because it involves the fear of the loss of others' love juxtaposed with the human desire for acceptance. For Freud, civilization's renunciation of individuality, oppression of aggressive instinct and institution of guilt makes it a structure in which humans are incapable of happiness.

This author's view is that religion is one of civilization's sergeants at arms, enforcing its dictates. It does this many ways, three of which Freud mentioned are the admonition to love thy neighbor and the previously mentioned guilt and anxiety.

The Christian admonition to love thy neighbor is both admirable and risible. Certainly, if human nature could be taught to only love thy neighbor, many world problems could evaporate, like hate and war. The problem is humans are not wired to love their neighbors. It does not come naturally to them, and it causes many problems. This Christian ethic under the banner of civilization imposes duty, devalues those who deserve love and values those unworthy of love. It is an ethic that by restricting individuality and enforcing compliance only produces neurosis and unhappiness. Thus, for Freud, civilization is built on humans being neurotic, thus they are constitutionally unhappy in it.

Religious faith imposes guilt and the result is repressed human desires under civilization—mostly sexual desires. This guilt causes many maladies such as malaise and dissatisfaction, which results in remorse, contrition and artificial feelings. Faith is the driver of this irredeemable source of unhappiness and can only offer artificial help through religious redemption, which is just religion's way to assuage the guilt it imposed. The upshot of all this is that religion causes a tension between the individual and civilized culture that only makes for guilt and permanent internal unhappiness in humans. Humans cannot be happy in the broth of religion, faith and civilization.

The denouement of the religiously imposed admonitions and the guilt they engender only results in anxiety and neurosis. Anxiety is the Crockpot of human happiness for Freud, which makes man constitutionally incapable of happiness under it. There is no escape from this neuroticism, which makes faith an inexorable cause of human unhappiness.

David Hume is the other example of a philosopher who does not think faith brings happiness, although in a rather roundabout way. Hume was an unsparing critic of religion and notorious skeptic of organized Christianity. He believed religion is founded on ignorance. It is reason and not faith that can stand up to any serious scrutiny. He wrote that reason in philosophy may be ridiculous, but faith in religion is dangerous.

In his *Dialogues Concerning Natural Religion*, there is a serpentine progression from whether religious beliefs can be rational, which leads to whether the religious argument from design that God exists is true to whether God is good and the world is evil. If the world is evil, then humans necessarily will be unhappy.

To the first of the progression, Hume asserts, as an empiricist, that all knowledge comes from experience, which excludes belief. Thus, people cannot know God's nature. In the second stage, Hume endeavors to prove his point by disproving the religious argument from design, which intends to prove God exists. The religious reasoning is that the world is ordered like a clock, and like a clock then it must have a designer, which is God. Hume says this argument by analogy does not work because the universe and a machine are not analogous phenomena; the universe is a whole, and a machine is just part of it—part is not analogous to the whole. Thus, the idea that the universe is ordered does not necessarily result in an intelligent design, so God is not the intelligent designer.

So the religious effort to use reason to prove God fails for Hume. With this conclusion, Hume proceeds to attack with reason the religious beliefs that God is good. Through his characters Demea and Philo, he paints a rational, bleak picture of the universe. It is not a harmonious machine with a beneficent God but rather in reality a miserable place filled with evil. Its only goal is the survival of species and not the happiness of species. So, religious faith is irrational and cannot prove God exists or that he is good, and reason reveals the universe is miserable and evil so humans are not naturally happy souls. Thus, for Hume, faith does not bring happiness rather only illusions that paper over reality.

Many of the scholastic philosophers like Thomas Aquinas, St. Augustine and Blaise Pascal as well as some contemporary authors think faith brings happiness. Generally, their religious view is if people have faith, they will be happy. Aquinas believed that people experience perfect and unending happiness when they see the essence of God. To have faith in God requires morality, which for Aquinas brings happiness. Saint Augustine's *Confessions* exemplifies the conversion from secular worldly unhappiness to happiness from faith. He wrote about being unhappily ambitious, drunken, attached to material things and a slave to lust before his conversion. Once he gained faith in God, he discovered happiness because it restored his free will to choose grace. For Augustine, people seek not to understand in order to believe, but rather believe in order to understand—they need to believe before they can understand happiness.

Pascal strenuously argued for faith as a vehicle to happiness. He believed that heart and faith bring happiness because the heart has reasons that reason does not understand. His famous wager admonishes to believe just in case it is true. Writer Lev Tolstoy believed faith was a prerequisite for happiness. He explained that if a man lives then he believes in something, so if he does not believe he would not live. To live, one needs purpose, and without faith he cannot live.

It is undeniable that faith brings some people happiness in many ways. For some, the belief in an afterlife mitigates the fear of death. The dying cancer patient may gain a degree of serenity with the faithful idea of reincarnation. The belief that there exists an all-good God looking after a person can bring contentment because he is not abandoned or alone. One can feel that a benevolent God is embracing and caring for them. Faith can bring hope to the hopeless, which comforts them and makes them feel more secure. Religion can bring meaning to people by connecting them to both other people and otherworldly teleological ideas. They can feel a part of something more profound than themselves and not adrift in an existential void. For many, faith brings purpose in life, which fulfills them and makes them feel like they are achieving something significant when they pursue their purpose. Finally, faith engenders a sense of wellbeing because it satisfies a desire to believe in something beyond oneself.

It does not matter whether these faithful beliefs are right or wrong to the individual, only that they make one feel emotionally better and happy. Why should they discard their beliefs and face possible angst, depression and anxiety? The truth is faith, religion and spirituality bring many people happiness.

Philosopher Søren Kierkegaard, author of *Fear and Trembling* and *Either/Or*, is perhaps the greatest proponent of the idea that faith brings happiness. His reasons are somewhat strange and involve fear and trembling, anxiety, choice and freedom. Kierkegaard himself had a dissipated, unhappy youth that lead to a rather tormented life. His overriding purpose was to have people believe in the essential teachings of Christianity, which he believed would make them happy. Like Hume and Nietzsche he eschewed priests and organized Christianity. In some ways Kierkegaard's story of faith and happiness is not so much about how to find happiness but rather how to escape depression and anxiety, which he calls fear and trembling. The next few paragraphs endeavor to present a very short summary of his reasons why he believed faith brings happiness.

Kierkegaard first envisioned a progression of individual types that could be described as a progress to happiness. The lowest stage is the aesthetic person who lives through their passions, the next is the ethical person who limits the passion that constrains them and the highest is the religious person with unabashed faith. For Kierkegaard, the religious person with faith enjoys the ultimate source of happiness, and those that are not religious live in anxiety, which leads to fear and trembling.

Faith for Kierkegaard brings meaning to life because (pe) the nonreligious is alone and there is no one to raise him up and give him meaning—it is faith that brings meaning to individuals in a meaningless world. Faith also transcends reason as a source of happiness because it involves passion, which is an instinctual source of happiness for many—reason is cold and indifferent, whereas passion enlivens their spirits. Thus, to overcome the siren call of reason and its consequences, one must make Kierkegaard's famous leap of faith. Reason only brings resignation, depression and fear and trembling, unlike the leap to faith, which brings happiness.

Kierkegaard used the Biblical figure Abraham to illustrate his view. Abraham was ordered by God to kill his son Isaac in order to test his faith in God. Abraham had a choice, which was to do the task or refuse God. He resigned himself to the loss of his son, which decision he kept secret. Just before preparing to kill Isaac, God rescinded his request knowing that Abraham had the faith to complete the task.

This macabre parable demonstrates Kierkegaard's philosophy. Abraham went through Kierkegaard's progressions. He was first emotionally aesthetic, loving his son and fearing his loss. He was originally ethical, but then abandoned ethics because he was willing to kill his son. And finally, he was religious. Once Abraham had made the decision to take the leap of faith, he relied less on reason and more on an enlivened passion. This brought him a greater meaning in life. Before his decision to act on faith, he had experienced the anxiety and fear and trembling religious people without faith suffer from, but this dissipated when he decided to follow his faith. For Kierkegaard, Isaac is a knight of faith, which condition brings happiness.

For Kierkegaard, there are two kinds of people. The lesser aesthetic and ethical individuals are natural men ensnared in sin and worldliness. They live in hope, always desiring something "out there." The higher, who live in memory, find something in themselves due to their faith. It is the difference between the outer world of ethics, aesthetics and reason and the inner world of spirit.

Kierkegaard had a profound impact on how people view human happiness. His philosophy changed much of how people think about freedom and choice, and the result was existentialism, of which many consider him the father.

Under medieval predestination, humans were resigned to their fates, thinking that there is nothing they can do to influence their futures. Kierkegaard's existentialist emphasis on a spirituality that is borne in freedom challenged this paradigm. An inner world of spirit is possible only with freedom. Spirit is people's ability to define their inner world and mould themselves. With this new-found freedom, people can make the choice to be happy and thus fashion their actions and beliefs in such a way to achieve it. For Kierkegaard, everyone has choice in life, and freedom consists in using that choice. And, like St. Augustine, these choices reveal themselves as a means toward an end, which can be happiness. It was the ideas of freedom and choice that lead to existentialism, or a non-teleological world that people make. Kierkegaard said that people have it in their power to influence the future and choose to be happy.

The answer then to the question at the beginning is that faith can bring happiness but it can also bring unhappiness. Experiencing the anxiety and fear and trembling Kierkegaard described is not a prescription for happiness. It is not necessary because there are other sources of happiness. Further, faith can blinker people from other sources of happiness, as in the case of Believe at the beginning of this chapter. Use faith as a source of happiness wisely.

In this chapter, it was mentioned that Freud wrote humans are incapable of happiness because civilization represses their instincts. This may be true, but not necessarily so. The ancient philosophers,

Bertrand Russell and Kierkegaard say that happiness comes from within. People make themselves happy. This is a freedom of choice everyone has that neither civilization- nor faith-inspired fear and trembling can take away.

SOURCES OF HAPPINESS

CHAPTER FIFTEEN

SIMPLICITY AND NATURE
Do not fight time or nature

Agitated lives a rushed complex and artificial life. His days are spent looking at computer screens and navigating apps. He constantly surfs Facebook and Twitter for the latest celebrity pronouncements and trends. He talks with others almost exclusively through machines when he emails and texts and verbally through his cell phone—his mediators in life are machines. If he ever dates it is through a dating website brought by a machine using a matrix to find the right match, but the matches never seem to work. He is bombarded daily by ads, come-ons and web detritus. Agitated is always hurried, his life is always complicated and he thinks in short sound bytes or bits of condensed, often incomprehensible thoughts. He rarely goes out in nature, is unreflective and utterly ignorant of the real world. His job as an internet technician only intensifies his anxieties. Agitated has lost his self and is unhappy; without electricity, he probably would not know how to survive.

    People in advanced societies live far more complicated lives than their ancestors, which is both a blessing and a curse. On one hand, it is far easier to turn up the thermostat to a gas furnace than have to cut down a tree, split wood and build a fire for warmth. On the other hand, modern civilization creates a labyrinth of artificial systems that must be successfully navigated to survive. Using the internet, keeping a car running, remembering passwords and an array of numbers like social security, bank account and cell phone challenge many. Civilization has become fast and complicated, which the philosophers say is not a prescription for happiness. They believe, rather, that happiness comes from slowing down in life, living simply and within nature.

    American philosopher and thinker Henry David Thoreau admonished to (v) simplify, simplify, simplify to achieve contentment and happiness. For him (p) there can be no black melancholy to those who live in nature. When people live simply, they satisfy many simple instinctual desires, which brings pleasure. Civilization too often warps people's instinctual desires with artificial ones such as the lust for power and luxury. Russian writer and philosopher Leo Tolstoy believed living simply mitigates these artificial evils.

Fundamentally, humans do not need much to be happy. Cicero wrote that the happy life depended on little. Epicurus taught that the happy person should live simply and calmly knowing that life's needs are easy to meet. Stoic Epictetus observed that (p) his poor body is not injured by plain living, and because of this, he lives a happier and more untroubled life than the nobly born rich. Fundamentally, humans only need food, shelter and health and sex to satisfy their basic needs to be happy.

Perhaps the greatest deterrent in modern American civilization to living simply is its materialistic ethic. In its fast pace capitalistic environment, citizens come to think material wealth constitutes happiness, when in reality the pursuit of it often brings unmitigated unhappiness. The disappointment in not getting the car one wanted or envy felt when another has a fancier house are painful feelings for many. The very mindset of spending life seeking more money and obtaining better material possessions brings many angst and unhappiness. M. M. Kirsch in his book *How to Get Off the Fast Track and Live a Life Money Can't Buy* wrote that the happy life consists in raising one's aspirations beyond materialism. He wrote that happiness and fulfillment come from (p) living a life of simplicity that allows the individual time to wonder and appreciate the simple joys in life—to live the good life is to be able to control one's life and one's destiny and not be at the mercy of the marketplace.

Taking the philosopher's advice, unhappy Agitated decided to take a break in life. He quit his job, sold his condominium and moved to the Greek island of Ios for a year. He moved into a small room surrounded by real people in a slower society more attuned to the rhythms of nature. The life transformations from agitation to peace, fast to slow, artificial to natural and complex to simple worked magic on his state of mind. The electricity was erratic, and he had no machines. He slowed down and began living simply and peacefully within nature. It changed his life.

Like Thoreau, he began taking the time to wonder and appreciate the simple joys of life away from the demands of work. The slavery he felt toward his job evaporated, and he found himself appreciating what he had rather than striving for more. Living in a slower environment caused him to put his desires in perspective. He realized that the things he previously thought he needed to make him happy were unnecessary. He learned a new sense of gratitude that diminished his pangs of desire because he came to realize how really good his life was. Gratitude was the antidote for his paradigm of unhappiness.

Before his move he rarely felt contented because he was always concerned about something, anticipating problems, or just anxious. He was always thinking about what was wrong with things and not what was right. In the big picture his life was great, but he could not see this through his cybernetic fog. He came to realize how easy it is to live simply. He was living cynic Diogenes's comment that a man's happiness is measured by what he does not want.

Unlike his previous life looking a computer screens, surfing the internet, being bombarded by ads and thinking in bytes, he found himself in nature slowing down. Because electricity was no longer a factor in his life, his nascent self emerged, and he began devoting more energy to the really important aspects of life like reading, thinking and just enjoying living. He was living a simpler and happier life.

Nature is simple, and in it, the exigencies of time harmoniously blend with life—time becomes a thing and not the enemy. Things slow down to the evolutionary human pace, and people come to live in existence rather than outside it. It is a simple process that has made modernity forlorn because it eschews slowness. The ancient philosophers like Epicurus, the stoics, and Lucretius state that nature is easily satisfied. Seneca wrote that (p) reason tells one to live in accordance with nature, or to live simply and to avoid that is which is unnatural such as luxury and avarice because they take one's happiness. Contemporary philosopher Bertrand Russell echoed these sentiments when he wrote that the rhythm of life is slow, nature is slow and the happy life is the quiet life. Russian writer Ivan Turgenev believed that happiness comes when humans perform their natural functions in life, and, it is worth adding, within the scope of nature and its natural time. The slow monotony of nature is conducive to a quiet, happy life.

Perhaps the best example of human's detachment from nature is found in their conception of time. Jeremy Rifkin in his book *Time Wars* described how many have become obsessed with time. They are always in a hurry, busy and harassed. They think of time as an enemy to be overcome. To understand this, primitive natural time and modern unnatural social time must be explored.

Rifkin associated primitive time with the earthly rhythms of incoming and outgoing tides, the rising and setting sun and the changing seasons. It is a time characteristic of a pastoral way of life. It is an organic kind of time grounded in the slow circadian rhythms of nature. It is a time of gradually changing seasons and not hours. The concept of an hour, which was created by the Romans, commenced a change in conception of time and the beginning of detachment from primitive time. Although the hour was rarely used in medieval society, the Benedictine monks invented the clock, the machine of the modern age that sped up time. In the eighteenth century the pendulum was introduced, which measured seconds and ushered in the new word "punctuality." Now, the world has computers measuring milliseconds and nanoseconds, which has utterly detached humans from nature's primitive time.

Now, watches, computers and atomic time clocks have artificially sped time up beyond comprehension. These mechanical contrivances measure human existence, divide time in discrete, unnatural ways and create electronic impulses people cannot experience. This new quantitative mechanical time is fast-paced and efficient but has nothing to do with living a qualitative life of calmness. It is a time that values efficiency and predictability over romanticism and surprise.

This speeding up of time ruins one's experience of life. Lives become full of haste— breathless, urgent and filled with sterile moments. The true things that bring joy such as love, relationships and nature become diminished, and happiness fades. The evolved, computerized conception of time has become a kind of Frankenstein that has turned on its creator. The new creation of fast-time is the source of many of contemporary mental maladies such as anxiety, tension and depression and physical illnesses like high blood pressure, ulcers and irritable bowel syndrome.

Primitive natural time and modern computer time are different lenses through which people see reality. The former moves with people, and the latter moves faster than people. With the advent of the latter, people no longer have a calm perspective of nature and her slow rhythms. They are detached from nature's time, and their psyches and bodies have been disturbed, which makes people unhappy.

The solution for many philosophers is to listen to nature, live within her rhythms and stay physically fit. Doctors prescribe translations of these ideas in order to be healthy. They say to exercise, get enough sleep, watch one's blood pressure and cholesterol and keep maintain a proper body mass index. They also declare to eliminate bad habits like smoking and drugs and moderate others like alcohol. Few listen because these are the paladins people use to cope with the modern, fast-paced conception of time. The philosophers say to slow down, get more sleep, relax and be more reflective. People's minds agree and tell them to take a hike in the woods or vacation. Few listen, however, because they are swept up in the whirl of society, work, other's opinions driven by new mechanical time. Their watches are more important than their health.

What people need is to learn how to live within nature's time to be happy. This is a tall order in modern society, but it is possible by knowing computer time is artificial, keeping artificial time in perspective and not being its slave. Living within nature was a central topic of the ancient stoic philosophers, which will be discussed next.

The need to live in accordance with nature is a central stoic tenet. From this author's book *Stoicism, Enkrasia and Happiness*, it is the sixth tenet of stoicism that entails living simply, wanting the right things and being wary of common opinion. It also means that living outside nature is evil because people form artificial, wrongful, and non-natural beliefs and opinions.

The stoics taught that common opinion too often leads to destructive and self-defeating beliefs, or beliefs that are not conducive to human flourishing or happiness. Collective man creates unnatural needs and desires that are not found in nature. In civilization, one experiences grief if they are not respectable or do not achieve some position. Nature does not demand respectability or position—they are of no account in nature, so their loss cannot be lamented. Nature is simple and comforting. For the stoics, people who labor under human-made artificial opinion do not live within nature and are prone to unhappiness. Seneca, quoting Epicurus, wrote (v) if you shape your life according to nature, you will never be poor; if according to people's opinions, you will never be rich.

Two final stoic observations about happiness and nature involve the desire for things and time. Many who live in the opinion of others become infected with the desire to possess things. They think if they own things then they will be happy. They imagine if they only had a bigger house, a fancier car, a larger bank account or more sensual pleasure they would be happy. However, as mentioned earlier, it does not take much to satisfy nature. Humans can live happier lives with the bare necessities of existence unencumbered by the desire for more. Indeed, it is the desire for more that often causes them to live unhappily outside of nature. To repeat Seneca's admonition, (v) for greed nothing is enough; nature is satisfied with little.

Finally, to live in nature for the stoics means living in the present and not the past or future. Seneca wrote that (p) looking into the future only brings anxiety because when people live in the future they start thinking about controlling the future rather than adapting themselves to the present. People, in short, unnecessarily complicate their lives by focusing on the uncertain future rather than solving the real problems they face today. When living in the past, people too often get regretful and ruefulness over what they did not do or what they did wrong. Regret is the cancer of life because people mourn what they cannot change. Living in the future or the past is not a prescription for happiness.

The philosophers advise not to be Agitated, keep modernity's technology in perspective and live simply and happily within nature.

CHAPTER SIXTEEN

KNOWLEDGE AND EXPERIENCE
*Know thyself, seek the crown of happiness
and avoid the prison of others' opinions*

Famous English writer and philosopher Samuel Johnson wrote about an unhappy, disenchanted prince in *The History of Rasselas, Prince of Abissinia*. Rasselas grew wary of factitious entertainments, so he left his paradise kingdom to find happiness, but all he discovered is the futility of the human condition. He and his philosopher comrade Imlac encountered many life situations but in the end came to realize that human happiness depends on illusions under which all worldly ambitions for happiness are ultimately defeated. In the end, the prince abandons his search for happiness and is left a disappointed skeptic. Johnson's prince is not happy.

Rasselas is unhappy because he has not lived long enough to understand happiness does not come on a platter; rather, one has to work to attain it. Johnson wrote that (v) people grow more happy as their minds take wider range. That wider range comes from knowledge and experience, which are two significant sources of happiness.

The theme of this chapter is that knowledge and experience bring happiness. Youth is often unhappy because it faces reality without a mental library of knowledge or storehouse of valuable experiences. It is in a kind of void that must be filled in order to think in ways that bring a better understanding of the world and, collaterally, happiness. Youth often think they are the center of the universe unaware that, as Alexander Pope observed in *Essay on Man*, as individuals, they are a small part of a whole, or in Pope's case, a part of an unchanging and timeless *Chain of Being*.

A scholarly publication, *The Journal of Clinical Psychiatry* reported that people become happier as they age. The article offered numerous reasons including that they become wiser, peer-pressure loses its sting, they make better decisions, they are more in control of their emotions, they do things that are not just for themselves and they are more studious and decisive. The articles most incisive reason was as people age they come to know themselves better.

Happiness is all about self, so knowing oneself has much to do with how to how to achieve happiness. The thought to know oneself is an ancient Greek maxim used by many philosophers. Its origin is attributed to the presocratic philosopher Thales and was used extensively by Plato in his dialogues through the character of Socrates. Plato defined it as that which brings wisdom and temperance, that which teaches how to be good and what to know and that which gives greater understanding of human nature, including one's own and others'. Thomas Hobbes asserted that the more people study themselves, the more they come to understand the feelings that influence their thoughts and motivate their actions. Alexander Pope advocated knowing oneself because (v) the proper study of mankind is man, and Ralph Waldo Emerson believed one should know oneself because he comes to know God, as God is within each person.

The essence of the philosophers' message is that gaining knowledge of oneself encompasses all of these things which ultimately bring enlightenment and understanding and in particular knowledge about how to be happy. There are many ways people come to know themselves, but two essential ones are through knowledge and experience. With these one becomes more comfortable in his own skin. It brings a state of mind that appreciates people but does not need them to be happy. Knowing oneself is a kind of pretense-free independence. Those who know themselves are content being alone because they like who they are with.

First, this chapter will examine knowledge.

C. S. Lewis had his devil character Screwtape advise his minion Wormwood to darken humans' knowledge because it brings them unhappiness. He told him this (p) angers men when they think a legitimate claim of theirs has been denied. This encourages their idea of ownership, which arises not from pride but rather confusion. Humans' minds must be kept (p) in dreary flickering so they do not know what gratifies their curiosity. He tells him to beware of the learned who have read ancient authors because they are a source of dangerous knowledge. These kinds of people must be derided as simple-minded and full of bunk.

Perhaps the famous debate on the question of whether knowledge brings happiness was between Jeremy Bentham and John Stuart Mill, which was mentioned in the introduction to this book. Bentham believed that (v) it is better to be a happy pig than a miserable human being. Bentham is known as the father of utilitarianism, or happiness for the most, and he is saying that happiness is the ultimate human end, so just do what accomplishes that. Knowledge only brings ambiguity, dismay and unhappiness. Indeed, it is often said that the more one knows the less he knows. Mill retorted that it is better to be a human dissatisfied than a pig satisfied; better to be Socrates dissatisfied than a fool satisfied. Mull agrees with Bentham that happiness is the ultimate human end but adds that knowledge is one way to achieve it. The fool is forever doomed to his lot, whereas Socrates may improve it with knowledge. The life of an ostrich that buries its head in the ground will never improve; ignorance may bring temporary bliss but no enduring happiness.

Happily, most philosophers do not agree with Screwtape and Bentham and have many reasons why knowledge can bring happiness. Their central argument comes from Samuel Taylor Coleridge who wrote: (v) people are what they know. What are people but a physical body and a mind with knowledge? People have no choice on the body they inherit, but they can choose the information in their heads. Absent chemical or biologic influences, it is that knowledge that makes people who they are. So, they can choose to gain knowledge that makes them happy or that makes them sad.

Some kinds of felicity-enhancing knowledge include knowing nature, understanding kinds of knowledge and appreciating the power of knowledge. Understand nature, including human nature, is the first. Spinoza wrote that (p) contemplation of the whole machinery of nature and reflecting within the mind on the whole intellectual order of things is happiness. Knowledge also enables one to discern what Saint Augustine called practical and theoretical knowledge. He wrote that (p) people learn some things to do them and others to know them. Being ignorant of one is not a formula for happiness because, as Augustine pointed out, (p) practical knowledge sustains life and theoretical knowledge sustains souls. Finally, knowledge indeed is power, as Francis Bacon pointed out, and it is these elements of knowledge that give people the power to find Plato's crown. It has been said that (v) minds that have no knowledge but of the present moment are either corroded by malignant passions or sit stupid in the gloom of perpetual vacancy. This may be true as far as it goes but knowledge also brings an understanding of the tenses so people learn to not be distressed by the past or overly worried about the future. Knowledge allows one to live happily in the present.

Here are a few specific ways knowledge, and in particular philosophic knowledge, brings happiness. People would not be human without desire and passion, but unrestrained they can ruin lives and happiness. Knowledge is one way to control them. Spinoza believed (p) as people acquire more knowledge of nature, and therefore themselves as parts of nature, they necessarily cease blindly to desire, love and hate particular things, and they cease to be governed by their passions. Knowing Samuel Johnson's *The Vanity of Human Wishes* lets one understand what he means by saying that nature's gifts are conditional. He means that desires are unattainable because as they achieve one they lose another. They come to understand that desire is like a mirage that disappears as they approach it because their reason for wanting it fades. Knowledge allows one to put desires and passions in a detached perspective.

Social norms, conventions and institutions are important but sometimes they can confound and stifle people, which brings confusion and unhappiness. Knowing Twain, Melville and Emerson gives one a new outlook on these forms of convention and sources of conformity. For those who fear the religions admonition that people may burn in hell, Mark Twain's irreverent snips at religion in *Innocents Abroad* may be a source of comfort. When people read about Herman Melville's Billy Budd in *Billy Budd, Sailor*, they come to understand that (p) measured forms are not everything because sometimes they are wrong. Many judge others by the conventions of the day, which themselves change and are often injurious to individuals like they were to Billy. Knowledge tells one to judge by justice and not social convention. Conformity also often forces people to try and be what they are not, which is a great source of unhappiness for many. Knowing quintessential American thinker and nonconformist Ralph Waldo Emerson's emphasis on individualism, self-reliance and the need to avoid conformity is freeing.

Leibniz believed God made the world the best of all worlds, which Voltaire in *Candide* scathingly criticized. Knowing Leibnitz and Voltaire brings a balance to one's world view, which brings a kind of peace. They know there are many sources of inevitable unhappiness in the world like poverty, sickness and death so it cannot be the best, but they also know there are many good things about the world that bring happiness. People heal, love and have children. Knowledge helps people accept the inevitable but strive to overcome the evitable sources of pain. Knowledge helps people make the most of the world they inherit. Indeed, knowing Voltaire inspires people to work, which he wrote (v) keeps people from the three great evils of vice, boredom and poverty (and, this author would add, which brings happiness).

It was mentioned earlier that knowledge teaches people not to be distressed over the past and future. Emerson pointed out that with such distress people miss opportunities today because they (v) are fearful to take the step from knowing to doing. For Emerson, living is about doing, so one should not live in the past or future but rather the present. When one loses the fear to act, he gains the opportunity to overcome the many sources of unhappiness.

Many philosophers like Hegel believe humans' greatest aspiration is freedom. For them, freedom brings happiness, and it is knowledge that makes them aware of this truism. François Rabelais in his wonderfully outrageous *Gargantua and Pantagruel* invented a motto for humans: (v) do what you will. This is a motto for freedom that is manifest in Rabelais's essentially cheerful, good and perfect human being, and it can only be a source of happiness for those who know his writing.

It is a personal belief of this author that philosophic knowledge is one of the greatest sources of happiness. With it, one can step back and see the world in a more objective way. One can gain a broader perspective and see a bigger reality. Philosophy causes people to think deeper, more universally and from more perspectives. Its central goal to find truth is liberating because it challenges biases and frees the mind. Philosophy puts everyday problems in perspective and often makes them seem insignificant. It influences values, attitudes and beliefs that influence happiness; if people are what they know, then philosophic ideas that bring happiness are worth knowing. Philosophic knowledge offers ways to be happy and provides solutions to sources of unhappiness.

What are some of those philosophic ideas that can bear on one's happiness? Plato's universal ideals cause one to think beyond existence. Kant makes one consider the importance of duty in ethics and the nature of knowledge with his idealistic philosophy. Aristotle's doctrine of the mean teaches the importance of temperance and his virtue ethics the role of virtue in happiness. Diogenes the cynic causes one to ponder the insignificance of possessions and commonly held opinions. Epictetus the stoic and Epicurus the Epicurean offer contrasting ways to happiness centered around the question: Does happiness come from seeking pleasure or denying emotion? David Hume's idea that action does not arise from reason makes one question reason and the value of passion; he also asks one to question religious dogma and any fear of eternal damnation. G. E. Moore's naturalistic fallacy questions one's ability to know by asking whether the color yellow can be further defined, and Friedrich Nietzsche's independent and willful Overman causes one to deeply evaluate Christian doctrine. All of these philosophers work and challenge the mind in such a way that enables one to evaluate problems and circumstances better and create new solutions for the old ones that did not solve them.

One can read daily about political fighting and constant crime, and people all deal with perceived injustices. These are some timeless sources of unhappiness that are depressingly just more of the same, and people resign themselves to a perpetually unhappy state. But with philosophic knowledge to know all is to forgive all. People can achieve a state of mind above the fray that detaches them in such a way that brings happiness.

Personally, the stoic philosophy espoused by Epictetus, Cicero, Seneca and Marcus Aurelius seems the most liberating source of happiness. From these Stoic masters, one can learn to superintend emotions because when indulged they can be a great source of unhappiness, one can learn to remain indifferent to that which is beyond choice and one can live naturally and simply in accordance with nature, eschewing opinion and convention. For this author in particular, studying philosophy and particularly stoicism brought happiness.

One may think of knowledge as a timeless river that few humans touch. This river extends back thousands of years and forward into the unknown future flowing with ideas, theories, and perceptions—an ever-changing body of knowledge. The river consists of all the great thoughts the best human thinkers have thought—it is a metaphoric collective river of the best ideas humankind has to offer. It is a cumulative river where new ideas are built on old ideas, and the result is an ever-increasing river of better ideas that can make people happy. So, swim in the river of knowledge.

John Dickenson wrote that (p) experience is a better guide than reason (or knowledge) because reason often misleads because one does not begin with all the necessary premises, whereas with experience the practical man feels the effects of conditions, which the reasoned overlooked. On the contrary, Desiderius Erasmus believed it was faith that brings wisdom, so he naturally derided experience (and knowledge) as folly and as (v) the common schoolhouse of fools. The philosophers may not agree on experience's influence on happiness, but Wendy Lustbader in *What's Worth Knowing* makes a strong case that experience is an essential ingredient of happiness. Indeed, many of one's experiences are one's knowledge, which has a direct bearing on one's happiness. As one shall see, many of the ways to happiness that come from knowledge are grounded in experience.

Lustbader in her book endeavored to discern some of life's most important lessons. She did this by interviewing old people—people who had lived long lives. She asked them questions like: (v) How would you live your life differently knowing what you know now? What advice would you give young people just starting out in life? What are the keys to living a happy life? She was mining older people's experience in order to discern ways to live a happy life.

They gave five poignant recurring answers: to appreciate freedom, to not worry about things that do not really matter, that happiness does not come from buying things, to not fight things one cannot change and to accept each day for what it offers. Each of these sources of experience that brings happiness can be examined.

Many philosophers like Hegel, Heidegger and Fukuyama have written that freedom is humans' greatest aspiration. It is so because it brings happiness. People gain the freedom to think what they want, go where they want and do what they want. These freedoms bring happiness. One cannot be happy in servitude for many reasons, but one reason certainly is that one loses the freedom to fashion his life in such a way that makes him happy.

A human foible is to not appreciate what one has. Those without freedom yearn for it, and those with it often take it for granted. The latter are too often willing to trade their freedom for security ignorant of the short-term gains of security and long-term unhappiness with the loss of freedom. Benjamin Franklin was right when he wrote that (p) those who exchange freedom for security deserve neither. To be happy, one must appreciate freedom.

Humans often fret unnecessarily over unimportant matters like whether the mole will reappear in the lawn, whether Bill will marry Ann and if it will be sunny tomorrow for the picnic. People spend a good deal of their lives worrying excessively about unimportant matters. They create for themselves a virtual world of pressing imagined needs and duties and then fret over them. People blow small issues all out of proportion. They worry too much about things that cause unhappiness but in the big picture really do not matter.

It was mentioned earlier that the stoics said that people should remain indifferent to matters that are beyond their control. Humans feel emotions like envy when their rich neighbor buys a better car. Why should such a worldly difficulty bring the envy that causes unhappiness? They are fretting over an unimportant matter. To be happy, one must ignore unimportant matters.

Lustbader's interview subjects consistently said that they had learned in life that happiness does not come from owning things. Perhaps the pride of ownership comes from one's instinct to survive—if human's ancestors owned a good hut and ox, they were happy because they were better able to live. This sounds intuitively right. But today, a good hut becomes bigger houses with unneeded rooms, and the ox becomes a Land Rover with four-wheel drive that one never uses. Experience shows that little is needed to be happy—nature is easily satisfied.

The older experienced view to not fight change is a stoic thought. Earlier, from knowledge, it was mentioned that a central stoic teaching was to remain indifferent to that which is beyond one's choice. Fretting over what one has no control is a waste of time. This is not a prescription for resignation—one should always fight evil, but why fight death? People's lives are far happier ignoring that which they cannot control and endeavoring to better that which they can.

Lustbader's interviewee's final advice is to accept each day for what it offers. Ultimately, one cannot engineer what each day brings, so he should accept and make the most of what fate brings. Happiness comes from enjoying the present rather than dwelling in a past one cannot change or a future one cannot predict.

All of these prescriptions for happiness came from old peoples' advice due to experience. Now, the focus will shift to a few more sources of happiness derived from experience.

To be wary of convention and others opinions and to live simply in order to be happy are derived from knowledge but learned from experience. Ultimately, happiness does not come from social convention but rather from how comfortable one is in his skin. Convention creates artificial criteria created by other people that have little to do with one's self and one's happiness. Others' opinions can make people prisoners of their judgment, which is a source of unhappiness. People become unwittingly preoccupied with what others think in order to be liked, and the result is an unconscious effort to shield one's true selves from others. The truth is, to be happy one should accept the fact that some will not like him and live life accepting this truism. One should not fear what others think or their contemporaries' judging gaze. It is better to relax, be oneself and let the chips fall where they may. Finally, people are happier living simply. The demands to live a happy normal life in contemporary advanced Western civilization require a sophistication that ultimately is not needed. People can slow their lives down, live simpler and achieve a kind of priceless mental freedom that brings happiness.

Two final pieces of advice on experience come from Benjamin Franklin and his *Poor Richard's Almanac*. First, experience teaches that (p) when the well runs dry, people know the worth of water. Second, (p) he who is made cautious by the misfortunes of others is fortunate. One should be happy, appreciate and preserve what one has and learn from others' mistakes.

Knowledge, especially knowledge of oneself, and experience together are an unbeatable source of happiness, so cultivate them.

Chapter Seventeen

VALUES AND CREEDS
Take the Tolstoy Test of Values and avoid Pascal's Wager

Lev and Roger were pondering their lives. Lev had lived a good life, had much to ponder and is satisfied. He had self-esteem but not pride, he had been realistic in his critical life decisions, he had been virtuous, he had learned to take his own counsel, he was rational and found wisdom in philosophy, he had worked hard, kept problems in perspective, relied on himself, thought through the consequences of causes and never gave up. Roger, on the other hand, had little to ponder and is disturbed—he is still looking for life's answers. He developed poor values and creeds when young and was living the unhappy consequences. He pursued false gods like unworthy ambitions, he mostly thought of himself, pleasure was his central passion, he let what others thought of him drive his decisions, he was emotional and constantly dreamed of a better life that was just around the corner, he was inclined to view the supernatural and spirits as real, he worked but not hard and always believed things would work out for the best in the end, he expected others to solve his problems, was always late and rarely prepared and he usually quit when things got rough. In old age, Lev and Roger's lives are different because they their life values and creeds were different.

What people believe has much to do with who they are. What one values and lives by powerfully influences his emotional state and level of happiness. This chapter is about some values and creeds that the philosophers have taught that bring happiness. This is a catchall chapter that derives many important values and creeds from other chapters in the book. It is intended to demonstrate the relationship between what a person decides to believe and his happiness. In keeping with the character of this section of this book, this chapter will focus mostly on the good values and creeds to adopt.

Values and creeds are similar but different. Values include that which people value—what they consider worthy, important or useful. They determine in many ways people's principles and standards.

Values influence beliefs. Creeds are beliefs, but they tend to be the set of principles and standards one lives by. Creeds deal more with actions. There are many values and creeds one can adopt, so the important point is to adopt those that bring felicity. Philosophers like Tolstoy, Cicero, Zamperini and Pascal encourage a few good values and creeds, many of which Lev adopted and Roger failed to recognize.

The summary of some good values will begin with a story. Russian philosopher writer Leo Tolstoy wrote *The Death of Ivan Ilyich*, in which he delineated many good values. Tolstoy was an example of what he preached. He had given up his wealth and became a peasant because he believed the good life lies outside of society near the soil. He practiced what he preached and purposely chose a life of simplicity and humility. He wanted to avoid modern civilization with its courts, laws and wars. He wanted to escape civilization's values of power and luxury.

With these predispositions Tolstoy wrote about Ivan Ilyich. It is a story about an average man learning about values that bring happiness too late in life. Ivan's life had flowed pleasantly and properly. He had valued only how to advance in the Russian bureaucracy, how to rise in society by associating with the right people, how to get a raise and how to impress others with his wit, charm and appearance. He was married with daughters and a son, but he ignored his family, and particularly his son, who desperately wanted his attention.

In middle age, Ivan caught a fatal disease and began to die. His first reactions were self-pity, fear, anger, and depression. These were the natural consequence of his poor values because he had been so self-centered. Also naturally, due to his values, his family considered his death an inconvenience that upset their pleasantness. and his colleagues viewed his death as an opportunity for advancement.

Ivan pondered his death and was struck by the thought there is no purpose to life because death is the only reality. With this insight, he shed all pretense and his poor life-values and their consequences became conspicuous. He began to see things the way they really are. He came to realize that living conventionally away from the essentials of nature does not bring happiness. He saw the falsity of ambitions, meaningless preoccupation with money and pointless desire for correctitude and propriety. He came to realize how important values are for living a happy life. He thought to himself that these values must include living simply and naturally and valuing love, caring and the importance of close relationships with family and friends. He came to realize the artificiality of valuing money, power and prestige.

With this story, it is not hard to discern what values writer/philosopher Leo Tolstoy believes bring happiness. He says that one should accept death because it real and live free of the fear of it, live simply and within nature rather than fighting it, avoid false ambitions, correctitude and propriety because they are pointless, and not be preoccupied with money and vanity because they are artificial pleasures. Bertrand Russell echoed Tolstoy's take on vanity when he wrote that (p) self-absorption leads to inactivity and loss of happiness; rather, focus on external objects because it leads to activity and happiness. Self-absorption defined Ivan Ilyich before his disease.

Perhaps the significant value Tolstoy teaches is to value living. All people have is now, so they should adopt the values that make the most of living now. Two thousand years earlier, stoic philosopher Seneca, in an antiquated way, wrote similarly that (p) people should use proper judgments today because tomorrow they may be dead. For Seneca, every day should be welcomed as if it were the finest day imaginable—what flies past has to be seized. If one unconsciously thinks he is going to live a thousand years, it is unlikely he will develop the right values for living in the present.

One can do a mind experiment to test Tolstoy's values, which can be called the Tolstoy Test of Value. In this experiment, one should do his or her best to imagine being in the future, lying on one's deathbed with only a few minutes to left to live. Imagine one's state of mind at that moment, asking oneself what is valuable in life. If one can reach this mindful place, it is a state of total self-honesty because there is no longer any reason to deceive oneself. This could achieve a moment of truth uninfluenced by artificial societal values—a place to find one's own true values. That is the place Ivan Ilyich found himself, and he envisioned the kind of values that Tolstoy truly believed bring happiness.

Some other values that bring felicity include education because, as John Stuart Mill wrote, it is better to be a dissatisfied Socrates than a satisfied pig, Henry David Thoreau's advice to simplify, Marcus Aurelius's admonition that the happy life depends on little and Buddhist Suzuki's idea that people follow *The Way*, which is to rise above earthly attachments such as desire, ignorance and hatred and to work and be productive.

Finally, philosophers mention some good values that include rationality, maturity, philosophy and the Good. Unlike passion and emotion, for the stoics, reason allows people to conquer pain and grief and achieve tranquility of the mind and wisdom. The result is wisdom or knowledge of how to live in such a way that brings happiness. Much of happiness, for example, comes from one's adroitness in dealing with fortune's blows, which is why Seneca wrote that (p) all people need for happiness is a rational and elevated spirit that treats fortune with disdain. Reason's relationship to happiness is important. It, for example, connects causes with consequences in such a way that makes one think more broadly, which puts problems in perspective and thus has a calming effect. The importance of reason in happiness will be taken up in the last chapter of this book.

Extreme passions like anger and envy cause great distress. Some of Seneca's dialogues, for example, deal with the destructive nature of anger and how to deal with it. He has many suggestions, which include reason and maturity. His goal is to bring control of the passions and emotional stability in order to be tranquility. Naturally, the philosophers suggest valuing and studying philosophy in order to achieve happiness. Unlike the creed of religion, which often brings dogma and passion, valuing philosophy brings perspicacity, sagacity, and wisdom, which are sextants to happiness. Cicero's response to his daughter Tulla's death could be an example. In his *Tusculan Disputations*, Roman Senator Cicero wrote that when his daughter Tulla died, he became despondent and inconsolable. After much distress, Cicero turned to philosophy for relief. Reasoned philosophy told him that grief is useless and that distress is an indulgence and a matter of belief. He thought that his grief had nothing to do with his dead daughter rather only with his emotional state. With these ideas, he decided to harden himself. He came to think that people should ponder evils like the death of a child beforehand, which will deaden and alleviate the distress of the loss. He came to think that nothing should happen that has not been expected. People should willfully become more prudential in their thinking, pondering that which may befall them. This kind of philosophic thinking led him to take control of his life and distress. It led him to think that happiness does not reside outside but rather within. Happiness is an attitude or choice people all make; philosophy enables people to (v) live serene lives within their walls and smile at the raging storm. Cicero's believed valuing philosophy brings happiness.

This brings one to an interesting nexus of value, the Good and happiness. Valuing rationality, wisdom and philosophy enables one to understand Plato's Good, which itself brings happiness. The Good is a somewhat vague Platonic term that means to come to understand Platonic forms, which include justice, truth, equality and beauty. He compared it to the sun, which allows people to see things not as the sun that enables sight with light but rather as the source of sight itself. The Good makes things intelligible and gives people knowledge. It (p) gives truth to the things known and the power to know to the knower and is the cause of knowledge and truth. For Plato, the Good enables one to understand difficult concepts like justice. For Plato's intraocular Socrates, the good (v) is what provides knowledge and truth.

The interesting nexus is thus this: rationality, wisdom and philosophy bring the Good, which is a way of thinking that brings true knowledge and happiness. Indeed, Cicero wrote over four hundred years after Plato that (p) a man, who he described as a philosopher, has the chief good in his power and the power of a happy life.

Consider now how some values play out in creeds, or the principles by which people live, to achieve felicity. The common sense philosopher Louis Zamperini in his autobiography *Don't Give Up, Don't Give In* provided many prudential creeds to live by. His creeds had enabled him to overcome many difficult challenges in life like criminal behavior in his youth, being lost at sea and being tortured in a Japanese prisoner of war camp. As the title of his book presages, he believed that people should never give up. Perseverance is a critical creed to achieve happiness. Keep at it, never give in and do the best one can with what one has. Similarly, Theodore Roosevelt, who could be the epitome of perseverance, said "do what you can, where you are with what you have."

Other Zamperini creeds include to stay active, have character and reputation because they are all one has, have hope, accept things and move on, control attitudes such as hate that are personal decisions, choose how to view one's fate, challenge oneself intelligently, learn to adapt, forgive because it is healing, do not leave crucial details to others and listen because it is not a weakness. He advised to accomplish something because it brings self-respect and to be accepting because it brings contentment. He also preached preparedness, which means thinking things through in advance. It seems certain that if one adopted Zamperini's simple creeds, happiness could follow.

The next creed is faith, and the philosopher is a not a simple philosopher. Blasé Pascal was a seventeenth century French mathematician, physicist and religious philosopher who wrote *Pensées*. He believed adopting the creed of religious faith brings happiness. In response to the secular, often-skeptical philosophers, he argued that man is both great and abject, which secular philosophers do not account for. It is only religion that can achieve goodness and happiness for all. Indeed, Saint Augustine in *Confessions* wrote that people (pe) drink till their Christian faith is slaked and the result is never-ending happiness.

To advance his thesis, Pascal invented a wager that was intended to disarm the faithless skeptical secular philosophers. He wrote that (p) he intended to overcome the indifference of the skeptic by means of a wager. It goes like this: if God does not exist, the skeptic loses nothing by believing in him, but if he does exist, the skeptic gets eternal life by believing in him. In other words, the skeptic wins either way by believing because it just might be true. In short, believe just in case it is true.

This, however, is flawed reasoning because it can invest future happiness in beliefs that could be proven wrong. Ghosts, for example, cannot be proven so ought one believe in them just in case they might exist? In spite of Pascal's wager's deficiency, if faith brings one happiness, so be it. However, to achieve a truer and more stable happiness, a better wager is to take the reasoned philosopher's Tolstoy's Test of Values.

There are simply too many creeds that bring happiness to describe, so the focus will be placed on a few final significant ones. Virtue is a creed that brings happiness. If one treats others honestly and fairly, most will do likewise. It is hard to be happy when others treat one with disdain. Interestingly, the idea that civility brings happiness is rarely discussed. Manners are the oil in the engine that keeps it running smoothly. It costs nothing to be civil, and the benefits are immeasurable. Manners are more than etiquette, they are also sources of happiness. It is easy to dislike what another thinks and hard to curtail feelings with tolerance, but tolerance brings peace, which brings contentment and happiness.

Some people think small, and others broadly, universally or catholically. When one thinks small, everything is bothersome and one gets easily bogged down in unimportant matters. Life becomes self-seeking pettiness constantly being troubled by trivial misfortunes. The antidote is a creed that focuses on the big picture, keeps the small irritants in perspective and reminds one that everyone dies. A final creed is to pick battles carefully. Life is a contest, and some get bogged down in never-ending feuds of revenge that only bring unending angst and unhappiness. It is better to fight the important battles and do one's best to win them.

Zamperini in his book pondered about whether if he had a time machine to relive his life he would do it. His self-answer was no because, like Lev, he was satisfied with the life he lived. Zamperini and Lev do not need a time machine because they had lived happy lives due to their good values and creeds.

CHAPTER EIGHTEEN

STOICISM AND EPICURIANISM
Avoid the skeptic's dilemma, know that pleasure cannot be increased only varied and be an unsatisfied pig

Sextus the skeptic, Epicurus the Epicurean and Cicero the stoic each had a young daughter they loved who died. They were all struck with grief. Sextus's solution was to suspend judgment about death, which only brought a state of inertness but did not balm his pain. He had focused intellectually and not realistically on what actually happens when a loved one dies. Epicurus had focused on the joy of their relationship, their walks through the garden and wonderful conversations together, but he had no solutions after she died because she was gone. He had focused on what brings happiness now only and not what might happen. As a consequence, he also remained grief stricken. Cicero was also aggrieved, but he thought that some matters are beyond his control, like the death of his daughter as well as his own death, so he ought to remain indifferent to them. He thought, why be distressed by that which he cannot control. With this Cicero reconciled himself to his daughter's death and gained a certain degree of tranquility. Sextus and Epicurus remained in various degrees of despair, whereas Cicero, who actually wrote that stoicism was the only philosophy that saved him from the despair of the death of his real daughter Tulla, escaped it.

The ancient schools of skepticism, Epicureanism and stoicism have been described or referenced often in this book. This chapter will discuss their philosophies on happiness in greater detail. Emphasis will be placed on Epicureanism and stoicism and their similar views on how to achieve happiness.

In many ways each of these ancients' effort to craft a philosophy that brings happiness is a result of Aristotle's view that happiness resides within. In his *Politics*, Aristotle wrote that (p) men imagine happiness lies in external goods but this is like ascribing fine and brilliant lyre-playing to the quality of the instrument rather than to the skill of the player. These three schools endeavored to mould philosophies that would bring happiness from within.

Very generally, to create internal happiness, skepticism teaches that people should suspend judgment, Epicureanism that they should rationally indulge passion, and stoicism that they should control or suppress passion. Because chapter two was about skepticism and why it does not bring happiness, it will only briefly be described here. The bulk of this chapter will deal with the aspects of the latter two philosophies that bring happiness from within.

Suspending judgment may remove the pains of harmful beliefs, but it does not bring happiness. It is a nihilist view because with it nothing matters; nothing is left for which to care or hope. It offers no future and one cannot be happy living in a void. Skepticism is a manifestation of Shakespeare's comment in *The Taming of the Shrew* that one should let the world slip in order to forget the cares of the world and have fun now to be happy. This is a prescription for forgetting and not happiness. It was mentioned in the introduction that happiness requires effort. Happiness does not come by forgetting, escaping or suspending judgment. Skepticism only brings the skeptics empty dilemma, which is to be skeptical of their own skepticism. Alternatively, Epicureanism and stoicism provide a roadmap for happiness. This chapter seeks to describe these ancient philosophies and then reconcile their prescriptions for happiness in the conclusion.

Epicurus was a popular third and fourth century BCE Greek philosopher who wanted to live a good life of inner tranquility. His school in Athens, which was a garden, competed with Plato's Academy and Aristotle's Lyceum for adherents. His views on philosophy and wisdom were widely disseminated in the ancient world and were particularly popular in later Rome, where his philosophy was lionized by the poet-philosopher Lucretius in his *On the Nature of Things*.

Epicurus taught that happiness comes five ways. The first and foremost is that pleasure is the highest good and primary source of happiness. Much of Epicurus's philosophy thus deals with how to enhance pleasure. Inerrantly, this naturally leads to his corollary that happiness also means the absence of bodily and mental pain. Thus comes Epicurus's first maxim, which is: to achieve happiness, all actions must be directed to maximizing pleasure and minimizing pain. This may sound obvious, but Epicurus had more in mind when he said that pleasure cannot be increased, only varied, whereas when pain and suffering have been removed, pleasure can only increase.

This is a profound comment on the nature of happiness. What it means is that people should pursue pleasure but be aware that it has its limits. At some point, pleasure just becomes more of the same—try as people may, they cannot increase it unless they seek an alternate pleasure. But this alternate pleasure also has limits and cannot be increased. So how then do humans increase happiness? The answer is to limit pain. Pain and suffering are bottomless pits of human unhappiness, so the solution is to work at eliminating sources of pain. The more pain one eliminates, the less pain one feels. Happiness then for Epicurus is achieving maximum pleasure and eliminating as much pain as possible. Happiness is an equation that maximizes pleasure and minimizes pain.

Epicure's second maxim is to have virtue and limit desire. Pleasure and desire are different. The former brings good feelings and happiness, whereas the latter engenders passion for something. Passionate desire can bring unhappiness in a number of ways. People may desire what they do not need, and they are perpetually unhappy when they have not achieved an ardent desire. For Epicurus, the desire for external things like fancy clothing, wealth, high office or status portrays ignorance of the true sources of happiness. Virtue is character and belief that teach people how to live a happy life. Virtue restricts desires and makes people treat others justly.

His third maxim is that philosophy brings happiness. Philosophy brings happiness in many ways. It teaches virtue, how to act, how to achieve pleasure, how to avoid externals, and it frees the mind from superstition and anxiety. Death, for example, is a great source of fear for many that Epicurus thought was unnecessary. Philosophy teaches that one should not fear death because it does not matter if one does. Death should be of no concern to people while they are alive and is of no account when they are dead. Philosophy makes people aware that they really have only three needs: equanimity, bodily health and the exigencies of life—everything else is superfluous.

Epicurus's fourth and fifth maximums are to avoid public life and cultivate friendship. Public life and politics are strife with anxiety and suffering. They are the venues in which man becomes the greatest enemy of man. It is in the public arena that humans attack, accuse and calumniate one another, so to be happy it should be avoided. Prudence requires one to live a simple, serene life in the convivial company of friends. Friendship was very important to Epicurus because it brings people together and engenders pleasurable conversation, preferably in the tranquil Epicurean garden. It is a place of refuge from the world of strife where people can retire with those they like.

Epicurus believed there were three stages humans go through to achieve the good life. The first, which is to master desire, has already been discussed. At this stage, people come to realize some desires are natural and some illusionary. They come to realize that desires for externals and luxury are illusionary because they can be taken away. These bring only momentary and fleeting pleasure interspersed with long periods of anguish spent searching for the next sensual pleasure. The solution is to understand that the external world rarely meets expectations, so one should bring desires to the level of actuality.

This truism is will be reiterated eight hundred years late by oft-quoted Boethius. Boethius is in many ways an Epicurean disciple. He emphasized the use of good judgment, much like Epicurus's logic. Both teach that free-floating desire brings unhappiness. Like Epicurus, he wrote (p) if people covet money they will have to take it by force; if they want high office they will have to grovel before those that bestow it; if they want high honors they will have to cheapen and humiliate themselves by begging; if they want power they will have to expose themselves to plots and run dangerous risks; and if they want fame they will be worn out. With the human body, all that one admires can be reduced to nothing by three days of burning fever. He did differ from Epicurus on pleasure when he wrote that (p) if people desire pleasure, others will scorn them for being a slave to the worthless and brittle human body.

Epicurus's second stage is to perform one's duty. Rather than live a life of (v) long and diversified warfare with others, Epicurus taught that people are not detached entities but rather part of a whole.

To be part of that whole requires duty to others. Unlike animals, man understands the connection of things, which brings obligations in public business, marriage and children. It is duty that mitigates strife and maintains the whole, which engenders a communal feeling that brings happiness.

The third and final stage is to know the discipline of reason, which Epicurus called logic. Logic helps people detect deception and false beliefs and avoid rashness of judgment. With logic, people come to understand inferences, which prevent them from concluding more from a proposition than it proposes. When, for example, someone says (v) "I am richer than you are they" infer "therefore I am better than you." Logic tells one this is an invalid inference because nothing follows necessarily from the premise except (v) "I have more possessions than you." Logic brings critical thinking, good judgment and perhaps wisdom. With it, people avoid self-defeating beliefs that bring unhappiness.

Unfortunately, today Epicureanism is often confused with the ancient Cyrenaic and Hedonist philosophies, which taught pleasure alone is the source of happiness. Pleasure is the highest good in Epicureanism but not the only one. As discussed, the philosophy also emphasized logic, virtue and the limitation of desire. Epicureanism is a far more sophisticated and insightful philosophy of happiness.

Stoicism was a contemporary of Epicureanism in ancient Greece. Its founder was Zeno of Citium and later adherents include Cicero, Seneca, Epictetus and Marcus Aurelius. Relevant to this book and like Epicureanism, its objective was to bring human happiness and tranquility of the mind. Epictetus asked, for example, (p) to what end does one pursue one's studies? Is it not so that one may be happy? Cicero believed philosophy brings happiness and (v) it follows that the wise man is always happy, and Seneca wrote that (p) philosophy holds out to humanity help for the unhappy.

In the introduction to this book, it was asserted that happiness requires effort, and in the beginning of this chapter, Aristotle's view that happiness resides within was introduced. Stoicism melds the two. Epictetus believed that people are responsible for their happiness because god made them that way. For the stoics, people have all the tools at their disposal to bring happiness, all one has to do is use them. As to the second part, Epictetus wrote that (v) the path to freedom is not to destroy the tyrant outside but rather the one within, which can only bring inner happiness.

There are seven tenets of stoicism that relate to happiness. The first is that the world is as people make it. They may not be able to control outside events, as Epictetus wrote, but they can control what they think about them. People have many circumstantial masters that they cannot defeat, but they can master those within. Happiness is a choice, and people have the ability to make the right choices to make the world a happy place. Seneca believed happiness resides in choice because state of mind and attitudes determine whether people are happy or not. Ultimately, according to Epictetus, (v) the good life can be achieved by adjusting one's desires to the way the world is, rather than trying to adjust the world to satisfy one's desires.

The second tenet is to limit desires to be happy. Epictetus wrote that the man who rids his mind of desire will have an untroubled mind. Seneca believed it was the uncontrollable tyrants within that bring unhappiness. For Epictetus, one can never be pitied for being satisfied for what one has. The third tenet, which is to use good judgments to bring happiness, is a key stoic belief that was discussed in chapter seven. Judgments are the ideas people use to interpret the impressions they get from the world. People are not responsible for the ideas that are presented to them, but they are for how they react to them. Some of these impressions are good and others bad, but it is within one's choice to judge them such, and whichever way one does will determine one's happiness. People can judge poverty as disgraceful and demeaning or, like Diogenes, unimportant, because they need little to exist and be happy. It is within one's power to develop good judgments and eliminate bad ones in order to think and act in a way that brings happiness. Seneca wrote that people are daily in a battle with fortune that continually thwarts happiness and the solution is to use proper judgments about what is in one's control and remain indifferent to matters beyond it. So, remove those beliefs that are unhealthy and use preconceptions properly in order to be happy.

The fourth tenet is to avoid emotions and especially passion. Anger, envy, hate and fear are timeless human emotions that militate against happiness. With anger, for example, people burn for revenge, which only makes them angrier and unhappy. John Stuart Mill famously asked whether it is best to be a pig satisfied or Socrates dissatisfied. Metaphoric animalistic pigs live at the whim of their feelings, which causes them some pleasure but mostly great distress. A satisfied Socrates, on the other hand, understands the need to question the emotions and control passion to mitigate their propensity to make one unhappy. The stoics therefore would ask Mill's question differently; is it better to be a pig dissatisfied or have the opportunity to be a satisfied Socrates. For them, ignorant human pigs are dissatisfied because they have allowed themselves to be victims of their passions.

The fifth tenet is to remain indifferent to that which is beyond one's control. Fate brings uncontrollable fortunes. There are some things that bring unhappiness, which people have no control over, such as death. For the stoics, it is useless to fret over these matters beyond control, so people should be indifferent to them. People are like a dog on a leash. The dog does not have the freedom to go wherever he wants but he can go where he wants within the limits of the leash. Within the length of the leash, people have some control, and thus control over their passions and ultimately happiness, but beyond it, people should remain indifferent because it is outside their choice. They should just do their best and then leave the issue to fate. Why worry over that which will happen whether one worries or not? For the stoics, people are happier when they do not live in fear of fate—people should just accept fated matters and move on.

The sixth tenet is that happiness comes when people realize they are a part of humanity. This may sound like a strange thought from philosophers who think people should control their passions and remain indifferent. However, the stoics believed happiness comes from thinking of the self as part of a whole. Epictetus wrote that (v) a foot is no longer a foot when it is detached from the body, so a man is no longer a man when he is separated from other men. Like the Epicureans, the stoics believed people are all citizens of the world.

Finally, the stoics believed studying philosophy can bring happiness. Repeating the theme that happiness comes with effort and from within the stoic, Epictetus wrote that (p) philosophic knowledge is the path to freedom because with it people can, through proper judgments and choice, turn out the tyrants within themselves. Emphasizing choice, indifference and control of emotion for the stoics brings happiness.

Famous philosopher Hannah Arendt in the *Human Condition* criticized some of these stoic prescriptions for happiness. She believed that the stoic independence from the world is pain. Stoic happiness achieved in isolation from the world and enjoyed within the confines of one's own private existence can never be anything but the absence of pain. The absence of pain is not happiness but only a felt short intermediate stage between pain and non-pain; thus, the concept of happiness becomes the release from pain rather than its absence.

There may be some truth in Arendt's criticism; however, limiting pain has much to do with happiness. The Anna Karenina principle states that more things can go wrong than right. Thus, keeping in mind the Epicurean's view that pleasure cannot be increased only varied, it would seem the greatest threats to human happiness are the bottomless sources of pain. Indeed, it is hard to be happy when one is in pain. Stoicism may not give a comprehensive blueprint for happiness, but it does tell people how to prevent pain, which is a step toward happiness. Besides that, the stoics believed people are integrated citizens of the world and not isolated individuals, which was one of their tenets for happiness.

Stoicism and Epicureanism have much in common on the nature of happiness. They both teach that happiness is inner tranquility and to limit desire, have virtue, be rational, have good judgments, and remain indifferent to that which one cannot control. They also both teach that individuals are all part of a whole or citizens of the world. Not surprisingly, they both also say that philosophy brings happiness. The difference in these philosophies hinges on pleasure and pain. The Epicureans believe indulging the right desires are acceptable, whereas the stoics thought that people should avoid the passions altogether to be happy. It seems the Epicureans emphasize pleasure and the stoics limit pain.

The truth is both philosophies are right to an extent. Enhancing pleasure and limiting pain does bring happiness. However, as Epicurus himself admitted, pleasure at some point cannot be increased, thus increasing pleasure alone does not necessarily bring happiness. The stoics emphasized limiting pain but here also Arendt pointed out that the absence of pain is not happiness. Recall from the introduction that Cicero lost a beloved daughter, and the only way to alleviate his despair was to remain indifferent to that which he could not control, which is stoic advice that alleviates pain. To be happy, adopt both Epicurean and Stoic philosophies, but remember that the sources of pain are deeper and broader than the sources of happiness.

Chapter Nineteen

BLISSFUL IGNORANCE
Do not take life and its troubles too seriously, lighten up, see the big picture, put things in perspective and have a little fun through blissful ignorance

A man is going through an awful divorce, just got his third driving under the influence citation and was recently diagnosed with grade three prostate cancer. He feels depressed, overwhelmed and impotent in the face of fortune. He has come to experience reality's harshness that too often brings unhappiness. What does he do? One solution is to retreat from her lashing winds and find safe harbor in non-reality. Some such safe harbors are folly, illusion and ignorance from the nor'easters of existence. Rather than solve vexing problems, some philosophers suggest retreating into one's mind to achieve happiness. Knowledge brings happiness, but ignorance often diminishes the severity of occasional unhappy events.

One way to retreat is to adopt Desiderius Erasmus's advice from *In Praise of Folly* and become a folly-driven fool. After all, everyone will die some day, so ultimately nothing matters. Why not just be careless and carefree today? Erasmus wrote that (v) without folly life is sad, troublesome, graceless, flat, distressing and utterly without pleasure. In order to avoid this unpleasant state, he says people should accept life with its oddities and become ignorant, thoughtless, forgetful of evil coupled with a whimsical hope of good spiced with a dash of delight. They should revel in telling monstrous lies and tall tales and become preoccupied with hunting, building and alchemy. They should always be starting huge projects they have no chance of completing and then complain that they cannot complete them because their lives are too short.

Erasmus pointed out that (p) drinking only drowns sorrows for a short time, whereas folly is a spree that never ends. Its effects are complete and immediate—it does not require any bothersome preparations and is available to all. Indeed, those who are mad desire madness when they are cured—they have tasted sanity and madness and prefer the comfortable, tranquil and happy state of an insane fool. Fool-hood is the Holy Grail of folly because it makes life's difficulties bearable. Further, to become a fool is easy, one need only to acquire mere opinions and eschew rationality. Those with expensive educations that develop their rational powers are among the unhappiest of all, whereas it costs nothing to be a happy fool living in opinion. The price of happiness is low: it is no more than a bit of illusion.

For Erasmus, folly brings happiness in many ways. For one, it gives (p) less reason for living, and the less one wants to live, the more one enjoys life. It also enables people to ignore scorn. If a rock hits one's head it hurts, but curses, disgrace and shame hurt only so far as one feels them. What is not noticed is not troublesome. So long as one applauds oneself, what harm are the hisses of the world? And what about the happiness brought on by empty flattery? Praise and flattery make people all more pleased with themselves. It is an acceptable form of pleasure that produces a sense of happiness, like two mules scratching each other. It is the sugar and spice of human intercourse.

Folly also brings illusion, another great source of happiness for Erasmus. Indeed, (p) the saddest thing is to not be deceived. The truth is that people are only actors in the play of life in which they pass in various disguises. If they do not follow the crowd and quit the play, they unmask the actors and the illusionary charade ends. This only brings emptiness and purposelessness—a kind of existential nothingness. One's happiness depends on one acting one's part in life's artificial play. Similarly, people must maintain illusions on how they are regarded by others to remain happy. Indeed, the truth is if they could read others' thoughts, no one would have friends. Ernest Becker, for example, believed that the health of any society depends on the strength of its illusions, and without them, people would all be neurotic. Another way to perpetuate one's salubrious illusions is by daydreaming. When a person imagines, for example, that he is some great athlete, war hero, or scholar, or just making love to a beautiful woman, he retreats into a pleasant fantasy world that only brings felicity. What is the harm?

One good thing leads to another, and it so happens that foolhood-folly-flyers with the greatest illusions are the most ignorant, which is another source of happiness. Indeed, Alexander Pope in *An Essay on Man* wrote that man's very felicity depends on his ignorance of future events-ignorance indeed is bliss. Unhappiness does not come from that which is not known.

Perhaps the culmination of folly, illusion and ignorance can be found in Miguel de Cervantes's character Don Quixote—the happiest of all humans. Quixote is a mildly insane and idealistic knight who follows his dreams in the face of ridicule and adversity. He calls himself The Knight of the Mournful Countenance whose romantic vision is to right past wrongs, avenge injustices, protect damsels, terrorize giants and champion battles. He rides on his horse Rocinante and with his loyal companion Sancho Panza charges imaginary windmills. He is a man who follows his dreams. Most think he is crazy, but is he?

There exist inescapable tensions in life between reality and illusion, romanticism and pragmatism, truth and fact and material considerations and ideals. People live in a world of contradictions that if they allow to remain unresolved bring only consternation and unhappiness. Don Quixote chose a path out of these polar tensions—there was a method to his madness. He escaped convention and pursued his own vision, followed his dreams and ignored others' judgments. Significantly, doing so enabled him to ignore others' criticisms. Virginia Woolf once wrote that the eyes of others are prisons and their thoughts, cages. He simply ignored others' eyes, eluded their cages, and thus avoided the worst thing Camus said men must endure, which is to be judged.

Following his illusionary dreams also allowed Don Quixote to suppress unpleasant memories and the exigencies of the real world. He epitomized Erasmus's advice and became ignorant, thoughtless and forgetful. He gained happiness by imagining himself victorious over fabricated foes. Albert Schweitzer once said that happiness is good health and a poor memory—Don Quixote had both, and he was happy. In a sense, illusion and ignorance not only brought him happiness but moral grandeur and inspiration due to his unflinching fidelity to his own vision.

Mark Twain once wrote that it is impossible to be both happy and sane. To be happy, introduce a little folly into life, enhance illusions and seek a degree of ignorance. Do not take life and its troubles too seriously, lighten up, see the big picture, put things in perspective and have a little fun through blissful ignorance.

Chapter Twenty

FLOURISH THROUGH LOVE, ZEST, HOPE
Break the hard shell of ego, enjoy a conflagration and hope for the best

Ann loves people and parties. Socializing with friends energizes her and her family enlivens her. She has a zest for living and lives every day as if it is her last. When she faces inevitable life problems, she is always naturally buoyed by hope that they will be happily resolved. She is naturally inclined to optimistically envision a better future. Ann is a happy person because she is full of love, zest and hope.

Certainly, these personality qualities are variable—they can take one many places. People feel pain when they lose the one they love, become dull when they continually fail and sadness naturally follows when dreams are thwarted. Be that as it may, many philosophers and common sense reveal that people have a greater chance to flourish in life if they love rather than hate, feel zest rather than disenchantment and are inclined to hope rather than dejection.

The stoics believed that to be happy people should not depend on externals like property and power because they are things outside control. The benefit of love, zest and hope is precisely that they do not depend on externals—they come entirely from within. It is within one's power as an individual to adopt these attitudes and feelings, which makes happiness within one's power to achieve.

This is analogous to the ancient philosophers' advice on virtue. For Aristotle and the stoics, virtue, or *arête*, which people can achieve through will, brings excellence and wisdom, which in turn brings *eudemonia* or well-being. Love, zest and hope are like this because they also can be achieved by will. It seems certain that having virtue along with love, zest and hope can help achieve *eudemonia* or a state of personal welfare, contentment, well-being and happiness—a state in which humans flourish. So, how do love, zest and hope accomplish this?

Not all philosophers have considered love a source of happiness. The ancient stoics degraded it as an emotion and called it insanity and madness. Cicero in particular in *Tusculum Disputations* wrote that love is an excessive passion that should be avoided. He believed (p) it is a craze, it makes the wise senseless, it brings anxiety and eliminates all reasonable restraint. He described love as a mad passion in which helpless romantic poets wallow.

C. S. Lewis's Screwtape had a more nuanced criticism of love. Screwtape tells Wormwood that their enemy, God, has told humans that being in love is respectable and ground for a permanent state of marriage. This kind of affection is unacceptable to Screwtape because he wants humans in hell. To achieve this, he wants humans to believe that when one gains another loses. He wants selfish humans, where the stronger sucks the will and freedom from the weaker. He wants humans to compete and not affectionately cooperate. The enemy, God, Screwtape says, resists this formula for unhappiness by proclaiming the good for one is good for another and calls this love. The enemy wants to change competition to cooperation. To counter this, Screwtape says people must promote desire and diminish affection, champion competition and destroy cooperation. This strategy can destroy humans' concept of love, destroy the institution of marriage and drive the human race into hell.

There is a little truth in Cicero and Screwtape's observations on love. Certainly, losing the person one loves to another and being forsaken by the person one loves are great sources of unhappiness. However, there are no guarantees in life, and these are the risks one runs with love. Better advice comes from Alfred Lord Tennyson who wrote that (v) it is better to have loved and lost than never to have loved at all. Those who love just might find the happiness it brings, whereas those who forsake the risk never will.

Bertrand Russell in *The Conquest of Happiness* wrote that (v) love brings happiness, and Seneca wrote, (v) if you wish to be loved, love. Love brings happiness in innumerable ways. When people are in love they feel elated, they are not alone in the world, they find another human valuing them, they connect with another human on a primal emotional basis and they experience passionate affection. Love brings an expansive and generous attitude toward others who reciprocate it, which engenders goodwill. Love is also the precursor to great sources of happiness such as marriage, reproduction, children and family that have been described elsewhere in this book.

Love breaks down the hard shell of ego and competition and sends people into a sensuous world of delight that brings joy and happiness. When people risk loving another, happiness will find them.

Zest is an odd characteristic for happiness. Indeed, people often think of zestful people as artificial, insincere and overzealous. But zest entails enthusiasm, which is an essential ingredient for success. It is enthusiasm that urges people to get an education, be good in sports, procreate a family or start a business, all of which may bring happiness. Happiness does not come from pursuing these life-goals in a plodding and grim manner.

A zest for living brings excitement and gusto, which results in a lively enjoyment of life. With it, people become more interested in things that animate them, which makes life more exciting. Life becomes one more of adventure than obligation and actions become more spontaneous than regulated. A zest for life brings happiness.

Bertrand Russell in *The Conquest of Happiness* wrote that civilization restricts people's natural zest, which results in the malady of disenchantment. For Russell, (p) without zest, people are powerless, and events only become experiences; people take no interest in them and they make nothing of them. This only leads to an empty kind of resignation that shows that people cannot control fate, so why try.

The antidote is zest. Russell believed that (p) the most universal and distinctive mark of happy people is zest. With zest, one has more interests, which bring more opportunities for happiness. Zest arouses interests and frees one from a life of tedium. With zest, people are less at the mercy of fate, and if they lose one thing, they can fall back on another. Those with zest have advantages over those without it because they are more inclined to see the opportunities in life's challenges and struggles. They are the adventurous and zestful souls who (v) enjoy shipwrecks, mutinies, earthquakes, conflagrations and all kinds of unpleasant experiences. For Russell, natural zest like that found in children is the secret of happiness and well-being.

Philosophers are mixed on whether hope brings happiness. Many think it brings a variety of maladies, and some like Kierkegaard think it is indispensible. Plato (SEP) believed hope was a kind of gullibility. Aristotle's views were contradictory; on one hand, hope involves bravery, but on the other, cowardice. The stoics believed hope is a fear of the future. For Descartes, anxiety always accompanies hope, and for Hobbes hope is a passionate pleasure of the mind. Spinoza believed hope is irrational and only results in false beliefs that bring superstition. David Hume believed hope is a passion born from considering probable events, which results in uncertain beliefs. Schopenhauer called hope a (SEP) folly of the heart because it hinders the intellect to grasp the truth.

Perhaps the greatest philosopher critic of hope is Friedrich Nietzsche. He opposed all notions of hope and called it (SEP) the worst of all evils because it prolongs the torments of men. Albert Camus rejected hope because it distracts from using one's energies to solve problems now. The philosophers' views against hope are varied but could perhaps be summarized with the view that idle hope is the crutch that the lazy man indulges in rather than working to better his future.

These philosophers' views may contain some truth, but the question remains, are those without hope happy? Certainly, those without hope may never be disappointed, but are they happy? Camus may believe that hope distracts from the challenges of this world, but he also believed that (SEP) it is impossible to live without hope, even if one wishes to be free of it. Likewise, humans fear death, so Saint Augustine wrote in *City of God* that hope for an afterlife is a significant source of comfort.

Unlike Nietzsche, Søren Kierkegaard could be considered the greatest philosopher advocate for hope bringing happiness. He believed that hope transcends understanding and is the antipode to despair. For him, (SEP) a person's whole life should be the time of hope. In contemporary practical terms, philosopher Richard Rorty endorsed hope because it enables people to reject divisive political models and seek agreement.

So the philosophers are divided on whether hope brings happiness. Be that as it may, it seems certain that hope does comfort those in misery and that it does bring a degree of happiness. The weight of fate bears heavily on humans. People lose loved ones, get sick and die. The Stoic advice to ignore that which one cannot control may bring a release from pain, but it does not necessarily bring happiness. Hope is that additional ingredient that can bring happiness. Wishing for things to aright is itself a happy thought. Thinking that there is a life after death, whether true or false, is also a happy thought. Just wishing or thinking things may get better is a happy thought. These kinds of hopeful thoughts cause one to imagine something desirable happening in the future, which makes one feel good. Those who despair have no hope; they are destitute and have no aspirations because they have nothing to hope for. They are like animals living inert, barren and resigned lives.

Those who hope live happier lives. They create an image of a potential better future that just may come true. Kierkegaard was right; hope is the antipode for despair as well as its antidote. Hope compels the hopeful to activity. Hope animates them to seek a better alternate future. The hopeful try to improve their lives. Those who only expect the worst will never be happy because they are forever expecting the worst, whereas those who hope for the best are happy because they live in anticipation of a better future.

It has been said that the one who hopes is often disappointed, whereas the one who does not is often pleasantly surprised. However, the one without hope has given up a vision of a better future in exchange for tolerating unhappy circumstances today. They sacrifice their future and, as Henry Sidgwick wrote in *Prudence*, (p) a man should care for the good life now as a whole and not sacrifice a distant good for a nearer one. Certainly, Ann's hopeful disposition may bring her disappointments, but with hope she lives a happier life now.

Do not delay happiness for some questionable tomorrow—have love, zest and hope today.

Chapter Twenty-One

PURPOSE
Be a ship with a rudder

Vain is a woman living a shallow life expecting to be entertained, always seeking petty pleasures and expediently doing what needs to be done to be happy. She is not a deep thinker but rather an emotional whirlwind, following her feelings wherever they take her. When young, life was a thrill, but as she aged, she began feeling pangs of worthlessness, ennui and a vague sense of emptiness. It was only when novelty had run its course and reality began to set in she began to ponder her values and came to realize she had lead a purposeless life with no objectives. She had been an aimless pinball bouncing between passions with no goals, just drifting through an unthinking and meaningless life. It occurred to Vain that she had done nothing significant or important in life. Her life had been a waste.

Vain lived a purposeless life. She never established a framework of values that would have brought her life goals and objectives. She never took the time to deeply ponder life and what might make a good one. She was like a ship with no rudder aimlessly sailing the seas with no port of destination.

In philosophy, teleology, which derives from the Greek word *telos* meaning end or purpose, is the study of purpose, directive principles or simply goals. Philosophers break teleology into extrinsic and intrinsic purposes. Extrinsic purpose is purpose imposed by humans, like using a hammer to drive a nail or a fork to eat food. These kinds of purposes are significant, but they do not give people ultimate purposes to live by. Intrinsic purpose is a universal and timeless purpose that is irrespective of human use or opinion. It is the kind of purpose Aristotle referred to when he suggested that the purpose of an acorn is to become an oak tree. These are the best kinds of purposes, and without them, people live aimless, meaningless, random and empty lives prone to unhappiness.

Teleology naturally initiates the interminable philosophic debate between determinism and free will. Are people's lives determined or do they have free will to choose? Hegel proposed a historic dialectic that teleologically progresses in a predetermined way, ultimately ending in human freedom. Others, like Kierkegaard, who opposed Hegel, argued for free choice principally because he believed that people become what they choose. Kierkegaard's free choice naturally segued into Sartre's existentialism, a philosophic theory that emphasizes free individuals and responsible agents determining their own development through acts of will. Existentialism presupposes a non-teleological universe with no ultimate purpose. For purposes of this chapter, it will be assumed that existentialism is true and free will and choice are possible. Note that with free will people are free to choose intrinsic purposes.

So, if existentialism is true, the universe is a void, and if people have free will, then the only purpose for existence must be chosen, which makes one the source of purpose in one's life. Purpose, whether extrinsic or intrinsic does not come from nowhere—it comes from an individual. This is significant because a person's level of felicity depends on his ability to discern some purpose for his life. Certainly, some could be satisfied with simple extrinsic purposes, but the greatest happiness comes from identifying some intrinsic special purpose and achieving it. Philosophy teaches that doing so brings meaning to one's life. This is a meaning that people create and cannot be taught.

Imagine life without the meaning purpose brings. In it, people would live like an unthinking animal, passively existing. Dogs are happy with the goal of chasing a ball and sheep happy procuring and raising their lambs, but dogs and sheep do not ponder existence like people. They do not ask what the point of life is like people. Humans are uniquely cursed with the knowledge that they will die, which precipitates questions about the reason for existing. People answer this unique question by creating purpose in their lives that brings meaning and, collaterally, happiness.

Unlike rudderless Vain, with purpose people are ships with ports of destination along with a captain, sextant and rudder, which naturally help to reach the destination. People establish a goal, which is to get to a port, engage all aspects of life and circumstances, apply themselves and hopefully achieve their goal. They arrive safely at the port having succeeded in an objective. They created a purpose and fulfilled it, and the result is meaning and happiness. Along the way, people also hopefully collected some admiration, respect and self-esteem. With purpose, they discover a reason for living and a sense that life is worth living. The result is happiness. Vain has none of these and often wonders if there is anything to live for.

Some purpose-objectives can come from various sources, including from society and from oneself. Heidegger believed that reality is a social construction; thus, purpose could be a social construction. The problem with this is that the societal purpose may not be personal purpose, and one could end up pursuing that which one does not feel is meaningful. For purpose to be meaningful, it must be virtuous, salubrious and from within. Masochism and Sadism are not good purposes because they cause harm and diminish happiness. But a carpenter who extrinsically believes using the right hammer to properly hammer a nail and the philosopher who endeavors to justify intrinsic ethical theories that promote peace are good purposes that promote felicity. Both extrinsic and intrinsic purposes bring happiness, but the intrinsic ones offer the freedom to fashion a world imbued with purposes that are uniquely meaningful to an individual. Indeed, one such significant purpose could simply be to be happy. Some sources of determining and achieving purpose in life will be discussed next.

A significant way to create purpose in life is to establish goals—without purpose, goals are irrelevant. Purpose derives from attaching importance to something worthy, which is a first step to establishing a goal. If nothing is valuable in one's life, then nothing really matters, and one ends up like Vain, sailing through life like a ship with no rudder going nowhere in particular. So, to create purpose in life, develop goals. Goals should capture one's interest, further one's unique potential and do some good along the way. They should be realistic; ones an individual has the ability to achieve. They should be, as Emerson wrote, (p) aimed slightly above if one wishes to hit the mark. They should not be unrealistic, unachievable or easily obtained goals. They should be in proportion to one's ability and character.

One reason Vain had difficulty deciding on a goal was because she feared limiting herself. She wrongfully thought that when she established a goal, she limited herself to that one objective and collaterally missed other opportunities. This is a common human problem because many believe that they are better off keeping their options open because it will bring more opportunities. Experience tells otherwise—once people pick a goal, not only do they advance an objective but also open up other possible goals. The world is full of those endlessly searching for some purpose with no goals going nowhere in life and feeling worthless.

Once one picks a goal, many unknown sources engage. Others who know the goal often want to help, and when one knows the goal, one sees more opportunities. Modest, who is not rich, always wanted a swimming pool, so he made a goal of getting one. One day he was driving and saw a sign that said, "Fiberglass boat free if you can move it." Modest thought a fiberglass boat hull could make a great swimming pool, so he acquired it, installed it and now has a pool. If Modest had never established the goal of wanting a pool, he never would have noticed the sign or connected fiberglass boat with pool. It has been said that the world works for people with a goal, like Modest.

It seems that people are naturally inclined to set low and easily obtainable goals. They may naturally be wary of newness, feel uncomfortable outside their ruts or be fearful of the unknown. Indeed, Shakespeare wrote that people (v) would rather stay with those ills they know than fly to those they know not. But these inclinations do not bring enduring purpose in life or happiness—they just bring more of the same. So, what is needed is courage. Settling on a purpose in life with specific goals is not an easy thing to do because it takes people out of their comfortable ruts. To have a purpose means to muster the courage to have it.

Existence is a smorgasbord of potential goals and resulting purposes. One could decide to be great at a sport, an erudite scholar, a good teacher, or the best doctor, lawyer or businessman. Although less durable some could find meaning in establishing extrinsic goals to become rich, powerful or prestigious. Certain enduring biological goals are to find a mate, have children and raise a family. Intrinsic goals such as those found in faith and Christian love can be intensely purposeful. For the practical, it could simply setting the goal to be happy, and for the wise, it could be to have virtue. Whatever the goal, the important point is to have one.

Multiple goals and purposes sometimes support one another and other times conflict. Having conflicting goals can be a problem. Making a goal to be a great athlete on one hand and indolently carefree on the other is contradictory and only results in an ambiguity that lessens the meaning of the goals. Consistent goals bring focus on what one wants, which brings happiness.

Establishing life goals is not a one-time event but rather an ongoing way-of-life process that becomes a habit. If one wants to be happy, philosophy teaches that establishing goals is a good habit to have because they bring purpose.

Similar to goals, having interests is another way to establish purpose. When people have interests they attach importance to something and thus determine something to be valuable. Significance and value are two sources of goals that, as was described earlier, often become purpose. In this respect, purpose in some ways derives from desire, because when people desire something, achieving it may become a purpose. Reading and education are examples of this. Reading gives new ideas that multiply—one interesting idea leads to another, and before one knows it, one has multiple interests that one finds important. With this, reading and learning become a purpose. Readers are lifelong learners, and learning inspires activity and prevents ennui, which brings happiness.

Interests can be personal or impersonal. Personal interests deal with the self and often one's feelings, instincts and desires. One wants to get rich in order to be secure, so wealth becomes an interest and ultimately a purpose in life. Personal interests are better than no interests, but they can be narrow, less fulfilling and isolating. Interests beyond one's selfish sphere can be far more enduring and significant. Two impersonal interests, for example, could be to eradicate cancer and bring peace. These kinds of impersonal interests tend to take people out of themselves to other-regarding moral places. They also tend to connect people with others, which often results in more exceptionally meaningful purposes.

There are many benefits to having interests in life in addition to goals and purpose. Interests have a way of leading to other interests, and thus multiple interests. To use an earlier example, reading is a labyrinth of winding intertwined interests that often segue unnoticed into another. If one reads, one will most likely develop interests. Other benefits include challenging the mind and a kind of zest for life. Interests that lead to goals and purpose infuse an enthusiasm for living. So, if one wants to be happy, the philosophers say, find interests, develop goals and have purpose.

It should be mentioned that goals and interest are of little value without effort. The most worthwhile things in life require effort. If anyone could become a tennis champion or scholar, then being a tennis star or scholar would lose its value. Any purpose in life derived from valuing and achieving goals through effort would be irrelevant. Only a few with talent and tremendous effort can achieve these goals, which means it is effort that provides much of the purpose in life. It is a strange irony that industry, which can be burdensome, is a source of purpose and happiness, which can be so pleasing. Indeed, many indolent are the least happy.

Two final thoughts on purpose are to avoid false gods and use good judgment. Some purposes, like maximizing sensual pleasures, have little past and future enduring value. The satisfaction derived from false gods is in the present, which makes them fleeting and somewhat empty. They tend to bring only short-term gratification and not long-term meaning. Choosing long-term intrinsic purposes brings greater satisfaction and thus happiness. It is also critical to use good judgment when choosing purposes. Purposes derived from sentiment and whimsy tend to be ethereal, capricious and short-lived. It is better to follow the Stoic advice to employ reason in the process of choosing purposes in order to arrive at the right ones.

Ralph Waldo Emerson wrote that (p) the high prize of life and crowning fortune of man is to be born with a bias to some pursuit which finds him in employment and happiness. Philosophy teaches that to be happy, one must endeavor to develop purpose in life. Otherwise, one will drift through life as a rudderless ship like Vain.

CHAPTER TWENTY-TWO

HEALTH
Health enables people to worry

Sloth and Vigor live different lives. Sloth smokes, never exercises, eats anything he wants and has a body mass index that is off the chart. He indulges his appetites and pursues his passions with abandon. His perspective on life rarely goes beyond the present. He thinks things are good now, so why worry about the future. Vigor is different; she thinks more about the future. She watches her weight, exercises, eats in moderation and avoids bad habits. Many contrasting worldviews emanate from these two stereotyped personalities, but the most significant one is about health. Vigor connects health with happiness, and Sloth does not. Being healthy is a prerequisite to happiness.

Curiously, philosophers historically have said little about the relationship between health and happiness. The ancient presocratic Pythagoreans taught the importance of caring for the health of the body. They believed that people should not neglect their bodies. They described different types of exercise with the view of improving strength and health. They believed people should attend to their bodies and maintain conditions not too lean or fleshy. The Greek Stoics went a step further by insisting that people are in control of their health by asserting that they are their own physicians. Cicero wrote that people (v) have the power to be their own physicians, and Marcus Aurelius wrote that (p) if they pay attention to their health they have little need for doctors or their applications.

Even thought there is a paucity of philosophic thought on the relationship between health and happiness, it remains certain that health is a prerequisite for happiness. It stands to reason that if one is sick, one only thinks about getting healthy. Indeed, it has been said that health enables people to worry. So, the theme of this chapter is to attend to health like Vigor in order to be happy. This means both physical and mental health because they are reciprocal. Physical maladies diminish psychological happiness and mental disturbances interfere with physical fitness. The first part of this short but important chapter deals with physical health and the second mental health.

It should be noted that many physical and mental illnesses are beyond individual will. Organic diseases, accidents, chemistry and genetics are sources of ill health beyond one's control. For these, people must look to the doctors and scientists for solutions. This chapter deals with those sources of ill-health that people can influence.

Physical health is fundamental to being happy. It is exceedingly difficult to be happy when people are struggling with illness or are in pain. Much of people's physical health depends on their willingness to listen to their bodies. People's bodies speak to them constantly in many ways; some listen and some do not. When the body says that it is sleepy, fatigued or satiated, one should take a nap, rest or stop eating. Unhealthy people too often respond to the same body-messages by staying up, working through it or eating more. Bodies have a natural relationship with nature because they are nature. Thus, to be healthy, people need to maintain a harmony with nature. To be fit entails a certain naturalness where one is part of one's environment and not opposed to it.

Part of health entails relaxation—a time for ease. One's physical and mental state requires occasional rest. However, the concept of time is upsetting this natural need. Jeremy Rifkin in his book *Time Wars* described this disruption. Original human time was organic and grounded in the slow cycles of the seasons and circadian rhythms. The concept of an hour, for example, is a Roman invention, the Benedictine monks invented the clock, the machine of the modern age and in the eighteenth century the pendulum measuring seconds ushered in the new word "punctuality." As a result, many have become obsessed with time. They are always in a hurry and think time is something to be overcome. Now people have computers measuring milliseconds and nanoseconds and become entirely detached from nature's time.

This speeding up of time ruins one's experience of life. Lives become full of haste, breathless urgency and sterile moments. The true things that bring joy such as love, relationships and nature become diminished, and happiness fades. The concept of time is a human invention, and like a Frankenstein, it has turned on its creators. The new conception of fast-time is the source of many physical maladies such as anxiety, tension and depression.

The solution for many philosophers is to listen to nature, live within her rhythms and stay physically fit. People know the doctors' prescription translations of these ideas in order to be healthy. They advise people to exercise, get enough sleep, watch their blood pressure and cholesterol and maintain a proper body mass index. They also advise to eliminate some habits like smoking and drugs and moderate others like alcohol. But few people listen to the doctors because those habits are the paladins people use to cope with the modern fast-paced world.

Of the physical maladies people endure, Bertrand Russell focused on fatigue as a major source of unhappiness. He explained that (p) those who love excitement and easily obtained superficial pleasures are the ones who wear out their nerves and become susceptible to fatigue. These unhappy people become accustomed to anxiety, are too tired to be capable of enjoyment and are constantly restless—all of which leads to fatigue. They are people who worry excessively about their problems, which for Russell is a form of fear that produces fatigue. Indeed, famous football coach Vince Lombardi once said that fatigue makes cowards of all.

People all make innumerable decisions daily that affect their happiness. Consider how Russell's explanation of fatigue would play out with Sloth and Vigor. Sloth encounters his problems over and over with no solutions, incapable of making a decision that might help him be happy. Instead he makes no decisions because they might negatively impact his future. His inability to make decisions is exhausting, and he becomes stuck in time, unable to act; the consequence is fatigue. Vigor is different. She considers her problems like Sloth but then, unlike Sloth, continues to think. She uses her will and mines her imagination and proactively asks herself what her solutions and what their worst scenarios are. She intelligently discerns those fears that will burn themselves out and courageously decides to act on those that might improve her future happiness.

With this, Vigor is energized and immune to the fatigue that Russell believes brings unhappiness.

In his youth, this author was caught in a similar trap as Sloth, driven by time, not listening to his body and increasingly listless. His physical and mental health were degrading, which made him unhappy and depressed. Unlike Sloth, he took advice from Vigor and sought a solution that freed him from his self-imposed prison. The solution was to quit his job and move his family to the Greek island of Ios. His book *Aegean Summer* describes his experience and how he was able to recapture peace, health and happiness. Following are brief excerpts from that book describing his experience:

> I quickly settled into a daily routine, which was to get up late in the morning after a long and restful sleep and have my coffee on the veranda overlooking the bay in a state of total peace. I learned that long and deep sleep is an essential ingredient for happiness. It made me rested, relaxed, and serene. After breakfast I would walk the path to the white sandy beach and go swimming in the warm, crystal clear Aegean Sea. The rest of the morning I would sit on the veranda and read. I felt supremely healthy and happy.
>
> My intellectual curiosity was challenged and fulfilled. I was talking about and thinking about the things I never used to have the time for. I was living in a way that fulfilled every need my body and psyche demanded for happiness.

Philosophers advise people to attend to their health because it is a necessary ingredient of happiness. So now their various views on mental health and its relation to physical health and happiness will be discussed.

Sloth and Vigor's characters, attitudes and habits have much to do with their physical health. The same is true of their mental health. Sloth is a lazy thinker, is ruled by his passions, sees only parts of reality and not the whole, has an inaccurate view of himself, is never sure if he fits in, has vague goals and objectives and is aimless. Vigor on the other hand is sharp; she is ruled by her reason, sees herself accurately, has clear goals that she is striving to achieve, feels like she fits in society and is insightful and focused. Vigor is better able to navigate the daily varieties of challenges to mental well-being than Sloth. Her character, attitudes and habits work to mold reality in a way that brings her not only success but also mental satisfaction. Sloth has none of this and is thus more susceptible to ill mental health than Vigor. What people think has much to do with how well they are mentally and consequently whether they are happy.

This precipitates two questions. The first is what mental health is and the second is whether philosophers are qualified to suggest prescriptions for it? Why is one characteristic considered abnormal at one time and normal another? It was once thought that atheists were nonconforming sinners but now they are common secular thinkers. Why are the hermit and eccentric considered less mentally healthy than the city dweller and conformist? Don Quixote was considered insane for being a dreamer of dreams pursuing windmills, but why is pursuing one's ideals not normal?

In many ways, mental health is an average. It is what society deems mentally correct at any one time. There is a kind of collective herd mentality, often called political correctness, where a majority of people endeavor to impose on a few their view of what constitutes mental health. But this makes reality a capricious perspective that changes with time—a changing societal construct that is right only in its time. True enduring mental health entails a benign form of happiness. It means being comfortable and satisfied in one's mind without fearing others' judgments. Some, mostly ancient philosophers, have suggested some ways to achieve this, which will be discussed shortly, but for now one can accuse the bulk of philosophers of offering poor advice on this subject.

It must be admitted that philosophers are not the best sources to help one achieve mental health and happiness. The reason is there are just too many flawed, unhappy and unsatisfied philosophers with unrealistic perspectives on reality. How can one who thinks deeply and is troubled teach others how to be mentally well and happy? This chapter will examine a few of the troubled ones first and then end with a few that say something useful.

Ben-Ami Scharfstein in his *The Philosophers, Their Lives and the Nature of Their Thought* wrote that the Bishop Berkley and Georg Hegel were the only philosophers who were normal, happy people. From his perspective, philosophers are detached individuals. Descartes lived in solitude and was emotionally distant; Spinoza lived a solitary and lonely life; Locke was secretive; Leibnitz was solitary and emotionally detached; Kant was wary of obligations, did not need friends, and lived a repressed and inflexible emotional life believing man is evil; Nietzsche lived in solitude and was lonely; and Santayana, who was detached and withdrawn, also lived in solitude.

Scharfstein described Voltaire as being manic depressive and Rousseau as masochistic; Kierkegaard had disgust for life, Russell had many affairs because he did not think a woman could love him, and Sartre learned to scent, fear and hate males. He describes Schopenhauer as melancholic, miserable, unbearable to live with, full of ill-humor and contemptuous of humankind. Wittgenstein had no sense of self-worth, was moody, and was also contemptuous of people and perpetually suspicious. He noted that philosophers rarely marry and some, like Schopenhauer, Nietzsche and Wittgenstein, were misogynists. Some courted death, and many perpetually warred with themselves. It seems certain that such an august group of flawed thinkers could have little to say about how one can achieve mental health and happiness. Perhaps at least they teach one what not to do.

But there are other philosophers, mostly previously mentioned ancients, who do help. Their views involve the need to be physically and mentally healthy in order to achieve happiness. The presocratic Pythagorean and Stoics' emphases have already been mentioned. Physical health is critical for three reasons. First, it is hard to be happy when one feels bad or is in pain. Second, to be happy, people must be able to act, which physical ill-health impairs. Translating thoughts that can bring mental health and happiness requires action. Finally, when people feel poorly, their mental faculties are used less and sometimes impaired. To be mentally well, people need to be able to nimbly think about their lives and how they should live them. They need to be able to intellectually discern that which brings felicity and that which does not.

Drug addicts and advanced alcoholics are good examples of this. These addicts are typically not happy. They are physically ill and often in pain. They are frequently incapable of acting to escape their addiction, and even if they could, their minds are so impaired they cannot figure out how. Physical health is in many ways a necessary condition of mental health. To be mentally healthy, many philosophers tell people to attend to their bodies.

Although their ideas also relate to other matters, Plato, Aristotle and Cicero espoused philosophies that provide frameworks for mental health. Because this book discusses each of their theories in detail elsewhere, they will only briefly be described here.

Plato believed mental health and the happiness it brings entails morality—people need to be moral to be happy. He described the moral harmony of the soul that includes the four cardinal virtues of wisdom, courage, moderation and justice. Wisdom enables one to rationally understand reality and apply useful knowledge to daily life. Courage helps one face adversity and to act on convictions in order to achieve happiness. Moderation, self-control and temperance mitigate desires, which free people from a source immorality and unhappiness. And justice is when one's reason rules one's appetite, thus avoiding another source of potential unhappiness. For Plato, the individual who attains these cardinal virtues is fulfilled and at peace—mentally fit and happy.

In his *Ethica Nicomachea*, Aristotle envisioned a theory of mental health from a different perspective. For him, well-being is achieved in his Doctrine of the Mean where virtue is attained by a mean between two extremes. An athlete's fitness, for example is maintained by not too much or too little food—rather through a fitting amount of food that just satiates. Similarly, the extremes of pursuing money become either prodigality or meanness, between which the proper mean is liberality—save enough for oneself and then help others.

Cicero, like all Stoics, emphasized the need for proper judgments to achieve mental health. When judgments and beliefs are in harmony, or when people see the world accurately, they attain a kind of harmony. He believed this harmony of the soul is virtue and mental health.

Plato, Aristotle and Cicero's philosophies on mental health entail two things: harmony and avoiding excess, which are two sides of the same coin. Harmony mitigates excess and excess violates harmony. The moral then from these philosophers is to avoid excess because it leads to mental disturbance. Sloth and Vigor are good examples of this advice. Sloth tends to extremes by indulging his appetites, whereas Vigor moderates and controls them. Vigor exemplifies Aristotle's moderation, Plato's cardinal virtues and Cicero's proper judgments to achieve mental health, and Sloth does not.

All of the causes of physical unhealth described earlier now become manifest in Sloth's mental unhealth. Sloth suffers from anxiety, which has become a habit; he worries constantly about his problems, which he cannot solve. He is indecisive, which causes him unrest. He lives in paralyzed fear of his future, unable to act and perpetually in pursuit of excitement and pleasure, which only brings him fatigue. Sloth is a paradigm for a mentally unhealthy and unhappy person.

Too many people live lives like Sloth in quiet desperation. They suffer from physical self-imposed illness along with depression, anxiety and fear. They live lives that perpetually verge on mental illness. They live unnoticed because they all wear masks to cover their pride. They are the suffering unseen of this world, and they are unhappy. To be happy, the philosophers urge people to attend to their physical and mental health and be a Vigor, not a Sloth.

Chapter Twenty-Three

REPRODUCTION
*Escape the isolated and barren prison
of self and reproduce*

At sixty years old, Bill and Hugh are living different lives. When young, Bill married the woman he loved, had children and raised a family. It was a daunting task, but now at sixty, he is reaping the rewards. His life is full of family, children, grandchildren, birthdays and holidays with family. At sixty, he is living in a web of human familial good feeling, which is a fountain of happiness. Hugh did not marry the young woman he loved. He did not want the obligations marriage and family bring. He preferred to pursue his own interests. He now has some money, his own business, flies his own plane and excels in tennis and golf. But Hugh has no intimate family, no wife and no children. He lives alone. At sixty, Hugh's greatest regret is that he never married and has no children. It has been said that regret is the cancer of life. When young, Bill took a risk and reproduced; he assumed reproduction's responsibilities and shouldered its obligations. Hugh did not reproduce. He avoided the risk, eschewed its responsibilities and never shouldered its obligations. Bill is happy, and Hugh is unhappily regretful.

Certainly, this is a simplistic characterization, but the point is that great happiness is born in the crucible of a man and woman in love. It is a crucible that entails affection, intimacy, sex, marriage, children and family. It is an age-old story of instinct-driven reproduction—a story people are biologically wired to perform. It is this instinctual crucible that for some philosophers is the greatest source of happiness.

But this crucible of marriage and children is not easy. In America, over half of marriages fail, and it is estimated that over a quarter of families are in poverty due to divorce. Divorce itself is an ugly affair with arguments, anger, recriminations and heartbreak. As for the children, it is estimated that it costs a quarter of a million dollars for a middle class family to raise a child in America in 2015, which is itself a daunting task. To make matters worse, the children raised are usually rebellious, the teenage daughters going through puberty are churlish and some children are failures and forever blame their parents for their life problems. Some children turn to drugs and become lifelong addicts unable to contribute to society. Some children never come to appreciate their parents' sacrifices. Parentage entails risk, children's recriminations that are sharper than a serpent's tooth, the loss of individual freedom and unending obligations. To make matters worse, biological families are shattering today in America, further stressing their ability to perform their function. Indeed, Bertrand Russell wrote in *The Conquest of Happiness* that one of the greatest sources of unhappiness today is due to families becoming derailed and disorganized. The risks of reproduction are endless, but its benefits outweigh them if they can be achieved.

There are several benefits of marriage, children and family. The first is very basic—it fulfills and instinct, or biologic urge. Humans have two fundamental instincts, which are to survive and to reproduce. As people live they fulfill the first, but if they do not reproduce, they do not fulfill the second. Fulfilling an instinct is a source of happiness because it satisfies and makes one feel human and whole. It is a primordial source of happiness that reproduction taps. Indeed, satisfying the instinct to reproduce is one of the few ways to satisfy an instinctual urge.

The second is that marrying and having children imbeds one in an unending chain of human history. It is like a river of life that flowed before one was born and continues to flow after one dies. People are given the opportunity to participate, or dip their toes in this river of life. They are the product of their ancestors, and with reproduction, they create descendants, many of whom are like them—people reproduce versions of themselves. Participating in this human chain of life brings meaning, purpose and great happiness.

The third is that children themselves are a great source of happiness. Children are spontaneous, touching and loving beings. They are just fun to play with. As a parent, it is fulfilling to watch them grow and deal with life's problems, and to help them surmount them. It is exceedingly rewarding to see them succeed in life with avuncular parental guidance. Life offers a few deep relationships with others such as close friends, parents and siblings, but the deepest ones are reserved for one's spouse and children—they are relationships that entail giving in to something bigger than self. These are not artificial relationships one can engineer but rather biological relationships that organically emerge. Bill is experiencing these relationships, and Hugh is not.

Marriage between a man and woman can be another source of great happiness. It is a unique relationship in that it produces children, unlike other relationships. It is a singular relationship because it creates life in the crucible of love. It is a life-long relationship with the person one will get to know better than anyone else. It is a life partnership with many shared experiences. It is a relationship with the person one loves, lives with most of one's life and grows old with. It is also one that brings great sexual pleasure. Studies show that married people enjoy far more sex than single or cohabitating couples. In addition to the frequency, sex becomes far more meaningful because couples are procreating—they are having sex for a reason and not just an orgasm. Saint Augustine in *Confessions* described when he was young how he surrendered himself to lust, which to him was just sowing seeds that bring crops of grief. He wrote that he (p) learned that reproduction is more than a sport but rather intended to beget children. He lamented that his youthful "surge" might have been calmed and contented by the procreation of children in marriage. It is eminently more satisfying and meaningful to make love with those one loves for a purpose.

Reproduction creates families, which Bertrand Russell believed is one of the greatest sources of happiness. Family is an institution created for men and women to beget, support and raise children. In a cold and indifferent world family brings intimate relationships, a sense of belonging, mutual support and love. For those who participate in this web of meaning, life is richer and happier. Those with broad and deep family relations are lucky indeed because the very feeling of love within a family brings happiness.

Russell wrote that (p) happiness comes from affection and intimacy, which qualities families can engender. Those who feel themselves unloved sink into timid despair and become self-centered and insecure. They become introverted and melancholic. Looking outward and valuing others for their intrinsic qualities, like one's spouse and children, is the antidote. Valuing others turns people away from themselves and allows them to focus on others. Russell said that the capacity for genuine affection for another is one mark of the person who has escaped from the isolated and barren prison of self.

Finally, Bertrand Russell wrote in *The Conquest of Happiness* that, though parenthood can bring some of one's deepest pains, it can also bring the greatest joys. For him, parenthood has the potential for the greatest and most enduring happiness life has to offer. It does so because it ties generations together and makes them less isolated and better people. For parents, the future is important because their children are part of it, and for grandparents, children are important because they revive and perpetuate their past. They tie both together because they are their legacy.

For Russell, with children, (p) people are not isolated individuals but rather part of a stream of life flowing from some original germ to some unknown future. Without children, people isolate themselves from this stream. Children also have a way of making one a better person because one has to put aside selfishness and think of their children's interests. What happens in the world no longer happens to just the self but also one's progeny. It is hard to be selfish as a good parent. Russell wrote that marriage and children take one out of oneself. They force one to be other-regarding, which is a maturing process because one comes to learn to care for others. With parenthood, people also must set a higher standard for themselves if they want their children to have higher standards. There is little room for selfishness in parenthood, and those like Hugh who never became parents often remain (v) isolated, selfish, small and boorish.

Bill both learned and experienced these life lessons about marriage, family and children. He married his life companion, and he came to appreciate both her and the importance of having someone significant with whom to go through life. He recognized the stream of life and the family dynamic that unleashes incredible benefits, including happiness. He discovered the deep happiness that comes from living within a group of people who love one another, like the family. He experienced the joys of companionship, closeness, warmth, and support that lie latent within the family. At sixty, Bill had lived these lessons, which made him less isolated and happy.

C. S. Lewis in *The Screwtape Letters* had the devil Screwtape advise his minion Wormwood to make humans avoid fertile marriages because they lead to happiness. He said to (p) use a man's sexuality against him so he perpetually pursues it rather than marriage. Doing so will be his undoing and lead to an exquisite and lasting unhappiness. With this advice, Screwtape is revealing one source of unhappiness. Pursuing sensual pleasures, romance and parties soon become more of the same. They may bring temporary pleasure but not the long-term happiness that comes from making a commitment, shouldering obligations and creating a family. Screwtape understands that reproduction is one of the most purposeful and meaningful things humans can do in life, whereas its counterfeit leads to emptiness.

Bill at sixty also pondered why he was drawn to his family. He began asking what its significance is. He thought that people are born, live and die, which progression was not enough for him. He asked himself if he had eschewed having a family and lived a life pursuing the gods of money, security, prestige, power or sensual pleasure, what would he have today that is worthwhile? It would have been a life of just more of the same, and he would die a forgettable human, having added nothing much to humanity. With this, what he had always suspected emerged as an epiphany—he realized how marriage, children and family change this historic equation.

Bill also pondered his children and came to realize how much they were a part of him. He realized how they had come from him and will perpetuate him. They are that eminently meaningful link in the chain of human experience. To have them, to get to know them, to fashion them in his image and to love them is the real stuff of life. Hugh never learned Bill's life-lessons about wife, children and family, and at sixty was left only with his empty prison self-shell.

One should find a lover when young like Bill, make a commitment, marry, beget children, create a family and be a parent. Do not put off this most important thing in life because it is one of the greatest sources of happiness.

Chapter Twenty-Four

THE MEAN
Avoid the Law of Undulation and embrace the mean

Politically, Sally and Donald are at opposite ends of the political spectrum. Sally is an ultraliberal Democrat who cannot tolerate right to lifers, becomes incensed with Medicare cuts and thinks polluting corporations are evil. Unbeknownst, she is a collectivist Marxian socialist who believes from each his ability and to each his need. Donald is a conservative Republican almost Libertarian who hates his progressively high tax rate, believes the federal deficit will sink America and is convinced non-originalist judges are tyrants. He believes in self-reliance, independence and individual freedom. Sally and Donald are unpleasant, always irritated, angry individuals constantly complaining about something. They hold deep resentments and grudges because things often do not go their way. They are unhappy people.

Sally and Donald are unhappy because they are extremists who never heard of Aristotle's famous Doctrine of the Mean. This chapter is about the Sallys and Donalds of this world, the mean and happiness.

The devil Screwtape in C. S. Lewis's *The Screwtape Letters* advised his protégé Wormwood to practice the Law of Undulation on humans in order to make them miserable. Humans, he explained, have a tendency to experience peaks and troughs, which brings them pride, hatred and emotional crises. They are particularly vulnerable in their troughs because their inner world becomes (v) drab, cold and empty, and it is in this state that they are most susceptible to sexual temptation, lust, alcoholism and sudden emotional crisis. Extremists Sally and Donald are Screwtape's inerrant fools, unwittingly obeying Screwtape's Law of Undulation's trough.

The solution is Aristotle's doctrine of the mean. Aristotle, one of antiquity's greatest philosophers whose ideas form much of Western Civilization, wrote about moderation in his book *Nicomachean Ethics*. It is a theory about happiness, or, in his words, *eudemonia* or well-being. It involves avoiding extremes and cultivating a mean in life. It should be mentioned that Aristotle's theory involves many things such as virtue and *arête*, but this chapter will focus on the mean and its relationship with happiness. But first the stage should be set with the good and rationality.

The good is a Platonic term, which means something that exists for the sake of itself and not others. It is not something that brings a happy state of euphoria but rather something desirable for its own sake. For example, the good is not cold and indifferent money but rather something like love, which is inherently good. More importantly, for Plato, participating in the good enables people to see and understand. Mentioned earlier, the good makes things intelligible and gives people knowledge. For this chapter, it enables one to understand the importance of moderation and that the end of the good is *eudemonia*.

Aristotle also taught that the human soul is made of the rational and irrational. Irrationality involves appetites, which have been described in this book as a significant source of unhappiness. Alternatively, the rational is calculative, which brings virtue, which will be described in chapter twenty-six as a major source of happiness. Rationality that brings virtue results in practical wisdom, which for Aristotle means having character, knowing the right thing to do and desiring to live as one ought.

The point of all this is that the good and rationality help people appreciate the importance of a mean in life. The good by pointing the way to knowledge and well-being, and rationality by teaching the right things to do. Together they tell one to be wary of Screwtape's Law of Undulation and to embrace Aristotle's doctrine of the mean.

So what is the doctrine of the mean? It is that in people's beliefs, attitudes and characteristics, they should follow a mean between extremes in order to be happy. In Aristotle's terms, it is a virtue attained similar to an athlete's fitness that is maintained by not too much or too little food. One example is facing death. One could rashly fear death and another cowardly ignore it. Neither one could achieve peace of mind in the face of death. Another example is courage, which is the virtuous mean between rashness, which is a vice, and cowardice, which is a defect. With courage, people face death and overcome the fear of it. They do not get such courage through ignorance or caprice but rather by controlling appetites and being rational.

Other examples of Aristotle's doctrine of the mean in which the activity or attitude is mentioned first, then the excess, then the defect and finally the mean or middle course. On pain and pleasure, the excess is selfish-indulgence, the defect is insensibility and the mean is temperance; on money, the excess is prodigality, the defect is meanness and the mean is liberality; on honor the excess is empty vanity, the defect is undue humility and the mean is proper pride or self-respect; on assertion, the excess is boastfulness, the defect is mock modesty and the mean in telling the truth; and finally on giving amusement, the excess is buffoonery, the defect is boorishness and the mean is ready wit.

For Aristotle, the middle course is practiced by the wise and good man. The good man (v) sees the truth in each class of things, being as it were the norm and measure of them, and the temperate man (p) craves for the things he ought, as he ought, and when he ought—this is what rational principle directs. For Aristotle, understanding the good and being wise, rational and temperate bring a mean that engenders well-being and happiness.

Like Aristotle, Cicero also believed living by a mean brings happiness; however, he called it temperance. In *Tusculan Disputations*, he wrote that intemperance is the fountainhead of all disorders. Intemperance is a revolt from reason and slippery ground because once started downhill it cannot be stopped. For Cicero, the cravings of the soul must be guided by the reasoned mind, and the result is temperance or avoidance of extremes. Like Aristotle, Cicero wrote that the mean of bravery (or courage) does not need the assistance of the extreme of irascibility to succeed because it is (v) sufficiently equipped, prepared and armed.

Finally, Boethius believed happiness comes from having no wants or cravings. Wants and cravings unencumbered by reason often become Aristotle's extremes and Cicero's intemperance. For Boethius, extremism is a brew that takes happiness because it makes

(p) individuals other-dependent and weakened. With moderation, people gain true happiness, which makes a man (v) self-sufficient, strong, worthy of respect, glorious and joyful.

There is an old proverb that says it is never too late to mend. For distressed Sally and Donald, this means to abandon their intemperate, extreme, inflexible, ideological political views in order to be happy. Reality tells them nobody gets everything they want and expectations are not reality. Happiness requires a compromise like Aristotle's mean, so to be happy, they should adopt it.

Chapter Twenty-Five

APPRECIATION
Everyone can choose whether to view the glass half empty or half full—appreciate any volume

Mildred's husband snores and is honest, slovenly, industrious, loving and overweight. When she thinks of him, all she can recall is that he snores, is fat and dresses badly. She never recalls his honesty and hard work or the fact that he loves her. Mildred focuses entirely on his vices and not his virtues, which distresses her. Certainly, nobody is perfect, and she knows that whomever she married would have some faults—she knows she could have married someone worse. But she does not think this way. Why is it that humans naturally focus on the negative in life rather than the positive, which only brings them unhappiness?

Human's proclivity to only see the negative side of life is a major source of unhappiness. There could be numerous reasons why people do so. Perhaps it derives from the instinct to survive—those constantly on guard against dangers survive, and those who are not perish. It could be a defensive technique due to the fear of losing what one has like a loved one. It makes people feel better to distance themselves now from that which they cherish in order to avoid the pain of their eventual loss. It just makes people happier to count their woes than their blessings. It could be that people fear hope because it can bring disappointment. Alexander Pope wrote: blessed is the man who expects nothing for he shall never be disappointed. People figure that if they eschew hope, they will not be disappointed and thus will be happier.

It could also be that people's preoccupation with the future causes them to lose the appreciation of what they have today. C. S. Lewis's Screwtape, who is trying to bring evil to humanity, advises Wormwood to keep humans focused on the future because all vices are rooted in the future. Doing so inflames hopes and fears that engender fear, avarice and ambition. He tells Wormwood to bridle humans with the future to make them unhappy. When people focus on the future, which is what most humans do, they lose an appreciation of the present. They come to think they will only be happy at some time in the future due to the benefits it may bring and not today. The present becomes something to endure rather than enjoy and appreciate.

Focusing on the life's negatives may also be due to malformed values. People may value something worthless that may be attained rather than something of value, which they already possess but do not appreciate. Tolstoy in *The Death of Ivan Illych* described an unhappy man who valued prestige and money, which he did not have, rather than his loving wife and son, which he did have. It was only during his process of dying that he came to realign his values and appreciate what he had.

The inability to appreciate what one has infects all people whether they are rich, poor, young or old. Everyone's circumstances entail some reason to want something they do not have and thus lose appreciation of what they do have. The young have health but no money, so they devalue health and value money, whereas the old may have money but poor health, so they devalue money and value health. Certainly, the young may never get rich, but likewise the old may never regain their health. People face circumstances that cause them to not appreciate what they have now.

Happiness comes from appreciating what one has now. Stoic philosopher Epictetus wrote over 2,000 years ago that the wise man does not grieve for the things that he has not but rejoices for those that he has. Wisdom teaches to appreciate the water in the well, which one knows may go dry. Counting one's blessings and appreciating what one has now is a formula for happiness.

People must not take for granted what they have now because someday it will be gone—they should enjoy it while they can. They must not give into excessive passions and desires that only cause them to want what they do not have. They should not live exclusively in the future, sacrificing the joys of today for some unknown and unbestowed future benefit, but rather value what is important like human relationships and appreciate the good ones they have.

On a deeper level, people must appreciate the very fact that they can appreciate. To borrow from philosopher G. E. Moore and his *Principia Ethica*, appreciation does not come from the object but rather the observer. Appreciation resides in the human heart and not out there. In the case of beauty, it is not beauty itself that is important but rather the emotional contemplation of beautiful objects. Moore's theory can be recast to mean that it is the appreciation of another's attitude toward something that is the most valuable good people know. In short, it is the very ability to appreciate that establishes value, so to appreciate must be the most valuable ability of all. So, one must appreciate and appreciate that one can appreciate; it is one of the most valuable assets.

For the author's master's thesis, he once interviewed a young man named Jason Regier. Jason had been a philosophy student at Oregon State University in the mid-1990s. He liked philosophy because it dealt (v) with the big picture of life, and how one lives. He was a young man full of plans, which came to an abrupt end in 1996 when in a car accident he instantaneously became a quadriplegic. Within a few hours, this healthy young man found himself alone in a sanitary solitary hospital room paralyzed from the neck down. His thoughts were all negative, and suicide increasingly became his solution. If anyone has the right to not appreciate, Jason Regier would be the one.

But consider what happened to him over time. As he lay paralyzed and alone in his hospital bed, his thoughts turned to the philosophy he had learned at Oregon State. Amazingly, he thought it could have been worse—he could have died. As time passed, he observed that some with spinal cord problems in the hospital were born with them, and these people never had the experiences he had before his accident. He thought about his family and the many friends who had come to his side after the accident, and the new opportunities to become closer to those he formerly knew casually. He realized he still had his life and loved ones, so he was in many ways better off than he originally realized.

He realized that whether he goes (v) up or down in life from here depends on what he thinks about his circumstances. He knew he could go either way, but which way, he realized, was ultimately up to him. Which way, he thought to himself, depended on his mind-set and his ability to think about things for how they really are and not how they ought to be. This caused him to recall a quotation from Theodore Roosevelt, which was that people should (p) do what they can, where they are, with what they have, and with this idea he began (v) going up.

His thoughts gradually became more positive. He thought how useless it is to worry about the things he can no longer do, rather than the things he can. Jason came to appreciate the ability he had to control that which was within his control. He came to the understanding that there are things he cannot control, and he came to appreciate his ability to distinguish what he can.

With these thoughts, Jason thrives in life. He became a soccer coach, he traveled the world, he owns a business, he gives speeches around the country, he obtained an MBA, he has had girlfriends, and he plays quad-rugby, in which he won a gold medal for the United States in the 2008 Beijing Paralympics. He also is planning to go to Europe and hopes to get married and have children.

Jason Regier's story is an example of how philosophy, in this case stoicism, can bring appreciation for what one has and thus can bring happiness. The stoics believed that things are how people make them, and that people should be satisfied with what they have and live simply according to nature. Jason's quotation from Roosevelt mirrors the Stoic belief that people ought to remain indifferent to that which they cannot control. His story poignantly demonstrates philosophy's ability to bring happiness to all. If a quadriplegic can find appreciation, so can everyone else.

People take for granted their blessings. Søren Kierkegaard in *Either/Or* wrote that people never use the freedoms they have but demand those they do not have; people have freedom of thought but demand the government provide them a microphone so their thoughts are heard. Appreciating one's blessings and not pining over what one does not have is a significant source of happiness. Indeed, one may have many unappreciated blessings. One may have health, home, a career, friends, loved ones as well as important immaterial things like peace and freedom. Without these, life could be much worse. Assuming one had none of these benefits, that person would still have the aesthetic ability to appreciate beauty, which is everywhere to be found—many just do not recognize it.

Being grateful for what one has means to stop living in the future. It means to be less concerned about what bad things one imagines might happen. Doing so causes one to forever endeavor to engineer future outcomes, which will make a person miserable. Trying to control events and people only sets one up for unhappiness because people resist being controlled and fate is its own engineer. For happiness, it is better to accept the day for what it offers. Happiness begins when people stop struggling with shadows and accept things for what they really are.

There is a story about a man watching from the beach another man drowning and feeling joy. He was not feeling joy because the man was drowning but rather because it was not happening to him. In many ways, people are like the man watching. They recoil at the suffering of others and fear the sufferings they may someday endure—one should live life appreciating what one has now, like Jason Regier.

Each person can choose whether to view the glass half empty or half full—appreciate it with any volume. One must do what one can, where one is, with what one has.

Chapter Twenty-Six

VIRTUE AND JUSTICE
Do not be a Troglodyte—focus on the inner ring

Vice is a selfish, self-centered individual. He is out for himself in life and has little concern for others. He has no scruples and believes if he can gain at another's expense with impunity, all the better. He thinks people who are honest are suckers. He does what is expedient, not what is right. Yet he is troubled because everyone treats him with wariness and suspicion. Everyone is guarded in his presence and many distain him. Nobody is friendly or gracious. Vice often feels isolated like a pariah and unhappy. He is so because he eschews morality and is thus without virtue and justice.

Plato wrote in the *Gorgias* that people who are noble and good are happy unlike the evil and base. The evil and base are those without virtue. The Skeptic philosopher Sextus Empiricus believed that happiness cannot subsist apart from virtue. Ancient Roman philosopher Cicero was particularly convinced that virtue and happiness are interconnected. He wrote that (p) adequate support for the happy life is found in virtue. The happy life is bound up with virtue—the virtues cannot subsist without a happy life, nor a happy life without the virtues—the happy life is bound up with rectitude alone. In his *Tusculan Disputations*, he clarified that the seeds of virtue are inborn and if allowed to ripen, nature's own hand would lead to happiness. For Cicero, virtue is self-sufficient for a happy life.

Immanuel Kant 2,000 later echoed Cicero's observations when he wrote that (v) morality is not properly the doctrine of how people may make themselves happy but how they may make themselves worthy of happiness. People become worthy of happiness when they decide to become moral beings, which necessarily entails virtue and justice. Morality entails virtue, which, as Plato, Kant and Cicero presaged, makes people worthy of happiness.

So, what is virtue? It is a concept that evolved over time. In classical Greece, it was called *arête* and signified Homeric masculine aristocratic qualities such as courage, skill and competitive prowess that resulted in superiority. Plato used the term to denote the quality of human excellence attained through rationality. In the *Protagoras* he wrote that (v) no one willingly goes to meet evil, which implies humans are inherently good and commit evil only out of ignorance. Plato's concept of *arête* emphasized rationality and is deterministic in that it is goodness humans naturally seek. The concept of virtue further evolved to mean excellence in other softer qualities like justice, right, knowledge and self-control. Eventually it evolved further to signify an excellence in all things. Perhaps a perfect tree or the American militaries admonition to "be the best you can be" are examples of late virtue in the form of *arête*.

None of these classical definitions of virtue carried the connotation of moral uprightness that it does today. The contemporary concept of virtue means to be morally good or righteous, morally excellent, to have good traits like honesty and fairness or to have similar admirable qualities. Perhaps above all it means to adhere to honorable principles that regulate actions. Virtue is used here in its modern tense because it signifies moral potential and not militant or esoteric potentials. So, how does virtue bring happiness?

Montesquieu in the *Persian Letters* asked whether men were happy through the pleasures and satisfactions of the senses or by the practice of virtue. He answered this by describing an imaginary race of creatures called Troglodytes who live by sensual pleasure alone. In their culture, each man is for himself, shares nothing, is avaricious, steals wives and murders. He described them as a very unhappy race in constant tension, fights and competition. Troglodytes are unhappy because they indulge their pleasures and desires with little regard for others. Likewise, Plato in the *Gorgias* wrote that to do wrong is the worst for the wrongdoer. A tyrant, for example is the most miserable of men because he wrongs others—when he wrongs them, they wrong him. Montesquieu and Plato are describing virtue-less unhappy people.

Virtue is the antidote. When people are virtuous they treat others fairly so other virtuous people do the same. It is an old equation: if a person treats others right, they will treat him right. But it is more than this. With virtue, one lives with others in harmony rather than faction, engenders a society of goodwill and finds commonalities, which lead to friendships. Beyond this, one earns others' respect and trust, which enhances one's sense of self-worth. Treating others right makes one square with the world, which is a circumstance that brings satisfaction and happiness.

Friendship is one of the great sources of human happiness. Indeed, Robert Frost described the cold sense of loneliness and the warmth of old friendship. Philosophers say that the best kind of friendship is achieved through virtue, which was a problem for Vice. Aristotle in *Nicomachean Ethics* described three kinds of friendships: those based on utility (or what a friend can do), pleasure (what pleasure a friend can bring), and virtue. Utility and pleasure friendships come and go as others' usefulness wanes, but virtuous friendships remain because people value others for their own sake. For Aristotle, virtuous friendship is the most glorious attainment one can achieve and the highest form of friendship. It is a friendship where one honors another for their sake regardless of utility or pleasure. Aristotle described virtuous friendships as complete, between people who are virtuous, resistant to slander, long lasting and difficult to achieve.

With virtuous friendships, people no long feel isolated and alone. People feel valued and uniquely connected to someone who is traveling the lonely path of life with them. They find someone who knows them and still likes them. Because these types of friends are people they do not expect to gain from, they can come from any source including the old, young, a spouse, children or an old high school acquaintance or college roommate. Philosophy teaches to be happy, be virtuous and cultivate friendships.

There exists a long-standing debate in political philosophy between the relative merits of collectivism and individualism. Are humans essentially collectivistic or individualistic? This book does not intend to unravel this complicated debate but rather to relate it here to virtue and ultimately happiness. Certainly, people are collectivistic creatures; they are born into mothers and fathers, families and states, which are all interwoven collectivistic entities. However, if they remained in these nascent relations, they would become alike, conformists, cooperative and interdependent. They would take on the virtues of the group, which often are different than individual virtues. Virtue is a personal characteristic and not a social norm that deals with how people think they should act and not how others think they should. Certainly others influence people's thinking but virtue ultimately depends on their vetting life and its verities. There is a burden associated with becoming virtuous that involves limiting passions and facing potential isolation that one must overcome to be virtuous. So, in this respect, true virtue can only be achieved by the individual; only then can a virtuous relationship like friendship arise. Collectivism does not bring the personal virtue needed for Aristotle's friendships. Rather ironically it is individualism, or to become who one is individually that makes people worthy of friendship and ultimately happiness.

Montesquieu's Troglodytes who live by passion are Sisyphus's doomed forever to push the rock back up the hill. Passion brings temporary pleasures and ethereal happiness, and the solution is virtue, which regulates passion. With this, virtue avoids both the fleeting fate of passion-driven happiness and the despair it can bring. Indeed, Seneca wrote that (p) happiness and the good life comes from virtue in which good character is the only guarantee of everlasting and carefree happiness.

The ancient Stoics had much to say on this interwoven relationship between virtue, passion and happiness. For them, the conception of virtue was essential to mitigate the pejorative consequences of unrestrained passion. By adopting good characteristics through the use of reason, such as the ability to judge impressions accurately, passions that lead to unhappiness can be mitigated. Collaterally, with such characteristics, good passions such as the passion to acquire *sophia* can be accentuated, which bring happiness.

What animate these characteristics are salubrious principles, or fundamental beliefs people adopt that they live by. The effect of these principles limits passions that lead to unrequited happiness. Seneca wrote, for example, that (p) without principles people live without self-restraint in stormy and disordered lives, passing time in a state of fear. Certainly some are incapable of controlling their passions, but those who can enjoy greater enduring felicity.

The idea that virtue brings self-control is central to Stoic thought. With it, they believed people become more temperate and better able to control or desires and emotions. Cicero wrote that (p) virtue, by controlling passion, brings fortitude, control of emotions, delivery from distress and fear, temperance and lust. For Cicero, virtue distinguishes kinds, links sequences, draws just conclusions and discerns true and false. It opposes enervation and weakening due to false beliefs and evil habits. These put the chief good in a person's power, which is the power to be happy. Cicero believed that the happy life depends on virtue, self-restraint and courage.

Obviously, it is a little more complicated than this—there is more to happiness than just virtue. True happiness may come from virtue, but it also resides in a mean between virtue and the imperatives of reality. Aristotle wrote that (p) happiness consists in a complete life lived in accordance with virtue but also accompanied by a moderate possession of goods. Philosopher Mortimer Adler added that the complete life is a well-lived life and that the goods people acquire include some possessions and wealth. For Aristotle, virtue is fundamental but not all—one must keep an eye to reality in order to be happy. That eye-view is to intelligently draw a line between virtue and wealth, which means the desire for a moderate amount of wealth, or enough to satisfy bodily needs, is itself a right and virtuous desire. It is the pursuit of wealth beyond one's needs, or pursuit of wealth for its own sake that virtue teaches is the wrong desire because it cannot be ultimately satisfied. In its own way, virtue guides desires.

The stoics believed that virtue is in humans' nature, which brings happiness. Epictetus in his *Discourses* wrote that happiness and the good life come from virtue. Indeed, he believed that virtue alone constitutes human happiness. This is a central Stoic ethical claim. They also believed that people are born for virtue, which means happiness is within their will to achieve. This is why the philosophers teach that happiness comes from within. Epictetus wrote that man was born for virtue and not with it—humans have the capacity to be happy. Recall Kant's observation that morality, which virtue embraces, is what makes them worthy of happiness. Plato enhanced this point with his view that the lack of virtue is due to ignorance. He believed evil comes from ignorance, but with wisdom, a power within control, the virtue that regulates passions brings happiness.

The point of all this is that happiness comes from an internal state of mind that embraces virtue. Happiness does not come from without—externals are not what make people happy. It is not what one owns but rather what one is that constitutes happiness. This is another stoic tenet, which is similar to other Hellenistic ethical theories: it is what one is and not externals that determines one's happiness. Another tenet of the ancient philosophers is the need for practical reason to superintend people's lives to achieve felicity. Practical reason makes the necessity of virtue conspicuous, and with the two, people live in a state that both supports virtuous living and the material resources to facilitate participation in the actions that virtue calls for.

Like moderating desires, virtue also enables people to discern good and evil characteristics in a way that brings happiness. Virtuous characteristics impart good consequences, whereas their counterparts bring bad consequences and unhappiness. Stoics Seneca and Marcus Aurelius (in his book *Meditations*) listed numerous virtues including simplicity, integrity, dignity, hard work, self-denial, contentment, frugality, kindness, independence, simplicity, discretion, magnanimity, bravery, loyalty, modesty, restraint, thrift, mercy and self-control. Certainly, hard work brings prosperity, self-denial brings frugality, thrift brings austerity, magnanimity brings friends and admiration and loyalty bring fidelity. These are consequences that succor happiness. Now, consider the consequences of their counterparts. Idleness and indolence usually bring poverty, indulgence and prodigality bring dissoluteness, stinginess a reviled Scrooge and unfaithfulness brings duplicity and sometimes perfidy. These consequences bring angst and unhappiness. Indeed, Cicero believed that (p) with the virtues people can choose between good and evil, or between good characteristics and evil ones, and if they choose the good ones, they will live in accordance with nature and be happy. Further, according to Plato, reason shows the contrasting consequences of virtues and vices, which give people the right knowledge in order to distinguish good characteristics from evil ones. Virtuous characteristics enable them to participate in the good, which is a source of happiness.

Justice is a critical component of virtue, but what does it have to do with virtue and how does it bring happiness according to the philosophers? C. S. Lewis in *The Screwtape Letters* concocted a series of letters from the devil Screwtape to his minion Wormwood in order to turn humans to the devil. He admonished Wormwood to bewilder the human soul in order to undermine human faith and prevent the advent of virtues. He tells Wormwood to keep humans focused on the outer ring of fantasy because if they focus on the inner ring, or their conscience, they will develop habits and virtue, which is really fatal to the devil. Screwtape is worried that an inner virtuous ring will result in justice that is inimical to all the evil the devil wishes to spawn. One consequence of those evils is unhappiness, which occurs when the devil is able to separate humans from virtue and ultimately justice. If humans follow their conscience, virtuous and just habits ensue and happiness is the result. It is indeed strange to contemplate how conscience or inner reflectiveness leads to a sense of what is right or wrong, a concern for moral issues and a social conscience that leads to happiness.

Certainly, this is a literary parable by Lewis, but it contains a relevant point to this chapter, which is that with virtue, people live justly, and with justice, people are happier. Seneca wrote that (v) to act justly means upright dealings with other humans. When people treat others fairly, others do likewise, and the result is harmony. Conscience, morality, virtue and justice are the primordial soup of felicity.

Plato believed that some of these ingredients in the individual make for a good—and in this author's view happy—individual. In his discussion of justice in *Book Four* of the *Republic*, he finds three virtues in the individual along with their natural functions. The rational part is for thinking, the spirited part the experience of emotions and the appetitive part the pursuit of bodily desires. Plato believed that one is just when each of these three parts of the soul performs its function. Justice is the natural balance, or harmony, of these virtues, and injustice is their imbalance. The point is that harmonious virtues in the individual bring justice, which in turn brings goodness and happiness.

This author believes this is as good as far as it goes, but there is a more fundamental relationship between virtue, justice and happiness. Plato was discussing harmony within an individual soul, but virtue and justice are the critical components that maintain harmony with other people. Imaginary Vice in the beginning of this chapter was selfish, self-centered, had no scruples and acted on expediency alone. He was described as unhappy because nobody trusted him; he had no friends and was isolated. He was so because he was without virtue, justice and in disharmony with others.

There exist many competing moral theories that purport to define justice. Two significant ones are utilitarianism derived from philosophers like Jeremy Bentham and the social contract envisioned by numerous philosophers including Thomas Hobbes. Utilitarianism is the idea that morality is based on happiness for the most, so justice is what makes the most happy. As a consequentialist moral theory, it fails because it holds the seeds of injustice to the individual. The social contract states that justice derives from voluntary essential compacts people make that limit their freedom such as not to kill, steal or lie. This author believes justice is a human concept that arises as a consequence of the social contract ethical theory. When two humans strike a bargain not to steal from one another, they both walk away thinking *that was a fair bargain—both of us got what we wanted.* This is fairness—it was a consensual bilateral agreement where both individuals believed they were treated fairly—a sentiment that originates the good faith Cicero said is the foundation of justice. Consensual bilateral agreements, like obeying traffic laws, constitute justice—this is what is called fairness. Justice is a simple concept.

Certainly, artificial layers of civilization can and do get added to this conception of justice resulting in Rousseau's chains and Freud's constitutional unhappiness due to civilization. Indeed, both claim that these additions bring unhappiness. But in the simple state of the social contract, justice reigns and the result is happiness.

It is virtue, or having the character to agree and adhere to the compacts made under the social contract, that brings justice. With this morality people treat others justly, and a civilization of Virtue-like individuals arises unlike the dupe Vice. With this morality, virtue limits passion and people become just to all. It is the old equation mentioned at the beginning of this chapter: virtuous people treat other virtuous people fairly, and if one treats others right, they will treat one right in return. With this, people live happier lives because, to mention a few reasons, they become safe and do not fear losing property, and people tell them the truth. Vice's human counterpart Virtue lives a happier life.

Francois de La Rochefoucauld wrote that hypocrisy is the tribute vice pays virtue. Why do many think this is a truism? Why do most people think to be virtuous is better than living under vice? They do so because they think they live better lives when they live rightly and justly. The truth is that when people are virtuous they live in Platonic harmony with others, which brings happiness. To be happy do not be a Troglodyte living the outer ring, rather do what the philosophers say and be virtuous and just.

Chapter Twenty-Seven

COURAGE
Act on one's inner voice, be authentic and escape one's cage

Allen is an unhappy businessman because he always wanted to be a philosopher. When he was in college he took some philosophy courses that sparked his imagination. He took a class once on Martin Heidegger and read his book *Being and Time*. He was struck by his depiction of the inauthentic one who follows the herd and never lives life. He remembers coming out of philosophy classes elated at having learned something so new, true, exciting and meaningful. He was constantly amazed how the philosophers expressed his vague thoughts and feelings so insightfully and clearly—in terms he could not put in words. It was like reading the scholars of human nature.

But time slowly slipped Allen's aspirations away. After college he fell in love, married, started a family and began a career. His life became full of obligations and responsibilities. Allen was a good provider but secretly longed for the life of freethinking philosopher. So now Allen is unhappy because he does not have the courage to alter his life and pursue his dream.

This chapter is about how courage can bring happiness. To be happy one must often act in life, which takes courage. Indeed, the proverb says fortune favors the brave.

In chapter twenty-four on Aristotle's doctrine of the mean, courage was described as the virtuous mean between the vices of rashness and cowardice. Aristotle also believed that courage, along with generosity, justice, friendship and citizenship, was a virtue that brings happiness. Allen's vice was cowardice. If he had abandoned his family like Gauguin, he would have followed the other vice of rashness. His path to happiness then is to adopt the mean of courage and find a way to be both a family man and a philosopher. If Allen had studied Aristotle, he would have learned that if he courageously acted on his inner voice and adopted the mean of courage, he would be happier.

Courage brings felicity in many ways, the first of which is the courage to change unhappy circumstances. People all face circumstances in life that cause distress. Their bosses are tyrants, their spouses have affairs or they cannot pay off student debt. Many lack the courage to change these circumstances because they prefer the known ills of which Shakespeare spoke. But to change unhappy circumstances, one must summon the courage to change them—one must have the courage to act.

Gregg Easterbrook in *The Progress Paradox: How Life Gets Better While People Feel Worse* described a paradigmatic work rut in America in which makes many unhappy. Many American workers think work is their life so they painfully toil on unable to envision other ways of living and thinking. They get so caught up in competition and preoccupied with money they develop ulcers, stress maladies and die young from high blood pressure. In many ways, Easterbrook is describing an empty, meaningless and unhappy kind of life.

This way of living saps people's will and robs their human essence. The solution is the courage to change, to rise above the fray and survey life and alternate possibilities that may bring happiness. Courage enables new life possibilities and changes unhappy circumstances. What is needed—what Allen needed—was the courage to pursue them.

Happiness also comes through achieving one's dreams and aspirations. Humans aspire to be something or do something significant in life. Few are content living like a satisfied pig. Author George Plimpton, for example, endeavored to do many challenging things like be a quarterback in professional football, perform comedy at Caesars Palace in Las Vegas and play with the New York Philharmonic Orchestra. He did them all, and any photo of George shows a beaming, exuberant and happy man.

Achieving aspirations brings satisfaction and happiness, but the process of striving to achieve something itself is a source of happiness. Striving brings the satisfaction that one tried, which is an observation surrounded by innumerable shibboleths such as nothing ventured nothing gained, one will never succeed if one does not try and winners never quit and quitters never win. The point is that it is the striving—to do something new and change bad circumstances—requires the courage to act on one's aspirations. This is a source of happiness.

Alternatively, Cicero in his *Tusculan Disputations* wrote about the need for courage to overcome unhealthy desires that bring people unhappiness. His message was that some desires people have evolve into habits that cause them pain. With this habit itself becomes a problem because it (p) teaches people to endure, toil and despise wounds the desire-driven habits bring. The result is unhappiness. For Cicero, the solution is courage and to use one's will to challenge these pernicious desire-driven habits. With (p) courage, fortitude and virtue, people can master themselves and curb these reckless desires. For Cicero, philosophy and courage free people from those habits that bring unhappiness.

In college, Allen had learned about Heidegger's *Dasein*, which is the part of a person that eventually defines being. This *Dasein* is in a world with concern and guilt, and in particular the guilt not to be true to oneself. *Dasein* has the choice to be what they are, and those who choose not to are what Heidegger calls inauthentic. *Dasein* is like a conscience that continually reminds people when they are not being themselves, or authentic, and urging them to be so. For Heidegger, those that do not heed this inner voice betray themselves by giving themselves over to the "they," or others. Alternatively, the authentic acknowledge they need to be what they uniquely can, to see the they's successes and failures as unimportant and to become resolute in the face of death. By being resolute, people succeed in owning their situation and selves. The moral here is that Allen needed courage to stop following the herd or the "they"—to be himself and thus become authentic.

Many philosophers have echoed Heidegger's view. Ralph Waldo Emerson wrote about how others think people ought to live and the importance of becoming self-reliant and living how they think they ought to live. More bluntly, Ernest Hemingway wrote that it is better to die on one's feet than live on one's knees. To be happy, people must summon the courage to be authentic, be themselves and live on their feet.

Sophocles once wrote that it is a mistake to wait until the evening to see how splendid the day has been. Most people are like Allen, spending the best part of their lives chained to obligations, toiling at work and wasting the splendid day. They are people not living life to its fullest. Youth is the time to explore, strive, seek, experience and investigate the world. Instead the Allens of this world toil thinking life will be better sometime in the future. When they get old and feeble they find that they are less able to realize their potential and it is only then that they come to realize they have squandered the best part of their lives to endless unimportant obligations.

Courage helps people live life to its fullest now. To be happy, people need to summon the courage to take the chance to pursue their dreams. It has been said that the greatest regret of old people is not doing what they really wanted to do in life. Have courage and live life to the fullest now before it is too late.

The ancient stoics taught that people are like a dog on a leash, they have some control over their movements within the length of the leash but beyond it none. The beyond is fate—death is inevitable. Fear of fate is a significant source of unhappiness. Fear of sickness, lost loved ones and personal death can be fearful thoughts. People cannot change their fate, but they can change what they think of it. However, remaining indifferent to that which one cannot control is good advice but a tall order. How does one remain indifferent to the death of one's mother or father or the news that one has terminal cancer?

There is a difference between what might happen and what has happened; between the possibility of getting terminal cancer and being told one has it. The stoic's advice brings happiness in the former, but it is courage that brings a degree of acceptance in the latter. Seneca wrote that people (v) cannot change the conditions of their existence so they should adopt a noble spirit and bear up bravely, and Cicero in *Tusculan Disputations* that (pe) the man who successfully and courageously faces terrors will be happy.

Courage helps people remain sanguine in the face of fate's harsh blows. It has the quality of helping people overcome their fear of what is to happen. Indeed, Johann Wolfgang von Goethe wrote that people should (p) enjoy when they can and endure when they must. Courage is what enables people to endure what they must.

Freedom is a state conducive to happiness. The freedom to do what one wants unencumbered by social norms, society and morality brings happiness. Certainly, people may be constrained for good reasons, but too often the reasons are others' desires to make them do something they think they ought to do. Courage is the antidote to these stifling sources that silently rob one's freedom. Have courage to break through others' imposed chains and be happy. Indeed, Thucydides once wrote that (p) the secret of happiness is freedom, and the secret of freedom is courage.

Courage changes unhappy circumstances, helps people achieve their dreams and aspirations, overcome malicious desires, to be themselves, to live life to its fullest and to face fate. Have courage and be happy.

Consider what happens with the opposite of courage, or cowardice, to happiness. Not only do people face opprobrium, calumny, disapproval and loss of self-respect, but they also find themselves in a sense of listlessness, a life of fear and a feeling of helplessness. Homer wrote in the *Odyssey* that (v) what man believes in woes to come so long as valor and tough knees are supplied him by the gods. If people are courageous and strong, they ought not worry because they believe they will prevail. With cowardice people fear all woes to come, live in fear of the future and are often unable to act. They find themselves impotent and listless, fearing the future, which is a source of unhappiness.

Many unhappy people are like a bird in a cage with an open door. They are free to take the door and fly to freedom, but the comfort of the cage and familiarity of the bars strangely comforts them. They are fearful people—prisoners of their own thoughts. A few face their fears, summon the courage and escape the coup. The ones that stay remain unhappily locked in their self-made mental cages living inauthentic lives doing just more of the same. Courage enables people to escape their mental cages and be free.

Early in this book, it was mentioned that American philosopher Ralph Waldo Emerson wrote that society conspires against manhood and demands conformity. He discussed the collective group that thinks it knows what an individual's duty is better than he. For Emerson it is this collective group that makes people timorous and fearful. Subordinating freedom and independence to the collective group is a process that only engenders fear and cowardice. If people acquiesce to it, they let Heidegger's "they" superintend their lives, do their thinking and rob their natural human autonomy.

This loss of autonomy brings an unhappy state akin to a person unable to act when facing great danger. They are so subordinated and fearful they cannot decide whether to fight or flee resulting in a paralyzed state incapable of doing ether. The result is a feeling of helplessness because they have abandoned their instinctual defenses—they willingly and cowardly give their body to the collective wolf. This state of helpless fear due to lack of courage is one of abject resignation and unhappiness. It is the virtue of courage and not the vice-filled extreme of cowardice that maintains individuality, integrity and happiness.

Friedrich Nietzsche wrote that the higher man is distinguished from the lower by his fearlessness and his readiness to challenge misfortune. Nietzsche had in mind an Overman but his advice is applicable to all the Allens of this world. To be happy, people must have fearless courage to act on their inner voice, be authentic and escape their cages.

CHAPTER TWENTY-EIGHT

REASON
Do not be a dog, cultivate reason and avoid an empty mind

The year is medieval 1,340 ACE, and Regis, who is a dog, and Robin, who is a man, were both caught stealing. Regis stole a bone from the butcher and Robin stole some jewelry from a rich man. They were apprehended, taken to the magistrate, convicted and sentenced to sixty days in jail. People today understand jail for Robin, but putting a dog in jail for stealing a bone sounds preposterous. However, it was a common practice in European history up to the eighteenth century to ascribe moral responsibility to animals. Like humans, they were punished for their transgressions. Why does this sound outrageous today? It is because humans have reason and animals do not.

Many philosophers believe that it is reason that distinguishes humans from other animals. Indeed, most philosophers venerate reason. Some have gone so far as to assert that it is reason that brings happiness. Spinoza believed that supreme inner satisfaction, or happiness, arises from a rational peace of mind, and Immanuel Kant in *Critique of Pure Reason* called happiness (p) the state of a rational being that brings complete satisfaction of all one's needs and inclinations.

It should be mentioned that this topic has been alluded to throughout this book. It was, for example discussed in the chapters on Epicureanism and stoicism and habits. The assumption has been reason brings happiness. The admonitions, for example, to focus on one's problems in an adequate way and to be self-directed by reason assume reason brings self-introspection and enables people to be self-directed, which will bring happiness. Seneca, for example, said that to be (p) happy people must adjust and shape their own personality. So, these assertions will be explored along with an attempt to draw some conclusions.

Many philosophers believe reason brings virtue that brings happiness. Happiness comes from many things such as a beautiful landscape or something exciting people just learned. Virtue deals not with these but rather the happiness that arises from association with other people. It is about how to live with other humans in consanguinity. Reason orders experiences, education and intellect in such a way that explains how to live happily in a community. With this, reason brings morality and admirable traits like integrity and honesty. Reason does not teach vice. Humans appreciate virtuous people and reciprocate with integrity and honesty, which brings mutual well-being and happiness. With these virtues, people live happier lives with other human beings.

Aristotle in *Nicomachean Ethics* wrote that (p) happiness consists of flourishing in accordance with one's nature similar to plants and animals that function well according to their natures. For Aristotle, the proper functioning of a human is to reason, which brings both moral and intellectual virtue. It is reason that brings these virtues that are necessary to live well and be happy.

There are other explanations from the philosophers. It has been said that man is a wolf to man. Human instinct drives people to selfishness, which is a trait that makes humankind the enemy. Reason-driven virtue breaks this unhappy contest and causes people to voluntarily limit their inclinations, passions and instincts in order to live in happy peace with others.

Another perspective comes from Immanuel Kant, who believed reason brings happiness through his categorical imperative. Generally, for Kant, it is duty and the need to act in such a way as others would act that brings ethics and it is only reason that demonstrates this. Lying, for example makes people unethical and unworthy of happiness because others will lie to them. For Kant, reason makes people worthy of happiness.

Saint Augustine in *Confessions*, for example, wrote that he loved the peace that virtue brings and hated the discord that comes from vice. He concluded from this that in goodness there was unity, but in evil, disunion. For him, unity was the seat of the rational mind, whereas the disunion consisted of irrational life. For Augustine, virtue through reason brings peace, unity and happiness. Imagine two minds, one without inner harmony and another with it. The first, according to Saint Augustine brings evil and disunion.

Such a mind necessarily experiences tension and conflict, which bring unhappiness. The rational mind with unity, however, resolves conflict, experiences less tension and is thus calmer. Satisfaction is one consequence, and it, along with calmness, engenders happiness. Reason unifies and resolves inner conflict because with it people are able to step back from circumstances and observe from an objective point of view. Such a view not only puts the sources of conflict in perspective but also allows people to understand their causes, which they use to gain a better understanding of reality. This resolves issues and brings satisfaction and happiness.

Plato in the *Republic* wrote that there were three parts to the soul, which are reason, spirit and appetite, each of which had counterparts in society. He maintained that whether it is the individual or city, it is justice that determines that each part fulfill its function without interfering with the other parts. It is reason that brings justice, so it is reason that maintains this harmony in individuals. Without reason, the parts become unbalanced, and one may supersede another. Spirit can become superstition and appetite can become avarice, both of which have overridden reason. This kind of disharmony only brings an imbalance that results in unhappiness.

Reason is the critical component that maintains a harmonious balance within individuals and societies. When reason fails, societies and individuals become extreme, zealous and unhappy. This leads to the next allied point, which is that it is reason that superintends desire and the passions.

That wayward desire and passion bring unhappiness was discussed at length in chapter nine on desire and appetites in the section describing sources of unhappiness. This section is about sources of happiness, and this is about how reason brings it by mitigating the pejorative consequences of desire and passion.

An unharmonious soul is susceptible to excessive desire and inflamed passion. Desires, like the ardent pursuit of money or sensual pleasure are readily transformed into passions like envy, jealousy, love and hate. People desire money and when they do not get it they begin passionately hating those who do, and when a person desires a member of the opposite sex and they spurn that interest for another, the person feels passionate jealousy. Desire and passion are capricious sources of unhappiness and it is reason that controls, calms and directs them. Reason superintending desires and passions prevents unhappiness.

It should be noted that, even though this has been the prevailing opinion of philosophers throughout history, one prominent Scottish philosopher, David Hume, disagreed. Hume believed that reason can never cause people to act; indeed, he wrote that (p) reason is the slave of the passions. For him, if there is ever a contest between reason and passion, the latter will always win. Hume's perspective will be discussed later in this chapter.

Philosophers have written much on the need for reason to control desire and passion in order to achieve happiness. Plato wrote that (p) the man who is a slave to his appetites is master of nothing, and a man who is master of nothing is the most miserable of men. For Plato the man of intelligence uses reason to control his appetites. People should desire only what they should and be satisfied with what they have. Forever wanting more money, more prestige, a fancier home or car, or a better appearance will cause people to engage the vicious cycle of desire, which only brings unhappiness. To be happy, people need only fulfill the natural and rational desires and not imaginary or societally driven ones. It is, for example, rational to desire knowledge in order to avoid ignorance, but desiring all knowledge is irrational because it cannot be achieved.

Saint Augustine in *Confessions* described the constant pursuit of pleasure, which is source of desire and ostensible happiness. Although Augustine's motive was to proselytize for faith and reverence for God, he collaterally describes uncertain joy from pleasurable bodily senses. He wrote that (p) he has never been aware of joy through bodily senses, he has not seen or heard it, smelled, tasted or touched it. Desired pleasures do not bring ultimate happiness, and it is reason that demonstrates this maxim. As Epicurus explained, pleasure cannot be increased only varied, and it is reason that Epicurus used to explain this. This brings up the topic of why reason also mitigates the passions.

It was asserted that desires are often inflamed into passions. Saint Augustine wrote that (p) crimes are committed when the emotions are corrupt and rise in revolt without control. Sins of self-indulgence are committed when the soul fails to govern the impulses from which it derives bodily pleasure. The Stoics believed that uncontrollable passions are a primary cause of human unhappiness. Once a passion is initiated, it takes on a life of its own. Anger, for example, unless inhibited, naturally inflames and becomes unquenchable. Seneca wrote that anger (v) indulges itself, judges capriciously, refuses to listen and clings to what it has seized. Inflamed passions like anger for Seneca possess people; people do not possess them. Uncontrollable passions like anger are significant sources of human unhappiness.

Superintending reason is the solution. Saint Augustine wrote (p) crimes come from uncontrolled emotions, and for the Stoics like Seneca, it is reason that controls these corrupt emotions. For them, reason is the antidote to unrestrained passion because it corrects wrongful beliefs, corrects improper judgments and brings virtue. To be happy, bodily driven passion should be subordinate to the reason driven mind.

Aristotle observed that reason causes men to do many things contrary to habit and nature. Desire and passion are parts of humans' nature that often become habits. It is reason that brings the wisdom to direct people to do those salubrious things that are contrary to desire and passion. Hence, reason is a significant source of human happiness.

Two sources of human unhappiness that reason ameliorates are ignorance and religious superstition. Regarding ignorance, John Stuart Mill asked whether it is better to be a satisfied pig or Socrates dissatisfied. Which brings enduring happiness? The enlightenment and knowledge reason brings comes with a price, which many believe is too high. Some believe ignorance is a prerequisite for happiness. Erasmus wrote that ignorance is bliss, and in *The Good Brahmin* in the *Romances*, Voltaire described a knowledgeable unhappy Brahmin and an ignorant and bigoted happy woman. The Brahmin did not know (v) from whence he came, what he is, whither he goes or what is to become of him. The ignorant woman is utterly unaware of these kinds of questions and happily navigates life as a satisfied bigoted pig. Indeed, the author of this book in chapter nineteen argues that a little ignorance does bring happiness.

Would a person rather be happy or know the truth? Reason bringing truth does not always bring happiness. Some believe knowing the truth is tantamount to eternal bliss, but is it? Truth shows many painful sources of unhappiness from an adulterous partner to selfish human nature. Fortunately, there are more reasons why reason, knowledge and truth bring happiness than not.

Reason organizes reality, investigates matters and brings order to the disordered mind. It is reason that enables people to escape their cages of ignorance and provide the opportunity to be a dissatisfied Socrates. Humans naturally fear that which they do not know, and it is curiosity-inspired reason that examines why. It is reason that explains to people why they should not fear the unknown. It is also reason that enables them to escape being a slave to their passions. Passionate desires and appetite have been shown to be a source of human unhappiness, and only reason and the knowledge it brings prevents this. This observation is the direct opposite of famous philosopher David Hume's philosophy. Hume is wrong; the reason will be explained shortly.

Truth from reason may not make people immediately happy, but in time it does. As truth settles in, people realign their ideas and beliefs in such a way that makes them realistically happier. They divorce the cheating spouse and learn why Adam Smith and Thomas Hobbes believed selfishness brings great benefits. Undoubtedly, it is truth from reason that has brought better medicine, better food and better housing, all of which make people happier. Socrates was right: it is better to live the examined life because it brings happiness.

The ignorant are susceptible to superstitious beliefs that can bring great fear and unhappiness. Superstition invents imaginary enemies and fanciful demons that haunt and terror humans, blasting every enjoyment from life. God's wrath is found everywhere, and eternal pain in hell awaits. Ancient peoples, prior to the rise of reason, were particularly susceptible to these superstition-caused sources of unhappiness.

Lucretius in *On the Nature of Things* wrote that (p) humans must unshackle themselves from superstition, irrational fears and hollow pieties. They should not fear imaginary gods that punish them in the hereafter, inflict lightening, tempests, earthquakes and disease. Religious superstition for Lucretius is a powerful force that persuades people that evil is the cause of anxiety and war. Superstition brings false suppositions and generates paralyzing fear of death and natural phenomena, which limits and bounds limited ignorant individuals' minds.

The solution for Lucretius and Seneca is to avoid superstition through reason. Lucretius believed that (p) people must exercise reason and adopt a scientific mindset in order to avoid superstition. Seneca believed that the distinctive nature of reason allows people to conquer their superstitious fears. Rationality for Seneca brings wisdom, which conquers fears and brings happiness.

Why is this? How does reason undermine superstition? With reason people delve deeper into the sources of their fears. In this process it connects causes with consequences, with which they come to see that not all causes come from supernatural forces and that some consequences necessarily follow from natural causes. Reason explains to people that Mt. Vesuvius erupted because there was a buildup of pressure in the earth and not because a god was angry and that the destruction afterward is due to the physical consequences of an eruption and not because a god wanted vengeance. Reason enables people to understand the fear and pain caused by superstition. It allows them to transcend their passions, instincts and ignorance to be happy.

Regis the dog did not connect abstract causes with consequences and thus lived by instinct and passion alone. Robin, although uneducated, knew that if he steals and is caught there would be consequences imposed by the law. If Robin had listened to reason, he would be more inclined to be moral, avoid stealing, avoid jail and thus be happier. Whether it is morality or superstition, it is superintending reason that brings happiness through enlightenment.

Humans are daily surrounded by sources of fear that bring anxiety, misery and unhappiness. It begins when an infant is born into anguish, weakness, impotence and distress, which herald a life in agony and horror. As people age they find terrors within them—their body and mind. A poet once described them as (v) the intestine stone, ulcer, colic, frenzy, moping, melancholy, madness, atrophy, pestilence that only culminate in despair. Saint Augustine *Confessions* wrote about (p) the daily wastage of people's bodies until they come to an end. Even with good fortune, Augustine wrote that people still live in fear because they fear losing it. In human society, people are surrounded by enemies who incessantly seek misery and destruction. They face murder, calumny, theft, injury, war and intimidation. Man is indeed a wolf to man. People also face wild beasts, poisonous snakes and insects that carry disease. Other animals can also be a wolf to man. Many suffer from poverty and want, struggling for food and shelter. Finally, people face natural disasters like earthquakes, hurricanes, flooding, landslides and lightning that can harm them, which instill fear. And above all, they fear death. Not much will be said about this here because it was described earlier other than that Ernest Becker said it is human's greatest fear. For simple minds, life can be terror.

Perhaps humans' lot is best described by the poet John Donne in *Anniversaries, Epicedes and Obsequies*:

>The last long night
>The carcass of this world
>Outward storms
>The dangers of disease and old
>There is no health, the physicians say just enjoy neutrality
>But knowing that we are never well
>Born ruinous
>Our parent marriage is our funeral
>The shortness of life
>Dangers and diseases of this world

But this does not have to be humans' lot. Reason enables them to understand and overcome these sources of fear. It explains that they can overcome impotency, they can understand and ameliorate the sources of mental and bodily pain, they can form philosophies and institutions that protect them from other people, they can design weapons to subdue animals, they can learn a job that brings sustenance and they can plan to avoid natural disasters. On death, it explains the need to accept it in order to avoid fearing it.

David Hume in his *Dialogue's Concerning Natural Religion* wrote that (v) reason teaches that life is not so bad, and the stoics taught that reason allows people to conquer sources of unhappiness like (v) pain, grief, and fear of death. For them, reason allows people to mitigate their passions, avoid misguided opinions, achieve proper judgments of impressions and be virtuous. They believed that human evil and error come from incorrect reasoning and not from evil itself. Reason enables people to overcome the fears that bring unhappiness

To briefly digress from this chapter's theme that reason brings happiness, it was mentioned earlier that reason enables people to influence those passions and desires that bring unhappiness, and that David Hume disagreed. He wrote in *A Treatise of Human Nature* that (v) reason is and ought only to be the slave of the passions. Indeed, for Hume, reason is a mild passion itself that can never cause people to act in such a way to bring happiness.

Cicero and Seneca do not agree with Hume. From chapter nine, Cicero lamented luxury, the love of good living, riches and the pleasures Romans pursued as sickly and disgraceful. Seneca was also dismayed with Roman luxury, which he believed was due to indulgence in pleasure due to the passions becoming reason's master rather than servant. So, who is right?

It turns out that Cicero and Hume agree on the solution, which is that, even if reason cannot control actions, it can influence passions, which can. Hume himself wrote that (v) reason can influence conduct when it excites a passion by informing people of the existence of something that is a proper object of it, and when it discovers the connection of causes and effects so as to afford people means of exercising any passion. Indeed, Hume ultimately believed that people achieve good ends when lively beliefs are mixed with good sense, or reason. It is reason influencing the passions that helps people obtain their proper desires, mitigates pain and accentuates happiness.

There has been a historic tension between passion and reason. In the case of happiness, most philosophers come down on the side of reason. They claim this because reason brings wisdom, which guides people to happiness. Seneca, for example, believed rationality brings wisdom, which itself brings happiness. If this is true, then one prescription for happiness is to become a philosopher. Philosophy focuses on happiness by (p) stripping the mind of empty thinking according to Seneca. For Hume, knowing things pleases people, which brings happiness.

Reason brings happiness in many ways, so order the mind and be rational.

CONCLUSION

Philosophers have said much on the sources of unhappiness and happiness. It seems certain that any rational person absorbing their wisdom would be happy. They have many specific prescriptions for felicity, but perhaps three incisive observations are that people are what they know, they are made for happiness and happiness requires effort. It is people's knowledge and beliefs that determine their happiness, so they can achieve happiness by embracing the beliefs that bring it. However, felicity requires effort, because as Epictetus explained people are born for it and not with it. So, know the source of Plato's crown of happiness and be happy.

ABOUT THE AUTHOR

John L. Bowman lives in Portland, Oregon, where he raised three daughters with his wife Kathy. He is the author of numerous books on philosophy, real estate, politics, sports, words, stoicism and humor. He received a Bachelor of Arts degree in 1973 from Whitman College, a Bachelor of Arts degree in philosophy in 1993 from Portland State University and a Master of Interdisciplinary Studies degree in philosophy and history in 2010 from Oregon State University. His master's thesis, titled *Stoicism, Enkrasia and Happiness*, surveyed the ancient philosophy of stoicism and particularly the famous Roman Stoic Seneca. A complete list of his books follows.

The author welcomes reader comments, observations and rebuttals. His books and biography can be viewed on his website at www.johnlbowman.com from which readers can e-mail him, send him an e-mail directly at author@jlbowman.com, or comment on his blog at www.johnlbowman.com/blog/. You can also view his Amazon Author Page at:

https://www.amazon.com/-/e/B001K6KNDW.

Thanks for reading my book; I hope you liked it.

John Bowman

BOOKS BY JOHN L. BOWMAN

Reflections on Man and the Human Condition

Selected Topics in Philosophy

Nobody's Perfect

How to Succeed in Commercial Real Estate

Socialism in America

God's Lecture

A Reader's Companion

Stoicism, Enkrasia and Happiness

Aegean Summer

The Art of Volleyball Hitting

Graduate School

Provocative and Contemplative Quotations

On Law

A Reference Guide to Stoicism

A Reader's Companion II

Democracy and Why It Will Fail in America

www.ingramcontent.com/pod-product-compliance
Lightning Source LLC
Chambersburg PA
CBHW051941290426
44110CB00015B/2062